About the Author

Ted Oliver was the first and only British federal bounty hunter to be working in the USA.

Drawing on a lifetime's experience as a marksman, sniper, martial artist, mercenary, wilderness survivalist, tracker, and an undercover FBI contractor, he pursued villains the length and breadth of the United States and beyond – in his truck, on horseback, and on occasions atop of express freight trains.

In a twenty-plus year career, he pulled in close to 48,000 skips. During that time, he was shot, stabbed, beaten, and on one occasion, kidnapped and left for dead. But mostly, he got his man.

Dead or alive? That was their choice.

Website: tedoliverbountyhunter.com
Facebook: Ted Oliver Bounty Hunter

Dead or Alive: Book 2.
How a British Bounty Hunter
took America by Storm

Ted Oliver AKA Dan Durass

Dead or Alive: How a British Bounty Hunter took America by Storm

Olympia Publishers
London

www.olympiapublishers.com
OLYMPIA PAPERBACK EDITION

A CIP catalogue record for this title is
available from the British Library.

ISBN: 978-1-78830-306-4

This is a work of creative nonfiction. The events are portrayed to the
best of the author's memory. While all the stories in this book are
true, some names and identifying details have been changed to
protect the privacy of the people involved.

First Published in 2021

Olympia Publishers
Tallis House
2 Tallis Street
London
EC4Y 0AB

Printed in Great Britain

Dedications

People in the States told me I would not live very long with the dangerous career I chose to follow. But here I am today, still alive to tell the real story.

I dedicate this book to my wife Irena, whom I owe so much, who has been at my side for over eighteen years, providing me with constant motivation, adding complete stability to my life, always believing in me, and convincing me that my story was worth telling, with the endless help and encouragement you gave me over the years, even when I had constant flashbacks and relived terrible nightmares, I know it was terrifying for you having no conception of what was going on with my sanity. Still, you held me and put up with it when you could have so easily walked away. I could not have survived on my own with what was going on in my mind.
Without you, I dread to think of what I might have become.

I also dedicate this book to my two sons, Cameron and Mindaugas. You have both helped me realise how important it is to belong to a family that I so much longed for. And of course, without you both, I would have finished this book ten years earlier. I truly love you both with all my heart, and I could not have written these books without your support.

In loving memory of my mother Phyllis and my father Ernest, both of whom I lost at a very young age.

Acknowledgements

No author has ever written a good book alone. Somewhere along the line, he had some assistance. This book is no exception. I want to thank Alan Wilkinson, who tirelessly spent many months unravelling all the handwritten logs that I was working on in the States and slowly putting them together to make some sense for the books finally.

I would also like to thank Clive Corner and Paul Brackley for all the help and guidance they gave me when I first started writing. They helped me get some ideas about how to put the books together. Thanks to my secretary, Jo Baxter, who, at short notice, tirelessly spent weeks helping to type up the chapters.

Thanks also to Hugh Byrne for the cover photographs for both books.

Likewise, thanks to Sandy Taylor of Taylor Investigations in Tacoma, Washington. She gave me my first job as an armed private investigator in the States. I relied on her for quick licence plate and information checks when on surveillance or tracking skips. Thanks also to my first bondsman Bernie who took me on to resolve my first-midnight run. This enabled me to find my way forward and helped me become successful in the profession I chose to follow.

Gratitude to the many attorneys — Harvey G. McCraw J. Razan R. and Steiner B. who all helped to get me out of many sticky situations unscathed and without serving too much jail time.

Thanks to the many doctors and nurses that treated me in life or death situations. They helped me pull through.

Special thanks to Dr. Starzl.

I would also like to thank Ramon, Papa Joe, Zoot, Randy, Crusher, Hondo, and all the instructors, who taught me skills to allow me to get through all the challenges I had to complete in sniping, combat training, and other courses I studied, even though at times I wanted to give up, thinking your teaching was wrong. I now know you were right, and your punishments, skills, and challenging training helped me survive in dangerous situations.

Thanks to my Sensei[1] Hirokazu Kanazawa Soke.

Special thanks to all the good friends and acquaintances I lost along the way, and to all my team members who were killed in shoot-outs in this dangerous occupation, standing by me in good and bad times, notably in life and death situations. Again, I thank you all from the bottom of my heart. You will never be forgotten and will remain in my heart forever.

---

[1] See glossary

This book is also dedicated to all the FBI agents I worked closely with and those that covered my ass on many occasions. Without your help, I would not be here today.

My admiration to all the FBI undercover and street agents worldwide, who make the FBI what it is today, the best investigative agency in the world.

Appreciation also to the FBI. I took all your comments on board when writing these books.

Thanks also to America's professional gang investigators[2] and the intel[3] they shared with me. Also, to the sheriff's office, federal agents, DEA[4] agents, and law enforcement, that helped me with information on the cases I was working on. Without your help, it would have been a lot more challenging to resolve my issues. I cannot name you for security reasons, but you will know who you all are when you read these books.

To all my friends out there who are still bounty hunters, and to all the agents I do not personally know, who are still continually involved in this dangerous job. Keep up the excellent work, be careful, don't take unnecessary risks, and definitely shoot first! Ask and answer questions later. Be safe and remember it's your life that's always on the line.

---

[2] See glossary
[3] See glossary
[4] See glossary

There is no hunting like the hunting of man, and those who have hunted armed men long enough and liked it, never care for anything else thereafter.

Ernest Hemingway.

***

Accept me for who I am now, not who I was then.

Ted Oliver

***

Remember wearing a black belt doesn't mean you are invincible; it means you never gave up; you worked past the pain, overcame the disappointments, and faced your fears. It's not about being better than somebody else; it's about being better than the person who you used to be.

Sensei Ted Oliver (Shichidan) 7th Dan

Contents

Prologue 21

Two Rides 23

Not Today, Dewayne 44

Me? Ride Shotgun? 54

A Midnight Run 66

Down Below the Border 82

A Man's Best Friend 111

The Stripper 131

Did He Have a Gun or Didn't He? 148

Mother's Boy 159

Sha'Dawg 168

You May Run, but You Can't Fly 175

Wipe Your Own Damned Ass! 189

Sure, I'll Do You a Favour 198

Freight Train, Freight Train, ... 207

Goin' so Fast. 207

A City in Flames 221

Size Isn't Everything 228

Meet Dan Durass 237

It's Your Thanksgiving. 265

Not Mine. 265

A Few Facts about Bounty Hunters 275

Interesting facts: 279

How drugs were spread in the USA 279

Glossary of Terms 290

Coming Soon: 304

Cases to read in Book Three 304

Taylor v. Taintor.

Very few people understand that bounty hunters have wide-ranging powers granted to them in the nineteenth century.

In 1872 the United States Supreme Court recognised in the case of *Taylor v. Taintor* that crime was rampant and out of control, and that many bail bond agents had to forfeit their bail bonds when defendants failed to appear in court, and that it was the common-law right of bondsmen or their agents, to arrest the defendants that had undertaken a bail bond contract and skipped their court date. This meant that at any time during the existence of the sureties' agreement with the defendant, they may arrest them without resorting to any new judicial process. This law remains in place today.

The following court ruling gave the sureties' and its agents (bounty hunters) sweeping rights to recover the accused that had skipped bail. This made the sureties exempt from 'due process,' giving them the power to break and enter a residence without a warrant, unlike law enforcement.

US Supreme Court Ruling of 1872: *Taylor v. Taintor, 83 U.S. (16 Wall.) 366.*

When bail is given, the principal is regarded as delivered to the custody of his sureties (bail bondsman). Their dominion is a continuance of the original imprisonment. Whenever they choose to do so, they may seize and deliver him up in their discharge; and if that cannot be done at once, they may imprison him until it can be done. They may exercise their rights in person or by agent (a bounty hunter). They may pursue him into another state; they may arrest him on the Sabbath; if necessary, they may break and enter his house for that purpose. The seizure is not made by virtue of a new process. None is needed. It is likened to the re-arrest by the sheriff of an escaping prisoner.

Confidential and Sensitive Matters.

Some of the chapters you are about to read in this book took place while working as an undercover FBI contractor in the United States. These cases may be of a personal and sensitive subject. My job was to track down and bring back defendants that had fled from justice. In those days, most federal agents were under extreme pressure to produce arrest results in certain American States.

Working undercover ranks as one of the most terrifying and dangerous things you could ever choose to do with your life. The assignments may be classed as classified, so you cannot discuss or tell anybody what you are doing. When you report in on a completed assignment, you had to phone in a secret code attached to that specific case. That code was also linked to me. Then you would have to complete a confidential full detailed report. Later at a secret location, that report had to be given in person to the federal agent that the case was assigned to, or you were informed to leave the information at a dead drop. When I was working undercover, I knew that I was out there on my own in the no go areas, with no police or the feds for backup if things got dangerous. I also knew I was expendable, and therefore they could quickly abandon or destroy me whenever they needed to cover their tracks. Even now, today, I am always looking over my shoulder.

You cannot imagine what the fear of death feels like until you are standing there right in front of it. I had to make split-second decisions; some paid off, some failed, and some almost cost me my life. I was living on the edge, and I knew it. It took its toll towards the end, physically and mentally, on my health. But before I left the States, I completed a personal hit list. And now, I have a new private list of all the people that fucked me over here in the UK. Remember, I am not a forgiving person, never have been, never will be. So never mistake my long silence as a weakness. Smart people don't plan big moves out loud. Is this normal? Well, I think it is. This is how we were trained to remove and deal with any problems that got in our way, think, and do things differently than the average person would never dream of doing.

In the States, I was using so many different aliases and Identifications in the undercover work I was doing. I had four passports with other names that I used to travel out of countries at one stage. Sometimes I would even forget my real name, as I had to memorise and remember my alias names and details without hesitation. After I left this dangerous business, it took me some time to go back to the UK to find normality. I wanted to belong in a family and live a normal life. I wished I could forget my past, but that's an impossible thing to wish for because it's with you every single day. You learn how to adapt to your new surroundings, how to mix and blend in. You try to look normal to other people, but the training is always there at the ready, waiting to take action at the first sign of any danger.

I never really knew if the information I was working on in the States was genuine or a set-up, or I was being lined up to be killed by someone I was tracking, or even the feds themselves to get rid of evidence and loose ends.

So, for obvious reasons, I have changed the names of the offenders and law enforcement officers involved in all the cases I have recorded here. In some instances, I have altered the locations and dates. Otherwise, all the incidents you will read in this book are real and happened to me in my work as a federal fugitive recovery agent.

Prologue

It's a familiar scene. A man all dressed in black is riding his horse slowly down Main Street. The streets are almost deserted; the only sounds you can hear are the clip-clop, clip-clop, clip-clop, of the horse's hooves as they walk on the hard stony road surface. The man's face is covered in stubble, he has dried blood splatters all over his arms and face, his hat is pulled low over his eyes, and he wears a sweaty bandanna around his neck. He holds the horse's reins with one hand; the other hand rests on a pistol that's placed in a holster at his side; he also has a rifle slung across his back, as he approaches the sheriff's office a gold badge on his chest glints in the sunlight.

Behind him walks a second horse, a pinto.[5] There's a large bundle across its back, hog-tied under the horse's belly. Flies are buzzing around a couple of dark red stains.

Some people passing by stop and stare. They glance at each other, then at the man in black. Who the hell is this, bringing a dead man's body into town in broad daylight?

A large man steps out of a bar to see what's cooking. 'Well, I'll be damned,' he says. 'If that ain't the feller I had breakfast with a coupla days back.'

Someone asks, 'So who the hell is he?'

The big guy stares at the horseman and then spits a wad of black tobacco juice on the sidewalk. 'Goddam bounty hunter,' he says and goes back into the bar.

---

[5] See glossary

The man in black has now brought his horses to a stop. As he dismounts, a UPS van brakes sharply, and a truck swings wide to avoid him. This is not the Wild West, after all. It isn't a movie scene being shot. It's just a modern-day bounty hunter going about his business. And this is his story.

Two Rides

'What you gotta understand is, he ain't like you and me.' The man sitting in the seat opposite looked around the café, lowered his voice, and leaned forward, so close I could feel the warmth of his breath on my cheeks. 'No sir, your authentic hillbilly[6] ain't fully developed as a human being.'

My chair made a harsh scraping noise as I shoved it back a few inches on the wooden floor and leaned away from him. It's a loaded word, hillbilly. If you've never been down to Appalachia,[7] it makes you think of all kinds of things. Just say it out loud, and people will bring up that movie, *Deliverance*. They hear that tune, *Duelling Banjos*. They see in their mind's eye a bunch of toothless, grinning retards ready to commit any outrage.

I was sitting in a breakfast place in Hicksville, West Virginia. It was just after seven in the morning, and I was digging into a man-sized portion of bacon and grits.[8] The big old redneck[9] sitting opposite shifted a wad of chew tobacco from one side of his mouth to the other, leaned back, and flicked a hand at a fly that circled lazily above the table.

'Yes sir,' he said, 'your genuine hillbilly's a low-grade individual. Part gypsy, part Indian, with a bit of Scotch Irish thrown in. Most like he'll have some kinda physical deformity. Won't have hardly no teeth, that's for sure.' He picked up a paper

---

[6] See glossary
[7] See glossary
[8] See glossary
[9] See glossary

napkin, wiped a dribble of black baccy juice off his lower lip, then said, 'Comes from the in-breeding, y'unnerstand. Cos that's all them mothers have to do all day. Like, fuck each other. When they ain't on a killing spree, that is. Birds, possums, wild hogs.... strangers.' He chuckled and added, 'Them ol' boys, they sure do like to kill things.'

I didn't say anything. I just let him talk – because he had plenty to say, and sometimes a guy like that if you let him speak long enough, he might just tell you something worth noting. 'So a word of advice, my friend. You planning to go up in them mountains, you be sure and watch yo' ass, and watch it good. Cos they'll shoot anything or anybody they find on their land. They take genuine pleasure in killing.' He nodded slowly and added, 'Yes sir, it's how they get their kicks, most on 'em.'

It was my very first visit to the Appalachian region. You might say I was just getting the feel of the place. The guy I was sharing my table with, soon as he heard me ordering my grub, he pointed at me and told me he'd heard my accent before and he bet I was from Australia. Told me he ran the bar across the road there, just by the sheriff's office, and I should look in some time.

I never told him where I was from. I'd grown tired of people asking me what a guy from England was doing in this dirtiest of trades, weary of explaining how I got to operate in the States, why I was doing so well, and how many men I had killed. I never said anything about working on a federal warrant. That was classified information. As far as this guy or anybody else in that town knew, I was just a lone stranger who was travelling through. So okay, he wanted me to be an Aussie. Fine. I've been called worse things than that.

The guy had an agenda, like so many of those know-it-all

bastards you meet in bars and diners in one-horse towns,[10] and once he heard I was headed towards the mountains, he started to tell me about the kind of people I might meet in the back-country. It took me a while to make out what the guy was saying, the way he mumbled out of the side of his mouth while biting a lump of chewing tobacco in his cheek, but in the end, I tuned in and started to get the gist of it.

'They's a backward people,' he said. 'They's dirty, violent, ignorant.' He thought for a moment and scratched the stubble under his chin. 'Yeah, I reckon that describes 'em pretty good.' Then he leaned forward and lowered his voice. 'Ya see, a hillbilly ain't what you or I would call civilized. Ain't hardly human, tell the God's honest truth. Don't even take baths, the half of 'em. They live off-grid. Eat roadkill. Possums, squirrels, raccoons, bobcats, I seen 'em eating rats – and God knows I ain't a man to lie to you. And work?' He shook his head. 'Work's a four-letter word, far as they's concerned.'

I'd arrived in town the previous afternoon. I'd driven all the way from Montana, fifteen hundred miles. I'd been hanging out on the Blackfoot reservation up there. Got involved with a woman, had a little too much fun, and found myself in trouble yet again. Lost my girlfriend of the time but came away with a new horse in tow. So it suited me fine when this gig came up. It was as if it was meant to be. When I got the green light to proceed from the feds, I hitched up the trailer and loaded the new horse, plus my pinto mare, and drove right across the country. It took me three days to get down to West Virginia, and it was late afternoon when I pulled into town. I found a room, then bought in the supplies I would need: extra feed for me and the horses, half a dozen large-scale topo maps, and a few cases of bottled

---

[10] See glossary

water. Then I stocked up on ammo: nine-millimeter mostly, for my pistols and the Uzi. All the other stuff I needed was already in the truck: camouflage suits, bedroll, body bags, and so on. In my line of business, you have to be ready to go any time, any place.

That night in my room, I went through my maps and tried to fix a picture of the terrain in my mind. I pulled out the Area working book and made a note of all the local sheriff's offices and numbers. The last thing before I turned in, I studied the photo of the man I was after. That's one thing you have to have fixed in your head, a picture of your target.

I was up early the next morning. I decided to grab some breakfast before I hit the road, and that's how I ended up sitting there with my red-neck pal. I let him talk some more, then I shoved my platter aside and got a refill of coffee as the waitress squeezed past. 'Yeah, that's really interesting,' I said. 'What you were saying about them, hillbillies.'

It was all the encouragement he needed. He was off on one now. He tapped a nicotine-stained forefinger against his temple. 'You take a people that's been inbreeding amongst their own kind for two centuries,' he said, 'then throw in the moonshine. Hell, it any wonder they're all fucking crazy?'

The man I was after, the man I intended to hunt down and bring back, had been raised in these parts. He'd been described to me as a red-neck hillbilly. He'd also been described as a crazy mothafucker. I didn't go along with that at all. Billy Bob Floyd, 'Bubba,' as they called him, had beaten, then raped a man and ass-raped his wife. Then he'd killed them both in cold blood. If you ask my opinion, those aren't the acts of a crazy mothafucker. They're the work of a perverted evil murdering bastard, pure and simple. Not for the first time, I asked myself, what the hell the American justice system was doing, letting a man like that out on bail while he awaited trial, but my job wasn't to ask questions.

My job was to track him down and bring him in – dead or alive.

As to going into the mountains alone, that wasn't my intention when I set out. The way I saw it, this was a two-man job that may need backup. I had a few contacts back east, and I called every one of them, but despite the high price on Floyd's head, I couldn't persuade anyone to join me. Maybe it was my reputation as a smart-ass Limey, coming over here and trampling all over their territory. I knew what they were saying about me. They'd read the newspaper stories about me. Who did I think I was? Rambo? The fact of the matter was, I did a better job than most of those guys, and they resented it. I commanded a twenty percent cut of the bail bond with a ninety percent recovery rate, whereas most of them only got the regulation ten. So they made their excuses, and when I pushed them, they told me this job was simply too dangerous. They laid it on thick.

Them hillbilly police, they told me, they won't be any damned help to you. They stick with their own. And now, just as I was taking out my wallet and getting ready to pay the waitress, my friend had a parting shot for me. He knew the area well where I was heading for, he said. He'd worked up there, maintaining the county roads, before he bought the bar. 'I seen a few strangers go up in them mountains,' he said. 'Thought they could hack it on their own. I don' believe any one of them ever come back in one piece.' He eased himself out of his seat and placed some money on the table. He told me he was off to the barbershop to get a haircut. Shook my hand and wished me luck. I wiped my hand on my pants and left.

I'd been driving for about an hour. Not long now, and I should find a dirt track that would take me into the woods. Low branches scraped the side of my truck as I made the sharp turn. I bounced along for a mile or so, then swung the rig into a tiny

27

clearing and checked the topo map.[11] I wasn't too far away from where I needed to be, according to the word I'd had from my informant. He had good reason to want to see the back of my man. Floyd had severely beaten up his sister one time then tried to rape her afterward; this guy was itching to get back at him, so his information ought to be good. We had arranged to meet at a remote rendezvous. He gave me the rough details of where Floyd's hideaway was situated. I gave him a down payment of two hundred bucks, with $1300 to come when I brought my skip out, so this guy had every incentive to provide me with reliable information.

I ploughed into the undergrowth forty; maybe fifty yards, then did a u-turn and pulled up. The weather had been warm, but there under the dense foliage, it felt damp and chilly. I got the horses out, and then set about camouflaging the vehicle and trailer with netting and broken branches. With luck, nobody would spot it – at least for the day or two that I'd be gone. I placed an 'X' on the map so that I would find the truck on the way back, and then tied markers onto trees nearby.

I saddled up my new horse. Two Rides then packed my gear onto the pinto. I had two mid-sized waterproof bags containing a bedroll for sleeping in, water bottles, a ghillie-suit,[12] camouflage, and all the other equipment I would need if I were to bring Bubba Floyd to justice. I had a Canon camera with a telescopic lens, a cellular phone – although I'd be damned lucky to get a signal out there in the boonies. I also had my vehicle tracking device and my first-aid kit – everything from ibuprofen to the needle and thread I would use for sewing up any open wounds. No good looking for medical help in that wilderness. If I was going to

---

[11] See glossary
[12] See glossary

28

make it, I'd have to make it on my own. I'd also packed enough meals ready to eat–'MREs'–to keep me and my skip fed until I got him out; these meals are high in protein and low in fibre; they also act as a natural anti-diarrheal, you get bunged up, and you don't shit that often. In places like that, you just don't go lighting up campfires. Plus a little extra feed for the horses. No telling what the grazing would be like, up there.

I was well-armed. Had to be. I had to be ready for any kind of combat or life-threatening situation, although I'd left my favourite Winchester repeating rifle at home on this trip. That was just too damn noisy for this kind of job. Instead, I had the sniper rifle with telescopic sights, an Uzi sub-machine gun, my 9mm pistols, and a revolver – plus silencers. From my belt hung my knife, handcuffs, canteen, spare ammo clips, a bunch of zip- ties, and all the other required tools of the bounty hunters trade.

I loaded up, mounted Two Rides, and with the pinto in tow, I followed a narrow track that snaked through the undergrowth. Soon as I could, I came off that; I then took a compass bearing towards my destination and started cross-country towards Bubba Floyd's location.

By my reckoning, I had a day's ride ahead of me and then some more, most of it through dense woodland. I kept away from the ridgeline and circled the occasional clearing. I rode on until the sun started to dip towards the west. According to the map, I'd covered about fifteen miles or so, still several hours' ride from my target. I found a spot where a little creek ran down the hillside and formed a pool among the rocks. I unsaddled the horses and let them drink, then set down a couple of tubs of feed for them. Later I would let them graze alongside the water. When they were settled, I ate one of my MREs. They call it food, but all it is really is fuel. It isn't designed to tickle your appetite, just to stop your gut from rumbling. Then I spread my bedroll on a bed of leaf-

29

litter.

It was a clear night with a big fat moon rising through the trees. It was quiet at first, just the relaxing sounds of the bubbling and rippling from the stream, then the occasional rustling from the undergrowth, the sound of the horses breathing slow and steady, and the whine of an occasional mosquito. I lay on my back, gazing upwards. I fell in and out of sleep. At one point, I woke up and saw a shooting star blaze across the sky and die. I found myself starting to think about what danger might lie ahead and immediately shoved the thought aside. Whatever happened, I would have to deal with it—no point in sweating. Instead, I relaxed and reflected on the life I was living, a life other men could only dream of doing. Guns, money, and sex-crazed women. Dangerous? Sure it was, but I could live with that. The danger is just the seasoning on a very tasty dish. It comes with freedom. You can't have one without the other.

Later on in the night, I was awoken several times by sudden noises, and each time I grabbed hold of my gun. But it was only critters – an owl, the yip and cackle of a coyote, a horse farting, and the bark of a cougar.

I was in no hurry the next morning. I couldn't imagine a retard like Bubba getting up at the crack of dawn. So it was around eight when I set off, mid-afternoon by the time I finally found his place. I came across it quite suddenly. I heard the dogs barking and then, as I brought the horses to a halt, voices, shouting. I dismounted and wrapped the reins around a tree. Then I smothered my face with camouflage paint and put on the ghillie suit, a sort of uniform with an outer layer of netting, interwoven with cloth leaves in camouflage colours – brown, green, khaki. With that on, I was just about invisible, impossible to spot. With my rifle strapped on my back, I lay on my belly and slowly crawled through the bracken.

It was hot as hell. The ground was covered with weeds, some of them very prickly – and I was continually looking out for poison ivy. At the top of a low ridge, I raised my binoculars to my eyes, swept left and right and left again, and there it was, the hide-out, in a hollow, very hard to see with all the trees around it, and it was just a few hundred yards away.

There were five makeshift shacks or cabins arranged in a sort of semicircle, with five maybe six old scruffy pickup trucks scattered around. To one side, there was an outhouse and a log-shed. In the open space between them was a fire with a spit over it. On the spit was a whole hog, fat dripping off it and bursting into flames as it splashed onto the hot coals. Around it was a whole bunch of odd scruffy people, some shirtless in britches and floppy hats, some holding and waving shotguns – may be in total, there were a dozen or so males and about eight females with kids. They were all singing and dancing. Staggering, more like it. One of them was swigging then passing around a gallon jug. Moonshine, most likely. Another two were playing fiddles – playing them pretty well, in fact. It seemed I'd nearly walked in on a hoedown or a rehearsal for the '*Beverly Hillbillies*' series.

I tried to make myself relax and think of how the hell I would play it in this situation; I was indeed outnumbered. Low as the sun was, the air was still stiflingly hot. I lay on the ground for some time, and then a gentle breeze brought the smell of roasted meat to my nostrils, making my mouth water and reminding me I was hungry. Maybe it was that, which added to my fatigue that brought on the drowsiness.

The sound of gunfire jolted me awake. I ducked down, grabbed my rifle, and lay very still, my face pressed hard into the soil, my heart thumping. Another crack followed a third, then a fourth. I waited, and then I slowly raised myself on my elbows and peered through the bins.[13] Down in the clearing, they were shooting into the sky, whooping, yelling, and dancing, all jiggling their asses. It could've been a bunch of good ol' boys partying with their gals. Except one of them was a dirty murdering bastard.

They stopped dancing and passed the jugs around. I soon spotted my skip getting out of a truck. Bubba looked just like he did in the photo, which isn't always the case. He was taller than his buddies, slimmer too, and his head was shaven. I looked at him through the scope of my rifle and got him right in the crosshairs. Tempting as it was to shoot him there and then, I lowered the gun. There was no way I was going to shoot him, then walk down and explain to his kinfolk that I was taking the body to town. What I needed was to somehow get this sonofabitch on his own.

I took out my camera, zoomed in with the telescopic lens, and got a few good shots of him holding and firing his rifle. It was one of the conditions of this boy's bail: No firearms. If I was going to take him out, I needed evidence that I was in some sort of danger. I snapped a picture of his truck, too, focusing on the licence plate. I'd learned a long time ago that you can't have too much evidence, especially if it ends up in court when some smart-ass lawyer comes chasing after your ass.

After that, it was just a matter of waiting. I crawled to one side to get under the shade of a big old hickory. An hour or so later, I heard a truck firing up and saw my skip drive off with a woman. Fuck, was that it? Surely I wasn't going to lose him after all this? There was no way I could follow him. A deep narrow valley separated us, and I would've had to make a big circle to get over to his side. Besides which, my horses were about played out.

---

[13] See glossary

I needn't have worried. Bubba and the woman were back within half an hour, unloading a few cases of beer and some groceries. That was good news: we weren't very from a town.

I laid there until it got dark, and the insects started biting. Down below, the party seemed to have petered out. They threw the bones of the pig carcass on the fire and left it to die down. One or two couples drove off; the others made for the cabins. My skip was the last to retire, dragged off by his gal, who giggled all the way to the door. Give them twenty minutes, and they'd all be too busy fucking themselves silly to worry about security.

I checked both my pistols, placing them both inside the holsters under my ghillie-suit. The Uzi I strapped to my chest in a combat sling. I filled a canteen with water, put it on my side belt, and then slid the hunting knife into the sheath that lay across my chest and left shoulder. Prepared, you have to be ready. Finally, I slipped the tracking device into a pocket on my trouser leg.

The sky remained clear, and the moon was up again. As I made my way slowly and quietly through the woods down towards the settlement, it was so light I was able to pick out each individual root that lay tangled on the ground. Approaching the clearing, I stashed the Uzi and the canteen under a tree near the cabins, where I could easily find them if I had to make a run for it, then crouched low and moved stealthily across the open ground. Reaching the truck, I rolled onto my back and wormed my way underneath the rear. I pulled out the tracker, switched it on, and placed it under the chassis. The sound as the magnet clunked against the metal made me stiffen. A dog started barking, but it was some way in the distance, maybe even in the next valley. Even so, I drew both my pistols, lay quite still, and took a good look around. Nothing. I worked my way back out and retreated across the open ground to the tree, guzzled about a pint of water; I took out my black rag and dabbed the sweat off my camouflaged face.

Back at my hide-out, I switched on the tracker monitor; the signal was excellent and healthy. Before I turned in, I had one last look at the clearing through the binoculars. There was no movement, no sound. Minutes later, I was in dreamland.

Did I say a dream? I meant a nightmare. A bunch of toothless hillbillies had surrounded me; they all had their tongues pocking out of the missing front teeth, leering at me, with their pants pulled down to their ankles, all standing around me with their dicks out, shaking them and shouting, 'Bend him over, fuck the little piggy make him squeal! Squeal, squeal, little piggy.' It was my own strangled cry for help that woke me up. I reached for my rifle, hoping to Christ I hadn't roused anybody else. I sat and watched the encampment for several minutes but saw no sign of movement, not even a light on in the cabin windows. The air was cooler now, and when I was satisfied, everything was okay; I burrowed back into my sleeping bag.

Dawn was breaking as I crawled slowly through the weeds to the low ridge. From there, I had an unobstructed clear sight of the clearing. It was quiet as a churchyard. I was about to work my way back and fix myself some breakfast when suddenly I saw a cabin door open, and there was my skip walking across to his truck, slinging a couple of holdalls and a rifle in the back. I wondered why he was up so early. Had he not gone to bed? Was he still drunk? Or had he popped some uppers? Maybe. He now looked very busy. His movements were swift. He was clearly fixing to leave this time. I quickly went back and rolled up the bedroll and loaded my gear onto the packhorse. As I saddled up Two Rides, I could hear his truck barking into life. I pulled out the tracker monitor. He was on the move, heading north-east. If he remained off-road or on the dirt tracks, I ought to be able to stick close enough to hold that tracker signal.

I started at a healthy trot, glad to be away from that hillbilly settlement. My skip seemed to keep stopping. I had no idea why, but it made my job of following a lot easier. That whole morning he never moved out of range. My only worry just now was that the tracker had limited battery life.

It got to late afternoon, and my man was still on the move. I was tired, hungry, and thirsty, and I wasn't happy about the weather: a breeze had got up, and dark clouds were spreading in fast from the west. Suddenly it started to rain. The signal was getting steadily weaker. I tried to stay calm. Surely the guy wasn't going to drive all day. No way.

I must have got distracted. Two Rides suddenly stopped dead with a steep drop right in front of him, almost throwing me off. The hillside had been felled a few years previously. The ground was uneven, with a dense covering of young trees and a lot of rotting stumps. The rain was starting to fall heavily. Looking down, all I could see way below me was a creek that snaked through the woods. My tracker told me that Floyd's truck had stopped and was but seven or eight hundred yards away. 'Good boy,' I whispered, leaning forward to pat my horse's neck with my gloved hand. I dismounted, wound the reins around the stem of a tree, and took out my binoculars.

I must have swept over the treetops three or four times before I spotted a thin plume of smoke torn, ragged by the wind. Below I could now just about see the outline of an old cabin, its roof covered with camouflage netting. Hard to spot in the fading light. This boy had his shit together. A few yards to one side, a sudden movement caught my eye. There he was, taking a leak against the woodpile, before zipping up and walking inside.

I untied the horses, gave them some feed, then retreated fifty yards or so to get under cover from the pouring rain. I got into my ghillie suit, ate an MRE, and stuffed a few granola bars in my pocket. If I had to make a run for it, I needed energy. I picked up my sniper rifle, checked that it had plenty of ammo in the magazine, and then grabbed a full canteen and a snack, then headed down the hill. I moved quickly between the saplings, taking care not to snatch at them in case my man happened to look up and see them shaking. Drawing closer to my prey, I now saw his truck, netted like the hut. I found a level spot on the sloping ground, cut away a few strands of undergrowth with my knife, and set up my rifle on its pod. Then I quietly cut out a few of the low branches that impeded my sight-line. By this time, my clothing was soaked, and I was shivering.

The question on my mind now was, had the guy come alone, or was the girl still with him? Or had he dropped her off en route? I guessed I'd find out in the morning. I doubted they would show themselves now that it was getting dark.

I returned to where the horses were picketed and got into my sleeping bag. I slept for several hours but was awake just before it got light. The sky had cleared, but everything was wet. My skip's truck was still where it had been the previous night. Surely it was now a matter of waiting. I checked the cell phone. To my surprise, I got a faint signal. I took out my map and compass and soon had my location figured. That town wasn't too far away, and it had a sheriff's office. Now to grab the items I needed, put my kit on, then head back down the hill to take up my firing position and wait for Bubba to show.

When he finally emerged from the cabin, it looked like he was planning to leave again. He had a rifle strapped on his shoulder and what appeared to be a .357 Magnum pistol in his waistband. He was carrying a large holdall in both arms. There was no way I could let him drive away, as the battery in the tracker was dead. I raised the sights to my right eye and got his head in the crosshairs. I took a deep breath, relaxed as I let it out, and then I squeezed the trigger.

Doof! With the silencer on, nobody but me was going to hear the shot, least of all my target. There was a couple of seconds' pause, then it hit, knocking him backward, the contents of his bag, clothes mostly spilling out around him as he fell hard on his back. 'Fuck it,' I mumbled. 'Missed, I should have brought the Winchester 300 grain ammo with me, for better MOA' (minute of angle accuracy). He was still alive but dazed. I'd missed his head but got him clean through the right shoulder, which was bleeding like crazy.

Bubba looked around, grabbed the revolver from his belt with his good left hand, and started to swing it right and left, trying to figure out where the fuck the shot came from. Before he could even fire off a shot, *doof!* I squeezed off another round that hit the gun and sent it spinning to the ground, out of reach.

The third round smashed into his hand as he clawed, trying to grasp his rifle. I aimed once again, but I could hear him screaming out his pain even from that distance. There was no need to waste another bullet. He couldn't reach the guns. I scanned the area around him. It was clear. Nobody was coming out to his rescue. I homed in on the shack and fired off a couple more rounds, smashing the window beside the door. Nothing! No girlfriend at the window with a gun, no door opening cautiously. The only movement was my skip, writhing slowly on the ground; the only sound was his screams of pain. I peered through the telescopic sights and centered the crosshairs again on his shaven head. Tempting as it was, but no longer necessary to kill him. I stood up and picked up the rifle, checked around me to make sure nobody was creeping up from behind, then picked up all my gear, walked back up the hill to my horses, and got ready to move in on my prey.

I didn't hurry. I wasn't going to take any chances for a worthless piece of shit like Bubba. I took my gold star badge out from the pocket inside my pants and pinned it on my chest. Then I tied the pinto to Two Rides saddle, I put on my black uniform cap and mounted up, with my sniper rifle strapped on my back; I made my way slowly and carefully down the hillside with my pony on tow, shuddering as the wet foliage dripped on the back of my neck. I held the reins in my left hand, in my right the fully loaded Uzi sub-machine gun. As I rode, I unbuttoned the front of my ghillie-suit to display my black bulletproof vest.

Bubba heard me coming. He rolled slightly onto his side to face me. His rifle and his pistol were still where they'd fallen, on the ground and beyond his reach. I raised the Uzi, cocked it, and pointed it at him and then at the shack, just in case someone was still hiding inside. It was a flimsy sort of thing, green mold covered boards warped by age.

'Help me, sir. You gotta help me; I'm bleeding to death.' I looked at him. He was shivering; his face was contorted in pain and fear. His voice was thin and shaky, and there was a large pool of blood on the ground beside him.

'Help me, sir,' he whimpered. 'My gal's carrying a baba.'

I pointed towards the shack. 'She in there?' 'No sir,' he gasped. 'Weren't nobody in there but me. I swear it to ya.'

I looked at his twisted features and evil little eyes, Then I raised the Uzi and fired a few more off at the building, taking out what was left of the front window. Then I dismounted and then walked over towards the cabin door. I gave it a loud kick and shouted, 'If you're in there, come out right now!' There was no answer. 'Or I'll shoot you dead and Bubba too.' I gave it a couple of seconds, then kicked the door open and poked my gun inside. A fat fly droned out and tried to land on my nose. I swatted it away then stepped inside; was a one-room place, scantily furnished. Just a rickety old bed, a rusting old stove, and a couple of shabby armchairs. It was a shit hole in there. Empty cans, discarded broken plates, cigarette ends all over the floor, and dirty clothing draped over the chair—the place stank – of rotten food, piss, and wood smoke. There was a tin mug on the floor. I picked it up and walked back to where Bubba lay on the ground, moaning and whimpering; his face turned again towards me. If I hadn't known he was a murdering rapist, I might have taken pity on him. I went over to where Two Rides and my pony stood and got my first aid kit and some bottled water. I put on my surgical gloves, picked up Bubba's guns, emptied them, and put them into plastic evidence bags.

Bubba was right. He was bleeding to death. I patched him up and stopped the flow of blood. For now, it was the best I could do, then I pulled him up and sat him up against a large tree stump; I tried my cell phone again. Nothing! Not even the faintest hint of a signal.

I took another look at Bubba. His head hung forward, and his breath came in short gasps. Before I tried to get him on the pinto, I cuffed his hands to the front. I could feel his warm breath on my face; it had a horrible sour smell like rotten teeth and gums. I filled the tin mug with water from my bottle and let him slowly sip. The sun was above the trees now, and I could already feel it warming my wet clothes. This was going to be a long day. 'Okay,' I told him, 'you and I are gonna take a little ride.' He didn't answer. As I tried to lift him to his feet, blood started oozing from his wound again. I could feel it on my cheek. I tried once more to stop the bleeding, with the last batch of the sterile dressing I had left in my kit, securing it by wrapping lots of duct tape around his body to pressure his wounds, which helped stop the bleeding for now. I lifted him up again and slowly walked him over to the pony; I struggled and barely managed to lift him onto the saddle.

He seemed to have a little strength in his legs but nothing in his arms. I placed his hands on the pommel.[14] 'You hold on,' I said. He grunted and leaned forward and hung his head down.

Sick as Bubba was, there was no way I was going to rush this. I'd already decided I would take him to that nearby town. It didn't seem to be above five or six miles away. I took it steady, but we hadn't gone far when I heard a loud thump and turned around to see that Bubba had slipped from the saddle and lay in the dirt, motionless. I dismounted and checked his vital signs, I tried to resuscitate him, but he was gone. I tried my cell phone once again. Zilch! I washed the blood from my hands in the creek nearby and then took the horses down to drink at the stream. I sat down and drank some water from my canteen, slowly ate another MRE, and then rested for a while; there was no need to rush now, I brought the horses back. Then I picked Bubba up, slid him across the packhorse, face down, and hog-tied[15] him to the saddle and under the horse's belly. Then I threw a tarp over him and secured it down.

About an hour or so later, I plodded slowly into town; I kept my black cap pulled low over my eyes and held my hand on my pistol in a holster on my belt. Just in case any of the local rednecks decided to challenge me, I slowly rode up to the sheriff's office. I drew a few curious stares from the town folks. I guess it wasn't the sort of sight people saw every day, even in deepest hillbilly country. I showed the sheriff my I.D and federal warrant explained the situation and what I was doing in

Appalachia. I then handed over the custody of the corpse.

He called two deputies out of the office, and we all carried the body inside. I handed over the bag of guns too and got receipts

---

[14] See glossary
[15] See glossary

for them. He told me to grab a coffee from his stove, then I sat down and started filling in a bunch of paperwork, as well as a full report of what had happened.

The sheriff was already talking on the phone to the FBI office and spoke to the agent in charge. Soon they would come here and take over, and that would be me finished.

The sheriff beckoned me over to speak on the phone, stating the feds want to speak to me. They requested my contactor codes:

'Delta ~ Delta ~ Charlie ~ 7707885 ~ Foxtrot ~ Whiskey~ 18937740 ~ Bravo ~ Bravo ~ Foxtrot ~ 10-79 ~ 10-39~ Delta ~ Oscar ~ Alpha ~ 10-24.'

Code translation.

'Delta ~ Dan **Delta** ~ Durass

Charlie ~ Contractor

7707885 ~ (My ID number)

Foxtrot ~ Federal **Whiskey** ~ Warrant

18937740 ~ (Warrant number)

Bravo ~ Billy **Bravo** ~ Bob **Foxtrot** ~ Floyd

10-79 ~ Notify coroner

10-39 ~ Current status

Delta ~ Dead **Oscar** ~ On **Alpha** ~ Arrival

10-24 ~ Assignment completed.'

***

The federal agent on the phone requested that I remain in the vicinity until they got there, which could take about two to three hours; I passed the phone back to the sheriff, got another refill of coffee, and sat back down at the desk to finish off my reports.

It was only when I went to the bathroom that I realised: I still had the dead man's blood on my arms and face. I cleaned myself up and then went outside to find the sheriff patting my saddled horse.

'That's a mighty fine animal ya got,' he said.

'Yeah,' I said, 'I reckon I lucked out with Two Rides.'

'Two Rides?' he asked. 'What kinda name is that?'

'Yeah, it's an odd one,' I said. 'I blame it on the girlfriend.' I didn't explain; without a backward glance, I raised one hand up as I walked across the road to the diner; I was grinning all the way. I'd first gone up to Montana with my girlfriend, the one who'd just ditched me. She was living on the Blackfoot Indian reservation at the time. She had a friend, Lori, a Cree[16] girl, voluptuous, and an absolute stunner who liked to walk around in short skirts. I mean real short miniskirts. And she had a thing about underwear – like never wearing any. She ran a little outfit that supplied horses for fun rides at events and parties. I offered to help out when I was free. Why not? I was into horses – and good-looking, sexy women, especially ones with big bums and tits. One afternoon she asked me if I'd feed the stock while she groomed them. My girl had gone to town for a couple of days to catch up with her folks. I went to the yard, hauled out some hay, grabbed a cold beer, and sat down in the big old barn where she had her mounts stabled. In she came a few minutes later with a currycomb, and when she bent down in front of me to start brushing, she gave me a front-row view of her cute, shapely, naked ass. I knew what she was after, and I made damned sure she got it.

It all ended in tears, as they say, but before it did, we had one hell of a time. Talk about animal passions. This was savage. As we lay there in the barn, exhausted from that first session, she told me about a mustang, a real wild one she had in the corral. Fresh out of the mountains and never been ridden. How could I resist?

---

[16] See glossary

It took a long, long time, but I eventually managed to get the reins over his head and finally persuaded him to let me climb aboard. He tried to bolt; he wanted to throw me; he reared up on his hind legs, but I hung on. Ride 'em, cowboy. By this time, one or two of the hired hands had shown up to watch the paleface at work. When I finally rode him around the perimeter fence, everyone clapped and cheered. I knew word would get back to my girl, but I never let someone else's feelings stand between me and a new conquest back then. Screw it; we weren't married.

Later that night, after Lori and I had fucked ourselves silly, she told me I rode like a true Native. Then she added with a laugh, 'I mean on the horse.' She told me the mustang was mine to go out on whenever I wanted. There was only one condition: whenever I came over, I had to ride her first. Later, when she realised nobody else was ever going to get on that horse, she gave him to me. I decided the horse needed a name – and there was only one choice, 'Two Rides.'

I took a different, longer route back to where I'd left the truck. Time wasn't so much of an issue now, and the fact was I enjoyed being out in the hills on my horse. Sure, it meant another dose of the MRE diet, but that wouldn't kill me. I had a big fat paycheque to pick up. I could then treat myself to juicy T-bone steak and a nice cold beer when I got back to town. Then a good night's sleep before the long drive back to Montana to see my gal if we were still talking. But the first stop on the way back would be at Lori's place, for maybe another long slow ride.

Not Today, Dewayne

It had been a stinking hot August day in the nation's capital city, the sort of day when you can change your shirt three times and still feel like you've slept in it. As darkness fell, the rain started pounding hard on the roof of my Chevy Blazer, and the temperature was down to the low eighties. Lightning was flashing across the rooftops in long, dazzling bursts, slicing through the mellow sounds of the car radio, the thunder following so fast that it all merged together in one glorious chaos of light and sound. It was quite a show, but I was in no mood to appreciate it. I'd been looking for Dewayne Rankin for several weeks, and now I was closing in on him.

I had parked under a burned-out street light, barely thirty yards from the old timber-framed apartments that Rankin had entered with a female, identity unknown, just a short while previously. If I'd been quick enough, I guess I could've taken him right there and then on the street. But it wouldn't have been right. The streets were choked with rush-hour traffic; people were splashing their way across the sidewalk, heads down under their umbrellas, colliding with each other as they sought shelter under the awning of a cramped little liquor and general store. And I knew damned well that Dewayne would be armed. One thing to take a chance when it's just my ass on the line, but you don't go provoking a shoot-out in the street when there are innocent bystanders around. The risk is just too great. The press may have been close to the truth when they labelled me as trigger-happy,

44

but I wasn't crazy. However, it was getting well into the evening, and the streets were more or less deserted. There was now barely any traffic, the sidewalks were clear, and the goods on display in the mom-and-pop joints were hidden behind steel shutters.

Meanwhile, the sounds of sweet romance flowed from the radio like maple syrup from an upturned jug. While I waited, I checked my paperwork to make sure everything was in order. The warrant was in place. That was the main thing. I tucked it into my pocket, then poured the remaining half cup of coffee from the Thermos flask. After I'd drunk the tepid brew, I adjusted the Kevlar baseball cap I was wearing. I knew I'd checked it maybe a dozen times already, but you do these things as a ritual, the same as a pitcher will tug the peak of his cap as he stands on the mound, waiting for the guy at bat to settle. Yet again, I unzipped my jacket and tightened the straps on the Kevlar vest I wore underneath. I reached forward and made sure that my snub-nose .38-calibre special was snug in its ankle holster. Pulling the Sig Sauer 9mm pistol out of my shoulder holster, I checked that there was around in the chamber. And then, ever mindful that I was on my own out here, no backup, no cops to surround the building, no cop cars riding to the rescue, I reassured myself that the two spare clips of ammunition were safely tucked away in my pouch on my shoulder holster. All of this was precautionary, and all of it was based on genuine and reasonable fears. It's a simple matter of your life and death. There were no excuses now—no last-minute checks not been carried out.

On station WBIG-FM, Jon Secada was crooning out some love song about a woman who'd left him. I flipped off the radio dial. A guy like that, he'd find another one soon enough. Then I opened the door and stepped out into the pouring rain to get Joseph Dewayne Rankin.

The boy deserved whatever was coming his way. Some

months previously, he'd walked out of his house on a Friday evening. He was packing a Saturday night special, .32-calibre,[17] semi-automatic pistol, so you can work out what his intentions were. He swung by his buddy Craig's place, and the pair of them headed for a liquor store just a few blocks from home. The cash register was sure to be full, they figured. Easy pickings.

It was Rankin's first attempt at armed robbery, and it wasn't the success he'd been hoping for. He and Craig came away with fifty-four bucks, a few candy bars, and a fit of raging anger. Fuck, this was meant to be easy pickings! They were hurrying along the walkway that led to Rankin's apartment when they ran into a woman who lived in the same block. She was on her way to the super's (superintendent) office to ask him yet again when the plumber was going to come and unblock the waste pipe from her dishwasher. She had popped out in her slippers, carrying just her front door key. The two failed robbers walked past her, then Dewayne swung around and grabbed her from behind. He clamped his left arm around her throat and held the .32 against the right side of her head.

'Gimme all your fuckin' money, or I'll blow your fuckin' brains all over the sidewalk!' he shouted.

'I don't got no money!' she gasped, half choking. And she held out her empty hands, open, palms up. 'Don' have no purse with me.'

Rankin wasn't sure what to do next. He pressed the gun tighter against the woman's temple. As she pleaded with him – 'Believe me, please' – Rankin relaxed his grip. And for the first time that night, he showed he might have an ounce of sense, refusing to take his buddy's advice. 'Smoke her,[18] man, smoke

[17] See glossary
[18] See glossary

her!' the other man was shouting. Dewayne stared at him, then let the woman go, calling after her. 'Yeah, run, bitch, before we put a bullet in the back of ya fuckin' head.'

As she disappeared into the stairwell, Rankin and his buddy left the building and ran across the parking lot. There they got lucky, running into an old man who'd spent the evening playing cards with the other old soldiers at the American Legion. He was walking away with a satisfied grin on his face, having just relieved his fellow vets (veterans) of some $350 at the poker table. As he reached his car and struggled with the lock – he'd won the worthless pile of junk at the tables only a month earlier and had cursed it out every day since – Dewayne and his buddy ran up to him and slammed him against the door, winding him. Dewayne pushed his .32 into the old man's throat.

This time he didn't even have to demand anything. The old man reached into his hip pocket and handed over his bulging wallet. Again, Dewayne's buddy wanted blood. 'Go on, do him! Blow the old fucker away!' he shouted, before whacking the victim across the back of the head and turning to run after his friend.

Later they headed for a neighbouring McDonald's, where they celebrated their big take with a double burger apiece before Dewayne picked a fight with the manager. He assaulted the guy before the astonished gaze of two uniformed cops who'd come in for a coffee. They took them off to be booked and locked up for assault.

It didn't take the cops long to identify Dewayne as the prime suspect in the two other assaults that had been reported that night, and within twenty-four hours, he was under arrest, facing ten years in the slammer. But despite the charges against him and his evident guilt, he would soon be let loose. A few days later, under the good old US of A's criminal justice system, Dewayne and his buddy were released on bail, posted at $125,000. Dewayne's mother, unable to believe that her darling boy could do anything so dreadful as robbing an old man, withdrew her life savings and handed over $12,500 cash to the bondsman. That was only the beginning of her commitment. To ensure that the nineteen-year-old would show up in court and adhere to the various conditions of his bail, she had to sign over the rest of her savings, her car, the home she owned with her husband, and all the valuables they could gather together. A mother's love: it knows no bounds.

Three months later, the Superior Court of Washington for King County reported that Dewayne had failed to appear for his court case. The Superior Court issued an arrest warrant and placed Rankins on the system. That's where I came in. They gave me the usual deadline and a sheaf of papers relevant to the case.

The first move I made was to go round to Dewayne's mother's place and impound her car. She came out of the apartment, shouting and raging and accusing me of theft. It happens all the time. People sign away their property and then forget all about it until their boyfriend, husband, or son goes missing, and then you call round to collect collateral. I explained to her that this was only the beginning and that I now had the power to impound any item she had put up as security – she would also incur storage fees and my recovery fees. She was distraught, as you'd expect her to be, and I had to explain that she had walked into this of her own volition. I added that I had the power to enter her house anytime and hold her at gunpoint while collecting any valuables that might go towards paying off the bond and that this would go on until her beloved son gave himself up. Next up, I told her, her house was in my sights.

Of course, my main concern wasn't to strip this woman of every asset she had worked all her life to accrue; it was to get my hands on Dewayne and bring him to justice. And here I got lucky.

A guy I'd once brought in on a warrant, a small-time drug dealer who had failed to show for a hearing and was in breach of his bail conditions. He was impressed – partly that I had been able to capture him so quickly, but mainly that I'd treated him fairly, as he saw it. So he'd stayed in touch with me, occasionally passing me useful bits of information. Now he called to say that he knew Dewayne had been doing a little trading on his own account. Better still, he knew where he was. 'Yeah,' he said, 'I think I can turn you on to the little fucker. Him and his girlfriend, they're shacking up at her place.' So here I was, a few days later parked across from the apartment house, at the address that my snitch had given me for a few bucks down. In the pissing fucking rain.

I got out of the car, pulled the collar of my jacket up, looked up and down the road one more time, and then crossed, making my way swiftly to the main entrance of the apartment block. There was a security lock on the door, but someone had destroyed it. My information was that the apartment I wanted was on the second floor. There was no elevator, only a single stairwell leading left off the entryway.

I can't deny that I get a bit nervous in situations like these. Ask any military veteran about going into battle. It's the same thing: if you aren't jumpy, there's something wrong with you— your heart's thumping. You suddenly feel like you need a piss, or worse. But, with experience, you learn this is normal. You know to forget it and get on with the job.

The rain was now hammering hard on the roof above me; I could hear it gushing down the over-flowing gutters and splashing to the ground below like the roar of a waterfall. I climbed the wooden stairs, two steps at a time, wincing as they creaked under my feet. I found myself in a long corridor lit by a single bare bulb, moving forward, the numbers on the apartment doors looming out of the half-light, 204, 206, 208, 210, a different

TV station blaring out of each one in turn. I stopped at 214. If my information was right, this was it.

I stepped carefully towards it and put my ear to the door. I could hear the TV, some sort of comedy show. Over the canned laughter, I heard a deep guffaw, joined by the giggling of a woman.

I stepped away, took a deep breath, and drew the 9mm from my shoulder holster. I gently pulled back the slide a tad once again to make absolutely sure there was a round in the chamber. With the pistol in my right hand, I took the doorknob in my left and gave it a very slight turn. Unbelievable! They didn't even lock the door. That boy Dewayne was even dumber than I imagined.

Slowly, very, slowly, I turned the knob. Just the clicking of the tumblers was deafening to my ears; thank God Dewayne and his girl was tuned to the TV, giving out another high-pitched laugh.

Pressing my thumb down, slow and steady, I cocked the hammer on the pistol. Boom! I crashed open the door, lunging forward with my right foot extended to make sure it didn't fly back in my face. I stood, arms straight out in front of me, holding the pistol in the classic double-handed pose.

'Freeze, Dewayne!' I could see his eyes widen as he turned to stare at me. 'You're under arrest. Now put your fucking hands up where I can see them! Now!' I screamed. The girl was facing me too, jaw hanging slack. 'You too, lady hands up!' Then I saw it, a .32mm pistol on the coffee table sticking out from under a newspaper. Dewayne, in shock, still sitting there like somebody had hit him over the head with a baseball bat.

'I said hands up and freeze, you fucking dickhead!' I stepped closer to him, aiming the gun at his forehead. 'Hands up high where I can fucking see them. Come on, fucking move it, dick-brain, or I'll blow your fucking head off! And you, lady, get 'em up! Up!'

They finally did as I told them. 'Now, both of you. Both of you – turn and face the wall. On your knees.' The girl had got the message, okay. She did what I told her to do. Dewayne still hesitated. I saw him glance towards the little table where the gun lay hidden. And then at the badge, I had around my neck. He wasn't sure what I was – a cop, fed, or what? Then his eyes went back to the gun.

'Go on, Dewayne, grab it up. Just try, I'll love to blow your fucking brains out all over the wall.' I could see him, weighing up his chances for a while, then the girl started to blubber. He soon realised the odds weren't good. When that realization hit him, he fell to his knees. As he assumed the prone position, I saw the crotch of his jeans were dark, soaked with piss.

'Okay, flat on the floor. Arms straight out in front! Now!'

As he assumed the position, I turned and kicked the door shut. Not knowing what kind of neighbours he might have in a dump like this.

I cuffed both of them, hands behind their backs, and zip-tied both their ankles together. Then I holstered my pistol and carefully placed the .32cal from the table in a clear evidence bag. I turned the TV off and said, 'Thanks for the cooperation, Dewayne. That's the easiest fifteen grand I'm gonna make this week.'

He didn't like hearing that one bit. 'You're dead meat, you mothafucka,' he mumbled, his face still hard-pressed against the carpeted floor.

I ignored the comment; you get used to the threats in my line of work; I double-locked their cuffs, put on my disposable latex gloves, and frisked them both, tossing the various items onto the table. Dewayne had a roll of 20 dollar bills, some change, a lock knife, wallet, keys, a bag of white powder, a knuckleduster, and two cell phones. After I'd checked the girl, I pulled them both to their feet and pushed them one at a time onto the sofa. 'Do not fucking move,' I told them.

All this time, the girl kept on sniffling and blubbing, but Dewayne was starting to come out of shock. 'Who the fuck do you think you are?' he began to say.

I make a point of never getting into a conversation with scum like him. 'Shut your fucking mouth, scumbag,' was all I had to say, but seeing him about to kick off again, I pulled out a roll of duct tape from my pocket and then sealed his big fat ugly lips for him. I didn't want to hear what the lowlife shit had to say. I took a good look at him— he fitted the mould okay, pale trousers, white shirt, neck-chains, chunky white tennis shoes. His girl was well presented, nice neat figure, a smart red top, and black miniskirt. I turned away from her and glanced around the apartment; there was a phone on the wall. I picked it up and dialled the local cops. I knew their number well enough. 'May I speak to Sergeant Steve Maloney?' I asked in my best English accent. They wanted to know who I was. 'Tell Steve It's Sherlock Holmes. Steve knows me; I'm a, yes, that's right, the English recovery agent.'

I heard the cop on the desk calling out, 'Hey, Steve, it's that limey bounty hunter on the line, you wanna take it?'

'Hey, cocksucker.' I could hear Steve's familiar voice, laughing as he spoke. 'Where you at and what you up to?' 'Just the usual – doing your dirty work for you,' I said. I gave him the address where I was. 'I'm enforcing a warrant for Joseph Dewayne Rankin,' I said, then fished out the warrant and read him the number.

'Yeah, terrific,' he said, 'we'll get a unit out to you right away. Everything okay there? Need me to send an ambulance, coroner, or anything?' 'No nothing, the skips are under control, alive and cuffed. Listen, tell your guys I'm armed, will you? I'll be ready with my ID and the warrant.'

Four cops showed up. Two of them pointed their guns at me. I held up the warrant and my ID. My badge was hanging around my neck. Satisfied that I was legitimate, they checked the captives' ID's then read them their rights. One of them radioed in to check if there were any outstanding warrants on the girl, but she had none. But they informed her they would be taking her in any way, for a statement and possible charges of harbouring a fugitive.

Two of the cops restrained Dewayne, and I retrieved my cuffs, then they put their own ones on him, the same thing with the girl. I also ripped the duct tape from Dwayne's big mouth. Then one of them signed my warrant. 'You have done good,' they said, 'another dumb fuck off the streets.'

They took the prisoners out onto the landing and down to the street. I followed. The rain had almost stopped now, and the atmosphere was steamy. I'd figured Dewayne wouldn't go quietly, but as he was led away to the squad car, he had one more shot for me. 'Hey, mothafucka. You're a dead man walking. You know that?'

I stared him down. 'But not today,' I said. 'Not today.' I then went right up to his face, so close I could feel his lousy breath on my cheek. I was whispering as I laid it on the line. 'You threaten me, Dewayne, and I promise you this. I will hunt you down and fucking kill you in cold blood,' He was still looking for an answer when the cop tugged his arm and shoved him into the vehicle – but not before I repeated out loud what I'd said earlier, with a broad grin on my face. 'But not today, Dewayne, not today.'

Me? Ride Shotgun?

I've heard it said that the harder a person works, the luckier he gets. There is some truth in that, but in my experience, you can give it everything you have – and in the end, you still need a slice of luck. When I first arrived in the States, I'd been working as a private investigator. It paid the bills, but it never looked like giving me the action and adventure I was after. When it wasn't some small business-man who suspected his employees were ripping him off, it would be a guy who thought his wife was cheating on him; or a family trying to trace a missing child. It brought home the bacon. But excitement? The thrill of the chase? No. Mostly I was sitting in my car someplace eating cold pizza, drinking tepid coffee from a Thermos, and pissing into the screw-top container I always had with me. I learned about that the hard way, having almost burst my bladder while I was waiting for some guy to break cover from his girlfriend's house. I didn't sell up a reputable business and crossed the Atlantic to live that way. I needed a break before I went out of my mind.

I was at Jack's Bar. I'd been in there about an hour. I was ready to call it a night and head back to my place. It had been a long day in the Seattle suburbs, staring at some divorcee's front door for eight hours, hoping she'd get off her fat ass and take a trip to the grocery store, the movie theatre, the hairdresser – any damned where so long as it gave me a change of scenery.

She never did, and when I saw her put her lights out, I gave it half an hour, then I was glad to call it a day. It was a beer I wanted, not company. But there was this guy sitting at the next stool who seemed to want to talk. He started with the ball-game on the TV. I never had any great interest in baseball, and I doubt I ever will, but I nodded and agreed with him, hoping he'd go away. Then the news came on, and he started on politics—the same result. I wondered why he was so interested in me. Maybe he was gay. I looked him over. He was tall, with a short haircut. Kind of muscular, except that he had a beer gut. An off-duty cop, I was thinking. I looked around the place and saw that the only other people in there were a couple on a date and some old fart sitting in the corner reading his newspaper, sipping at a glass of iced bourbon. Maybe he was plain lonesome.

'So what do you do for a living?' he asked me.

I hesitated before telling him. The last thing I wanted at that time of night was the same old questions; that people had asked me a dozen times before. Did I carry a gun? What was my most interesting case? Did I ever shoot someone? But he was cool. He told me he was in a similar line.

'Oh yeah?' I said, kind of half interested.

He reached into his pocket and pulled out a badge in the shape of a star. 'I'm a bail enforcement agent,' he said, adding that his name was Dale.

'What's that?' I asked. 'Like a cop?'

He laughed. 'Some people think so, but no – we're what the great TV-watching American public calls a bounty hunter.'

'I've seen them in the movies,' I said. 'Westerns, and so on.' I looked him over and added, 'Except they're usually mean, ugly bastards with long duster coats.' I wouldn't say Dale was handsome, but he was well turned out with regular features. He looked like a perfectly normal kind of guy. You could imagine him selling you a life insurance policy. Dale bought another round of drinks and explained what the job involved. He explained how a suspect could get released from custody, pending a trial in exchange for a sum of money. 'Bail – they can set it at five hundred bucks, but it could be half a million. More than that, sometimes.'

'And if the guy doesn't have the money?' I asked. 'What do they do, lock him up?'

He shook his head. 'The bondsman, my friend. They call in the bondsman. That's a guy who puts up the money and charges the suspect a ten percent fee. Then he walks free until the court case comes up.'

I thought it over for a moment, then said, 'And what if your suspect is guilty and decides to disappear? What then? The bondsman gets screwed, right?'

Dale laughed. 'You got it, bud. But that's where we come in. When a suspect skips bail, the court sets a time limit for him to be brought back into custody. Usually, it's between three and six months. After that, the bondsman forfeits his money.'

'Six months,' I said. 'That's a long time for a criminal to be out and about; he could even leave the country.'

'Yep. And the stats tell us one in four don't show. So let's say the standard bail is a hundred grand. It's generally way lower than that, but let's work on a hundred thousand dollars. So you're a bondsman, you've put up this sum of money, and the guy doesn't show up in court. You're pissed off, right?'

'Damned right,' I said. I could see where this was going; I was all ears. I had been writing to bail bond companies for years, without a single reply. I needed to play this naive and ignorant, so I could find out more about how this bail bond system works, then I might get a start in this business.

'So he hires a bail enforcement officer. If we bring the skip in, we get —'

'A rake-off?'

'Yeah, usually ten percent – plus expenses.' Dale leaned back and stretched. 'But I gotta tell ya, its long hours, you're out there on your own, and a lot of the work is – well, it's flat out boring.'

'You mean like surveillance?' I said.

'Yeah. I guess you know plenty about that.'

'Certainly do,' I said.

'But then there are times it gets pretty hot. Some of these guys you're chasing, they are desperate, they carry guns, and they're not afraid to use them.'

'And what about you?' I asked him. 'What about the bail enforcer?'

'Oh, we carry. Have to. You any good with a gun?' He replied.

'Handy enough,' I said. I wasn't going to tell him any more than he needed to know.

'Licensed?'

'Sure,' I said, 'so tell me about the rewards.' I was now getting really excited like a dog on heat; I could feel this tingle deep in my groin, a bit like I was starting to get a hard while watching a raunchy blue movie. It could be the break I had been searching for.

'Oh, there's good money to be made. Some guys can make a hundred to two hundred grand a year. It depends on how good you are. Listen,' he said, 'time to time, I get a job where I need backup. A guy with your experience, you ought to be able to handle it. What do you think?'

I wouldn't say I bit his hand off, but I made no secret of my interest. 'Okay,' he said. 'Gimme a number where I can reach you.' Then he ran through a list of equipment he recommended I bring with me. I already had most of it, but I made a note to buy a few extra items.

He called a few days later. Said he was about to bring a guy in and needed a backup man to ride shotgun. Was I free the next day? I decided that this was more important than anything in my diary and said, yeah, I was. I don't remember that we discussed money. It wasn't on my mind. All I wanted was to get a taste of it. I hardly slept that night. I was wound up like a watch spring, out of bed at five and getting myself ready.

I guess I should've had breakfast, but I was far too excited. I made do with a coffee, and then another one. I felt as if I was about to enter an action movie where I had a starring role.

After I'd got dressed and was ready to leave the house, I put on my mirrored shades, pinned my investigator's badge to my chest, and stood in front of a full-length mirror in my hallway. I pulled out my pistol and pointed it at my reflection, holding the pose for several seconds. I was embarking on a whole new way of life, and the realisation made my heart beat faster; I could feel that tingle in my pants starting up again.

As I approached the rendezvous, my excitement turned to nervousness. I found myself humming the same damned tune over and over, tapping my fingers on the steering wheel. We'd agreed to meet at some gas station, next to a big shopping mall.

There were no preliminaries. Dale was now businesslike and laconic, from being the chatty laid-back guy he'd been the night we met in the bar. He got into the passenger seat beside me and said, 'Okay, Ted. We'll go through the checklist. Guns?'

I patted my shoulder holster and tugged at my trouser leg, showing him the 38 caliber I carried around my ankle.

He smiled and then continued.

'Mace spray?'

'Check.'

'Handcuffs?'

'Check.'

'Binoculars?'

'Yep.'

'Walkie-talkie switched on?'

I double-checked the switch. 'Yep.' This was in the days before everyone had a cellular phone. The dark ages, you might say. A few people had them, but they weighed half a ton, and if you got a signal, you'd think yourself blessed by the gods.

'Vest on?'

'Oh, yes.'

'Coffee and food?'

'Just coffee.'

He paused, then asked, 'Piss bottle?'

I pointed to the rear seat.

'Okay, bud looks like we're good to go; just remember, don't use our real names on the talkies – just in case.' He pulled a street map from his pocket and showed me where the target's house was. '1625 Adams. It's maybe half a mile, no more. I don't know whether the guy's at home or what, but we're gonna go check it out. The plan's simple enough. I'll take up a position on the street at the front, you'll be at the rear – but we'll both stay well out of sight of the house. Yeah?'

'Got it. Close enough, but not visible.'

'Right. Now, here's our man.' He passed me a photo of a black guy, about thirty years old. He was tall and slim, with a great shock of dreadlocks. 'He drives a gold-coloured Caddy – big funky thing, about fifteen years old. So that's easy to spot. Okay, let's get to work. Talk soon, buddy.'

Two minutes later, I followed him as he swung off the main road into a residential area. It was a decent neighbourhood. Not fancy, but the kind where you'd feel safe walking the streets. Ranch-style bungalows, maybe forty years old, a few tall trees, four-foot wire and small picket fences around the yards, wide alleys behind. I drove slowly, keeping a reasonable distance behind Dale's car. When he turned right into Adams, I carried on past him and entered the alleyway that ran along the houses' back. I stopped fifty yards short of our target between a row of parked cars, switched off the engine, and climbed over into the rear seat. That was one of the first things I'd learned on surveillance, that when people check a parked car, they rarely look to see whether anyone's in the back seat. Then I spoke into the walkie-talkie. 'Are you receiving? – In position. – Over.' Dale grunted an acknowledgement. I placed the receiver on the seat, picked up my binoculars, and scanned the house. The blinds were down on all the windows, and I couldn't see a damned thing.

I was already fully prepared to sit where I was for hours if necessary. Surveillance is a waiting game – and no guarantee that anything will happen. So you learn to relax. Nothing you can do is going to change it.

I soon wished I'd had breakfast, but at least the coffee would keep me awake, or so I thought. As the sun appeared over the roof-tops, I got hot, then tired. I opened my flask and poured myself a mouthful, no more. Way too easy to scald yourself if something kicks off and you have a full mug. I screwed the top back and replaced the flask. And yawned.

The loud thump on the roof of the car nearly stopped my heart. I turned around sharply, reaching inside my shoulder holster for my pistol. Out of the corner of my eye, I saw a sudden flash of something black drop onto the hood. Shit! A cat. The clock showed nine. I'd been there two hours already. I shifted in my seat, working my toes and shoulders to relieve the tension that gave me a stiff neck and the start of a headache.

I've always had a problem ignoring my impulses. If there's trouble, I'm the one who still wades in first. When I heard the low murmur of a car engine and the crunching of loose gravel, I peered over the rear seat and saw a gold Caddy nosing its way around the corner and into the alleyway. By the time it pulled up, I'd slipped into action mode.

'Hey, Bud.' Dale's voice was low but urgent. 'Bud, do you receive? Over.'

'Receiving,' I answered.

'Keep your head down; a Caddy is heading your way.'

'Tell me about it,' I said. 'Caddy's parked outside the fucking house.' I slid down in my seat until my head was below the bottom of the window. My heart was already beating fast. I could hear the blood pounding in my ears.

'Bud, how many? Over.'

I raised myself slowly until I could just see over the dashboard. There were three males, one white guy, two black, and – 'Shit, it's him! The dreadlock guy, it's him. They're sitting in the car – no scrub that, they're getting out. Christ, one of them is carrying a gun. I think. Ah no, maybe a metal bar.'

'I'm on my way,' said Dale.

As I dropped the receiver on the passenger's seat, my legs started shaking, and my mouth was suddenly dry. I tried to bring to mind the calming techniques I'd learned in karate. But that was a theory, in the gymnasium. This was the real deal. There was every chance I was going to have to confront three armed men in a street shoot-out. I took in a slow, deep breath, held it a few seconds then started to let it out. I watched the men slam the car doors and then begin to walk the opposite way from the house to another parked car. Okay, I told myself, here we go. You wanted action; now, you've got it. I drew my gun, double-checked it for ammo, then pulled out my backup pistol and clipped my gold PI's badge onto the front of my vest, then hooked a finger around the door release.

After offering up a silent prayer to my mother in heaven, I got out and moved swiftly along the sidewalk towards some large

61

trees.

'Freeze, motherfuckers!' I bellowed out the order, and the sound of my own voice shook me. It had the same effect on the three guys. They stood perfectly still, then looked around. I was now behind the tree, peering out from around the trunk, both guns pointed directly at them. 'On the fucking sidewalk. Now! Hands up where I can see them. Look straight ahead, not at me!' I took a couple of steps towards them and shouted, 'Okay, I'm only going to say this once before we start shooting; I want you all on your hands and knees. Now! Fucking do it now! Okay, now lie flat. Move! We have you surrounded.'

I was in the zone, acting on instinct, high on adrenaline. I heard footsteps approaching rapidly and swung around; gun held high, ready to fire. It was Dale, standing a few yards away. He glanced at me, then at the three captives, prone on the sidewalk. 'Fucking Jesus,' he said, and then walked forward, training his pistol on them. 'Okay, keep these fuckers covered while I frisk them.' He said. 'Anyone moves, shoot them.'

The guy who'd been brandishing the iron bar was clean. The other two had pistols in their waistbands. I covered Dale as he snapped two pairs of the cuffs on, then I threw him a spare pair of mine. I heard sirens. Two patrol cars swept around the corner and into the alley. 'It's okay,' I shouted. 'The cops are here.'

The captives were seriously pissed off when they heard that. 'Goddam mothafuckin bounty hunters,' one of them said. It seemed the guy was okay with being taken in by the cops, but us? He figured we were a form of low life.

Dale had explained to me about the procedure when the cops showed up. Without him having to say a word, I lay down my guns and put my hands in the air. They checked our IDs, the warrant, and everything was cool, except me. I was awash with sweat and still trembling. So much so that when one of the cops said, 'You done good, feller,' and slapped me on the back, I stumbled and almost fell over. When he got on the radio, he had news for us. 'Those other two guys have warrants and also skipped bail,' he said.

Dale was in like Flynn. 'Which bonding company?' he asked, then nudged me in the ribs and said, 'Shit, we could get ourselves a nice little bonus here.' Then he hissed at me, 'I thought I told you, you were backup? I was waiting for you to call me in, you crazy limey bastard.'

I shrugged my shoulders. 'They were there, and I was ready,' I said. 'Guess I just acted on instinct.'

'Yeah,' he said. 'Yeah, I guess you did okay, but —' I think he was about to read me the riot act, but just then, the cop who'd been on the radio came across and signed the release warrant we needed to get paid.

'And the other two?' Dale asked.

'Sorry guys, but no deal,' the cop said. 'They're from out of state.' That meant he couldn't tell us who had put up the bond.

'Here are their names and warrant numbers if that's gonna help,' said the cop.

'Outstanding,' said Dale.

Suddenly I was feeling deep down good – and deep down hungry. The cops took the captives away, and we drove to a diner. Inside, I sat staring into space; it was like being injected with a drug; I was on a high cloud nine. At the same time, Dale ordered us both a super double brunch with coffee. It was when I saw him nodding appreciatively at our waitress, walking back to the counter, that I realised I hadn't even noticed her. 'Jesus,' I said, following his gaze and taking in her neat figure and sexy walk. 'What a little cracker. I must be losing my grip.'

'So how ya feeling?' Dale asked.

'You mean, apart from horny?' I said.

He ignored my answer. 'Cos I gotta say you handled it like a pro buddy.'

'You want the truth?' I asked. He nodded and grinned like he knew what I was going to say. 'I was scared shitless. I was sure they were gonna pull their guns on me and start shooting. Christ, I was shaking like a leaf.'

'Yeah,' he said, 'and it can happen, believe me.'

'But then,' I said, 'when I got them on the ground – whoa, that was a good feeling. Can't remember when I had such a buzz.'

'That too,' he said and then sniffed. 'Until one day you realise you've gotten used to it.'

We devoured our grub and sat awhile, chewing over the morning's events. I had a chance to study the waitress and made up my mind to ask her out. When Dale paid up, I gave it a go. Made his day when she smiled sweetly and told me she was married.

'Hey, never mind, tough guy, plenty more out there,' he said. 'We got to go collect our dues now.'

We both drove downtown to the bonding company office. It was in a crummy neighbourhood; Dale asked me to watch his car while he went inside and filled in the paperwork. I stood outside under the shade of the awning. When he emerged a few minutes later, he handed me an envelope. It was fatter than I expected, so I slit it open and flipped through a wad of hundred-dollar bills.

'Two fucking grand?' I said. 'For three hours' work?'

Dale just grinned and said, 'They ain't all that easy, trust me. Or that profitable. And if I get a bounty paid for the other two guys, you've got a big bonus to come.'

I walked to my car and opened the door. Then I turned and asked him the only question that was on my mind. 'How do I get into it, this bail enforcement game?'

He shook his head. 'It ain't easy, bud,' he said. 'Ain't easy at all. Listen, most bonding companies go for guys like me. Ex-special forces, ex-police, CIA, or FBI, and so on. In my case, I was in drug enforcement. Plus, they'll always choose a United States citizen over a registered alien. But hey – I can get you plenty more backup work if you want it'.

I thanked him for the offer. 'Yeah,' I said, 'that's fantastic. Give me a call.' But I knew I wasn't going to go down that road. I wasn't cut out to ride shotgun for anybody on this planet. I had my own way of doing things. The way other people work always pisses me off in the end. I needed to be a lone operator. I said goodbye, then got in my car and watched Dale drive off.

I celebrated that night with a few beers, a big juicy steak, and a hot little number I picked up at a club near my hotel. In the morning, after I'd bought her breakfast and sent her on her way, I sat down with the *Yellow Pages* and spent hours calling just about every damned bail bond company listed in the state of Washington. Out of state too.

By mid-morning, I could recite their definitive answer word for word. 'Sorry, we have our own enforcers standing by, but if you put a resume and letters of reference in the mail, we'll keep you on file.'

We'll keep you on file. Jesus, I was more than gutted. I was mad, mad as all hell. But I did as they said. Sent out dozens, maybe hundreds of letters, and waited, and fumed. Didn't they know what I had to offer? Had they got any idea what they were turning down? Just give me a fucking chance, guys; that's all I want. I was seriously pissed off. Working with Dale had got me all steamed up. You know how it is when you find yourself doing something and realise that this, *this* is what you were born to do? Like everything else you ever did in your life was just a series of stepping stones leading you to your true destiny? That's how I was feeling, and the fact that the road ahead was blocked – man, that pissed me off big time.

A Midnight Run

In the end, it was a phone call, and, like so many of life's big moments, it came from out of the blue. It was a guy called Mitch. Said he had his own bail bonding outfit in Seattle, and, glory be, he'd read my resume. Would I drive over for a chat? Drive? I would've fucking crawled there on my hands and knees if he'd asked me. We arranged to meet the following morning at nine. It was quite a way, maybe ninety minutes, two hours in heavy traffic. So I set the alarm for five-thirty and left home an hour later. No way was I going to be late for this. No way at all.

There was a tailback on Interstate 5 that had me banging the steering wheel in frustration and cussing out the other drivers, the highway system, and my damned luck. Then, as suddenly as it had formed, it cleared, and we got rolling at a steady fifty-five. I relaxed a little and took in the colours of a spectacular autumn morning as the sun started to burn off the early mist.

I arrived at the place with time to spare, parked up, and took a look around the neighbourhood. It was strictly low-rent. Metal grilles protected the premises that weren't boarded up. I'm talking thrift stores, loan companies, liquor stores, and fast-food joints run by immigrants, here and there a beer joint. Sidewalk's paved with broken slabs. There was trash in the doorways. Occasional pedestrians scurried by, heads down, despite the fact that the day was warming up nicely.

It was about ten minutes to nine when I walked up to the bonding company door and rang the bell. The door clicked open, and I entered a sort of reception area with a desk on the far side. The girl there took me through an office where half a dozen staff was working at individual desks. She went up to a kind of booth and knocked on the glass door. I followed her inside. A tall, slim guy got up from behind his desk and shook my hand. 'Good morning,' he said, 'I guess you must be Ted. Take a seat. And thank you, Jeannie.' He saw her out, then turned to me and asked, 'Coffee?'

'Sure,' I said. 'That would hit the spot.' He went to a little stove where he had one of those glass jugs brewing with coffee. I tried to act calm and self-confident. The fact was I was wound up like a clock spring.

He gave me a seat across the desk from his. As he poured the coffee into two paper cups, I looked him over. Yeah, he was slim, but he was well muscled. And his suit caught my eye. Nothing flashy, but well-tailored. Charcoal grey with a light blue pinstripe. He had on a white shirt and a dark blue tie, perfectly knotted. His hair was dark, and his skin sallow. Italian, maybe. I relaxed. Forget the neighbourhood: this guy was okay.

He took out a plastic folder and started riffling through the documents inside. 'Oh, I forgot to introduce myself. Mitch Sandford. It's Ted Oliver, right?'

'That's correct,' I said and shook his hand again.

'So remind me,' he said. 'How long you been in the states?'

'On and off, about three years,' I said, and then added, 'but I'm based here now. I've taken up permanent residence.'

He put the folder down. He'd found whatever it was he was looking for. Probably my resume, but I couldn't quite see. 'And you're working as what, some kind of PI?'

'Yes,' I said. 'In Tacoma.'

He picked up his coffee and took a sip. 'Well,' he said, 'I gotta say your resume looks very impressive.' He looked me up and down. 'Got a question for you. You stand what – five-eight, five-nine? A lot of guys we go after are big, mean, and very violent. Could you handle yourself – I mean, if someone gets violent? How would you be in that situation?'

'I'd be fine,' I said. I'd been half-expecting the question to come up and was ready. 'Number one, I work out every day. Strength and stamina, mostly.' I paused. I wanted to know that he was listening. 'I also run two-three times a week, fast – not jogging. I weight train, and I study martial arts.' I reached into the briefcase once more and pulled out my licence from the SKI – Shotokan Karate International, 'Here, I'm also black belt karate, third Dan taking my fourth Dan next month.'

If I had any doubts that he was taking this all on board, he soon answered them. 'You know, we try to bring these people in using no more than necessary force,' he said. 'We aim to get them to jail in one piece uninjured.'

'I understand that,' I said. 'And my skills are all about self-defence, not unprovoked assault. The people who have taught me are big on self-discipline. It's a huge factor in martial arts. Part of their philosophy.'

That seemed to satisfy him. 'Okay,' he said, 'can I see your licence to carry a gun and your concealed weapons permit – and your social security card?' He looked them over and then asked me what weapons I carried.

I pulled out my 9mm Sig Sauer from the shoulder holster, removed the clip, and ejected the round in the chamber before passing it across the desk. He seemed to like that. 'I can see you have been well-trained,' he said. 'Majority of Americans would pass you the gun, and then tell you it's loaded.'

'Not me,' I said. 'Never know if the gun will go off, accidentally or on purpose, then someone gets shot. Safety precaution,' I said.

He handed the weapon back to me. 'And uh – have you a bulletproof vest?' he asked.

'Yes. The best money can buy. Type 111A, American body armour. Guaranteed to stop .357 and .44 Magnum rounds.'

He wanted to know what other guns I used. I listed them all – the .38 snub nose, the Uzi sub-machine gun, 9mm Walther PPK and .45 ACP, or Automatic Colt Pistol, etc. After we'd dealt with the guns – this guy was thorough, and I liked that – he asked me whether I was familiar with American laws and how they varied from State to State. I was able to reel off a whole succession of courses I'd taken, along with my private studies, over the past few years.

Mitch seemed to have made up his mind. He went to his cabinet, pulled out a case file, and handed it to me. I looked at the name on the cover. Jerome Butler.

'Okay,' he said, 'this guy has been on the run for almost three months. He's bonded out on assault, firearms, and drug charges. Now, I've got six bounty hunters working for me, and every one of them is after him. And what have they got? Nothing. Not a goddam sniff.' He looked me right in the eye and said, 'We're down to seven days now. Seven days to find this sonofabitch, or I'm out fifty grand.' I was sitting up in my seat now. It sounded like this was a challenge, and I was up for it. Big time. A chance to show this man what I could do. Confidence in my ability: that's one thing that has never been a problem.

'What I don't want,' Mitch was saying, 'is to be landed with a lawsuit because of some trigger-happy cowboy's ego, exceeding his legal rights. On the other hand, I guess a dead fugitive is worth just as much as a live one. Do I make myself clear?'

'Clear as crystal,' I said. 'And how much do I get paid?'

He seemed surprised by the question. 'You get paid zilch – unless you bring him in. You do that, and I'll pay you twenty percent of the bond plus expenses. This is a commission-only business as far as you guys are concerned. You did know that, didn't you?'

'Sure,' I said. The fact is, Dale had mentioned it to me, but it hadn't really registered. I guess I'd been too excited to take it on board.

Mitch then passed me a document saying, "this is our standard bail recovery contract, please sign on the dotted line; I've crossed out 10% commission and added 20%". I signed on the line; he then went to the Xerox machine and gave me a copy.

'Okay, you do a decent job for me,' he said, 'and I can guarantee there'll be more work coming your way. But right now, I want you to concentrate your mind on Jerome. You have today plus...' He looked at a calendar on the wall beside his desk. 'This is what – the nineteenth? Yeah, we have until the twenty-fifth, midnight. Because once that clock turns twelve, my money's down the toilet – and you've wasted six days of your valuable time.'

'So, when do I get to meet your other six bounty hunters?' I asked. 'To maybe exchange information?' He shook his head. 'From my point of view, that's not a good idea. Not in this case, anyway. I don't want them to know I've got someone else on it. Not yet, anyhow. Here, take this file. Its got photographs and copies of all the original documents. Take it and get to work.' I rose from my seat. 'Oh Ted,' he said, 'one last thing. You ever killed anyone?'

'No,' I replied. 'Not yet.'

'You will,' he said, then paused before adding, 'so good luck.'

As I walked away from the office, I glanced at my watch. Shit, I'd been in there three hours. And what had I learned? Lots, including one major lesson about how the bonding company recovery racket worked. They get a whole bunch of people running around, like headless chickens on their own expenses, and the only one who gets paid is whoever brings the target in – dead or alive. I got in the car headed out of town, putting my foot to the floor as I hit the freeway. Always good to know the score, I thought.

Naturally, I couldn't wait to get started with this guy Jerome Butler. It could be my big break, and the clock was ticking, but right at this moment, I had a surveillance job to finish that I couldn't neglect. That took me most of the rest of the day but, exhausted as I was, I went home and spent the evening reading the files Mitch had given me.

There were many phone numbers in there, and I figured I might as well begin by calling them all. I brewed some coffee, sat in my favourite comfortable chair, and started at the top. I spent two-three hours on the phone and got nowhere. Some numbers were defunct; the rest didn't answer. I went into my little office and dug out my reverse directories.[19] These give you a list of all the numbers in an area, listed sequentially, and the addresses they relate to. They aren't cheap, and I only had ones in the areas I was regularly working, but that included most parts of Seattle and Washington State.

It must have been ten-thirty or eleven when I finished, but I now had a list of addresses for a whole bunch of Jerome's relatives and associates. Late as it was, I decided to go out and see if I could get a head start. I sat for a couple of hours outside his sister's house, watching the door and windows through my infra-red glasses. Nobody came, and nobody went, although the inside lights stayed on, mostly on the ground floor. I decided to raise the stakes, sneaking into her yard and fixing a tracking

---

[19] See glossary

71

device to her car. I also popped an eavesdropping bug on one of the windows. Big mistake. The bitch was into rap and heavy metal, and she liked the sound big and beefy. I had to sit with that shit assaulting my eardrums at 110 decibels until I was begging for mercy. When she finally switched that off it was MTV – and guess what was on. Yep, heavy metal, so even though I was pretty sure she was speaking on the phone, I wasn't getting a damned word of it. I tried taking out my catapult and firing stones at the door to see whether she'd answer. It's an old trick. Glass marbles or ball bearings work, too – although in this case, I guess the music was just too damned loud. She never showed.

Eventually, it went quiet, and all the lights went out. It felt as though I'd wasted the whole evening and half the night, but I reminded myself that the answer is to work harder when things go wrong. I have six days to prove myself, and for six days, I need to work my bollocks off. So I was up at five-thirty to give it another crack. I decided to go back to the guy's sister's house. Call it a hunch; call it dogged persistence. I just figured that was the way to go. If I were wrong, I'd have to try something else.

I'd been there an hour or two when I saw a woman come out of the house with a couple of kids and drive off. School, I guessed, and I was right – more or less. I followed her to the Teeny Tots Nursery and Kindergarten, then back to the house.

It got to lunchtime, and nothing had happened. I'd had enough. I wanted to go home and sit in the bathtub. I was stale, hungry, in need of a toilet, and feeling the effects of that early start. I thought about the fact that all this time, I was earning nothing. It occurred to me that this was why so many enforcers give up on cases. But in my experience, that's the difference between success and failure – the willingness to stick at it. The thought kept me going.

It was around one in the afternoon when the house door

opened, and out she came. She got into her car and set off. I followed at a safe distance. I assumed we were on our way to pick up the kids. Wrong. At the highway, she turned left instead of right. She kept going about ten miles, then pulled up at a run-down motel. Single-storey place, just a few beat-up cars, and trucks parked outside. This looked interesting. I cruised on by, stopped about fifty yards away, and fished out the binoculars. I got them focussed just in time to see her knock on room number; I adjusted the little wheel. Twenty-five. Soon as it opened, she had a quick look around before slipping inside.

She stayed in there an hour, got back in the car, and drove off. I decided to follow her far enough to satisfy myself that she was heading home, then returned to the motel. I parked the car so that I had a comfortable, unobstructed view of the room she'd visited and settled down for a long wait.

It got towards late evening time. I know I nodded off once or twice, but only for a few seconds. I was pretty confident I hadn't missed anything. As night came on, I started to wonder how long I could keep this up. Fortunately, there was a gas station about two hundred yards away, and I was able to use a toilet, buy a hot dog and a coffee cup. Again, fingers crossed that I hadn't missed anything.

A little later, I took out my air rifle from the back of the car, waited until I was sure nobody was around and shot out the nearest of the street lights. I didn't want anybody spotting me.

It must have been eleven o'clock when a large convertible came past me, low-slung with a fancy paint job and loud music pumping out. Music, rap – call it what you will, it was a fucking row. The driver swung in through the motel entrance and parked right next to room twenty-five. He and another guy got out, tapped on the door, and someone let them let in.

Then nothing. Sometimes this is how it usually goes with

surveillance. Minimal action, and just because one thing happens, it doesn't necessarily mean that there will be a follow-up. As far as I knew, those two guys could have been coming to spend the night. In this case, they weren't, but I didn't find that out for another two hours later. When they did re-appear, they had two other guys with them wearing hoodies, with the hoods over their heads. It was way too dark for me to identify any of them, but as they piled into the convertible and took off, at least I managed to get the registration number.

They headed for the freeway, and I followed at a safe distance. The car drove south a couple of exits and turned off into the downtown area. Their destination was a night club, a dingy-looking spot in an all-black neighbourhood. There was no way I was going to follow them inside. I'd most likely be the only white guy there. So I sat at the far end of the lot, and watched, and waited. It was a cold night; My legs and feet were frozen. Rather than sit there with the engine idling – not a good idea when you're trying to remain unobserved – I got out and did a few exercises behind the car. Then back in, trying to stay awake by recycling memories of – hell, girls I'd known, fights I'd had as a youngster.

Tonight was my second late night in a row, and it was a struggle to stay alert. Back to the girls and the red-headed waitress, I'd met a week or so previously. Sheila was a bit on the plump side – not usually the kind I go for, but she had something. I wasn't sure what it was until she asked me if I could give her a ride back to her place. Then it hit me. I mean ka-pow! The girl had energy. She was all over me as we made the short journey, unzipping my pants, and going down on me. I never even asked. The only time she let up was when we hit a junction in the road. 'Which way?' I gasped as she slid her tongue to the top of my erect dick. 'C'mon, before the goddam lights change!' Jesus, it was all I could do to keep the damned car on the road as she brought me to a monumental climax. Luckily for me, Sheila was a swallow-not-spit kind of girl.

We got to her place, went straight upstairs, and hit the hay. She had a super king-sized water bed, a mirror on the ceiling, the whole shebang. Christ knows how long we were at it before I collapsed, exhausted. 'Man,' I said, 'I need to catch up on some zees.'

'You're kidding me, right?' she said and disappeared downstairs. A few minutes later, she re-appeared with a bottle of chilled champagne and a tray of Italian antipasti – Parma ham, olives, fancy cheeses, all that good stuff. 'The chef set it up this afternoon,' she said, 'and then the people never showed up. He was going to throw it out.' She placed it on the dressing table then slipped back into bed. 'Now, how you doing, babe?' She was under the cover, talking to my dick, not me, lifting it between her lips. 'You surely didn't think the show was over, did you? That was just a curtain-raiser. Now, c'mon, let's wake up and stretch ourselves, yeah?' She dragged herself up to meet me face to face. 'So Whaddaya say you little horn dog?'

I put on my best English gentleman voice and answered, 'Whatever you want, my dear. Whatever you so wish. Let's get on with the jolly old show, what?' I almost laughed aloud, thinking about her. She was some woman.

Outside in the parking lot, everything had quietened down. The streets were deserted. There was still no action at the club. In all the time I'd been there, I'd seen maybe half a dozen people arrive, just one couple left. I was starting to wonder. Was I wasting my time? I still didn't know whether the guy I was after was in there. All I was doing was following a hunch based on a suspect's address. But at least I had the licence-plate number of the guy's convertible; I decided to call it a night.

The next morning I ran a check on that. Nothing positive

came up, so I decided to go and talk to the motel manager. He was immediately wary of me. He wasn't going to tell me a damned thing until I pulled out my badge and slammed it hard on the counter. 'You know, if I find that you've been harbouring a fugitive, you're gonna be in some fucking serious trouble,' I shouted at him. 'In fact, I can tell you right now; I'll come back and have this place swarming with feds. Oh yeah, I'll come back – and have this place searched and have you arrested. I'll have your lying ass put in the slammer.'

He didn't look too closely at my private investigator's badge and ID card – not that I gave him more than a few seconds before I withdrew it. The point is it worked. He immediately came over all co-operative, eager to help me. 'Okay,' I said, 'so tell me if you recognise this man.' I showed him the photo of my skip.

'Yeah, sure,' he said. 'He was in room twenty-five. But – but he took off this morning, real early.'

'Where to? Any idea?'

'Yuh, he – um, he mentioned a place along the highway. I mean another motel.'

'Called?' I snapped my fingers at him, like you would a dog, to keep him in line.

'Think I heard him saying to his buddy the Sunrise.' he said. He bent down and opened a desk drawer. 'I got the motel address right here. Yes, sir.' He pulled out a card and handed it to me. 'Anything else I can do for you, officer?'

I wrote him my cell number on a card and tapped the side of my head. 'Eyes and ears,' I said. 'Just keep your eyes and ears open, see or hear anything, call me, eh?'

I got back into the car and made my way to yet another parking lot, stopping on the way to buy a bite at some Mexican drive-through fast food joint. Well, at least it was daylight. If I got a sight of the guy, I'd be able to make a positive identification.

The sun was already blazing, the air had warmed up, and hey, it was another day. Who knows what can happen, I told myself. Think positive.

I hadn't been there five minutes. In fact, I'd only just started eating my bacon and egg burrito when a silver VW Beetle convertible pulled up beside me. I wouldn't have given it a second glance, usually. It's not your average gangsta car, but this one was blaring out some serious hardcore rap. As I looked up to see what the hell kind of idiot this was, I saw the most beautiful sight I'd seen since Sheila skipped across the bedroom, stark naked from the shower demanding one more fuck before I dropped her off at work. It was Jerome. Jerome fucking Butler. You beauty, I muttered beneath my breath, you absolute beauty.

There was no doubting the guy out there. I'd studied that photo in his file long and hard each day since the meeting with Mitch. Yep, this was my man – with two buddies in the car, and it seemed they were all about to get out. I almost had to shake myself into action. It's what happens when you spend days at a time hanging out in parking lots, hunched in your car, when the only exercise you're getting is between the sheets.

Did I weigh up the odds, or did I act on instinct? I couldn't say now, and I certainly couldn't have said then. I threw my burrito into the paper bag and just found myself sliding across to the passenger side of my car. I saw Jerome get out of his driving seat, looking straight at me. I pulled out my cuffs, clipped my badge to my top pocket, popped my radio earpiece into my ear; it wasn't connected to anything. I checked that I had the warrant in the glove compartment – I knew it was completed correctly and logged in the system.

The car door slammed, and Jerome was out, turning to lean back into the car and say something to the other guys. Was I edgy? You bet I was. I was in a black neighbourhood. Jerome was black, and his buddies were black. I needed to act quick, clean, and smooth. I didn't need any screw-ups, noise, or draw too much attention.

So decision time. Should I let Jerome go to his room, or should I go for it with his buddies in the car? I slid my hand inside my jacket and felt the reassuring shape of my favourite weapon, the Sig Sauer 9mm. Reliable, never known to jam.

I was out of the car, right behind him. Before he had time to turn, I'd slapped the cuffs on his left wrist and felt the satisfying click as the lock snapped shut. 'Jerome Butler!' I shouted the words right in his ear. 'You're under arrest.' Then I turned to the guys in the car. 'Everybody! Hands in the air or the snipers will take you all out. Up, you fuckers! I wanna see them hands.' As I barked out the orders, I had my hand inside my jacket. They only hesitated for the half-second it took me to withdraw the weapon. Then they all froze with their hands up. I could see one of them trying to make out what it said on my gold investigator badge. Was it 'police or feds'? He couldn't be sure; the others were looking around for the snipers.

I cuffed Jerome's other wrist, yanked him backwards, and pushed him into the passenger seat of my car. 'Nobody move!' I yelled into the convertible, pointing my pistol in their direction, turning to look around as I backed away. I was conscious of a couple of passers-by hesitating and looking in my direction. There was a young guy, maybe twenty, starting to move towards me from a car in the next row of the parking lot. I flashed my badge. 'It's all under control,' I said. 'Keep back.' He hesitated, looking at the brothers in the VW. 'The man is under arrest,' I shouted, flashing the badge once more. 'So stay back, you hear me?' I was in the car now, firing up the engine. I leaned out and shouted at the guys in the Beetle. 'Keep those hands up where I can see them,' I said, waving my pistol out of the window.' With that, I backed out, swung it towards the exit, and burned rubber as I accelerated away.

Oh man, did I feel good? Way beyond good. I was high as a kite, suddenly braking as I realised I'd crashed way through the speed limit. Slow down, I was telling myself. Slow fucking down. You've done it, baby, and hooked your fish. This was some kick, and I was getting a severe charge of adrenaline pumping through my veins.

As I drove towards town, I wanted to laugh like a maniac. You couldn't beat this feeling. All those hours, I was sitting outside Jerome's sister's house, freezing my nuts off while she tried to drive me insane with her fucking rap. Man, it was worth every minute for the high I was getting right now. And still to come – payday. Bring it on, baby. I glanced across at Jerome, sitting there grimacing as he wriggled around on the seat, trying to get into a comfortable position.

'You okay, Jerome?'

He looked at me, his forehead lined in perplexity. 'Sure I'm okay, man, except I near fucking pissed my pants. Where you taking me, bro?'

'We're taking a ride to the precinct, buddy boy. Then soon as I hand you over to the boys in blue and get my warrant signed, I'm back to the bonding company to collect my fee.'

'Aw shit, man, you a fucking bounty hunter? I thought you was a fed. Aw shit, pushed around by a fucking bounty hunter! I don' believe it.'

'Enough of the disrespect, Jerome. I'm doing my job, and you're going where you belong, so why not shut the fuck up and enjoy the ride, okay?'

But Jerome wasn't ready to shut up. 'So how much they pay you, man?' he asked. 'Three grand? Four? Five? Tell me, man. I'll double it! You take these cuffs off, and I'll take you to the cash right now. You can name your price.'

'I ain't dealing,' I said. 'I don't want your dirty stinking drug money. You can stick that up your fucking arse. My money's clean, and that matters to me.'

'Shit, man. C'mon,' he whined. 'Let's deal. We can do a deal. And who's gonna know?'

I braked, pulled over, and turned around to face him. 'That's enough,' I said. 'Any more of that, and you'll be licking the fucking glue off a strip of duct tape. You got that?'

We got downtown in silence. The paperwork took a lot longer than I'd expected. As this was the first time, I'd handed a prisoner in on my own. Soon as I had finished, I called Mitch. 'Got some news for you,' I said. 'Your man Jerome Butler? He's in the slammer. So, uh, do you pay cash or cheque?'

There was a moment's silence, then he said, 'Ted, tell me you're not putting me on here.'

'That ain't my style, Mitch, as you will no doubt learn. Trust me, the boy's behind bars, and I'm on my way to see you with a seriously itchy palm.'

'I'll be waiting for you.' Said Mitch.

When I showed up, he was still shaking his head in disbelief. 'God damn,' he said. 'I just got off the phone to the cops who are holding Butler. So tell me, who'd you have working with you? You get one of my other boys involved?'

'I don't get what you're asking,' I said. 'It was just me. You said not to contact your other guys. So why would I?'

'Now you are shitting me,' he said. He looked me right in the eyes, then asked, 'Aren't you?'

I couldn't help laughing. 'No, I'm not. I hunted, tracked Jerome down, and took him. Simple as that.'

'So you're telling me I've had all those bounty hunters,' Mitch said, 'some with years of experience, and in three months, they never even got close to the guy. Then you come along and what, in less than four days, and you nail the sonofabitch and on your own? Damn!'

The good feeling was lasting. It got even better when Mitch wrote me a check for ten thousand bucks, plus a few more for expenses. After he'd settled up, Mitch told me he would be away for a week or so at a bonding convention in LA – a sort of annual get-together for all the bail bond companies in the States. He said he'd get in touch with me when he returned and would defiantly have a lot more work for me.

I thanked him and drove home. He had only been away for a few days when my phone suddenly started ringing none stop. He'd been telling all his bail bonding buddies down in LA about this crazy Limey, new to the job and working wonders. Now they were all lining up to ask if I was free to work for them. I told some I might be. Others I kept waiting. Why not? Some of these were the same arrogant bastards who'd told me they'd keep me on file, months maybe years ago. And now, it seemed, I was a wanted man. I could more or less guarantee the end result. I was riding a wave of self-confidence. At last, Ted Oliver, the bounty hunter, was now open for business.

Down Below the Border

As a Federal bail agent working on FBI warrants, you try to work within the law, and you try your best to uphold the law. You don't step outside of the boundaries. Unless, of course, you are an undercover contractor working for the feds. Your work sometimes has to work outside the edges of the law, especially when something different comes up. Something extraordinary that takes you across the border to another country where different rules and regulations apply.

I mean somewhere like Mexico. I'd never been to Mexico, but I'd just done a job in El Paso and got talking to a few guys who knew how it was over the border. They made it sound like a regular playground. Hot weather, hot food. Hot girls too. And everything cheaper than back home. So when a bondsman that writes federal bail working out of Albuquerque offered me a job down there, of course, I would think about it. I thought about it for fifteen seconds and then decided I would turn him down flat.

'Why?' he asked. 'What you scared of?'

'Couple of things,' I answered. 'One, I've heard enough about the Mexican police. Bent as a nine-bob note, every single one of them. Number two, the jails – they're complete rat-infested shitholes, aren't they? And those perverted guards. People get thrown in those places, guilty or not, and just die.'

The bondsman listened to what I had to say, then started talking about money. 'Listen,' he said, 'I got two skips on the run in old Mexico, each with a $250,000 price on his head. If they stay down there, it could hurt me, big time.' He paused before adding, 'So I'm prepared to offer a little more. How would a twenty percent commission payday grab you?' Later, when my reputation had spread, I would always command that. Right now, it was a desirable proposition. It added up to quite a lucrative payday: $100,000 plus expenses.

I started to go through it in my head, thinking over the practicalities. It wasn't very long before I realised this wasn't something I could risk on my own. The problem was, finding someone I know who would put his ass on the line for a job like this? I'd got to know several other bounty hunters by now, and most of them I didn't care for too much. I mean the kind you had to go and clean up after – the gung-ho type who thought they knew it all, but they were nothing but a goddam menace. I'm talking about guys who like to work in partnership because they're crap at their job; they want someone else to do the brain work, take responsibility for the planning while they wave a gun and strut around looking like a superhero. But there were a couple of guys I felt I could trust.

One such guy was Hanson. I'd met him a few times, and he struck me as dependable. We'd traded information, worked with one or two of the same informants, occasionally relaxed over a beer when we came across each other at a bonding office.[20] I got the impression he came from the same mould as me, that he was a man who trusted himself better than any sidekick. There was an issue, however, and I was aware of it. Hanson was a short, stocky guy, with an even shorter temper. I'd heard through the grapevine that he'd made plenty of successful arrests, but also one or two where he'd screwed up, big time. The word was that Hanson would blow his top when the pressure was on. On the flip side,

---

[20] See glossary

he was one tough sonofabitch, an ex-Marine, and hard as nails. The more I thought about it, the more I saw him as a possible partner. This job in Mexico was the sort of gig that may require a team of three or even four, but I didn't trust groups. It's too easy for confidentiality to be breached and also too easy for communications to break down. So it would have to be Hanson and me – that's if he was willing.

I told the bondsman I was very interested but needed to see whether I could get a team I could trust together. Then I gave Hanson a call, and as luck would have it, he was free. I didn't give him any details, just explained that I had a proposition, a job we might do together for easy money. I didn't say how much at this stage.

He was keen to work with me. He knew that the word panic was never in my vocabulary. He was living in Las Cruces, and I told him I'd drive down. He suggested I come to a little town called Anthony, just north of El Paso. He told me he knew a place there, a mom-and-pop joint that served good Mexican food. I travelled early morning and met him after the breakfast rush, before the place filled up with lunch customers. We got a large corner table where I could lay out a few photos and documents, to give him an idea of what was involved. First, we sat and ate. Damn, it was good. I remember eating *huevos rancheros*, the eggs nice and creamy with plenty of good green chillies. Hell, they have vast fields of it down there; it ought to be good.

Hanson liked the look of the job – and naturally enough, the sound of the money. He was in for fifty percent of the bounty. We shook hands and agreed to meet up the next day at his place and start some serious planning. It was the first of several planning sessions. He put on a few beers and a big bowl of chips and salsa. The first issue I had to raise was the fact that we would be bringing these guys back across the border illegally. Did he

84

understand that? Did he have a problem with it?

'Lemme get this straight,' Hanson said. 'This is, like, we're kidnapping these motherfuckers?'

'I wouldn't put it that way,' I said. 'But yeah, I mean... they aren't gonna come willingly, are they? So sure, a little coercion will have to be involved.' 'So we're gonna bring them back across the border without – uh, without their consent?'

'That's what it's going to boil down to in the end. Does it bother you?'

'Hell, no. Just wanna make sure we're talking the same language here.' Hanson grinned at me. 'Tell ya the truth. It sounds like a regular caper.'

'Yeah. Just a little matter of taking two wanted, drug dealing US citizens across the border against their will. But hey, I enjoy a challenge, don't you?'

We started chewing it over. We both knew the high risks involved. The first thing we had to do was figure out the best way to transport our two skips – once we'd found them, that is. We soon came to the conclusion that they'd have to be drugged, tied up, and secured, in some case, pretty much the way you'd transport a consignment of guns. From there, it didn't take us long to come up with the idea of a special compartment on the floor of my truck.

We sat there, eating and drinking our beer, sketching out the dimensions. It was going to be a tight fit. It had to take two prisoners and not suffocate them. It had to look normal, even though we would be putting a pile of clothing, cases, etc. On top of the wooden case. The idea is to look like we were just a couple of regular guys returning from a vacation down below the border. So, ventilation: we needed to think about that.

Hanson wanted to know what else we'd be taking with us. 'Well,' I said, 'we can't take any guns. No way are we carrying them across the border in case we get searched.'

'You mean we buy them down in Mexico?' Hanson didn't look happy. 'Can we do that?'

'Don't worry,' I said. 'The bondsman's on the case. The guy we meet down there, he'll supply us. It's all taken care of.'

'And who's the bondsman? Do we get to meet him?'

'Monday. We're going to meet him on Monday. Guy called Ramon.' We also had to spend the next few days in a fully equipped garage I rented, refitting my truck ready for the job.

We eventually met him in downtown Laredo, at his other office. He was an American citizen but born in Mexico. He still had plenty of family – and contacts in Mexico. He explained a few Mexican law points, the first being that there's no assumption that you're innocent until proven guilty, and it's not uncommon to be held in jail for up to a year before they even get you a court date. On top of this, foreign nationals do not get bail. That was the bad news. The good news was the fee for this case, which, he confirmed, would be $100,000 plus expenses – and the costs would be considerable since a lot of palms had to be greased in Mexico. But we didn't need to worry about that side of things. His people were going to set all that up. They would also recruit a reliable scout, or guide, who would lead us to the skips and then back into the free zone.

The free zone is a swathe of land about twenty kilometres wide to the south of the border. The US and Mexican authorities have set up many factories there, with significant tax breaks to encourage cross-border trade. It's a kind of no-man's-land. Foreigners living there have far fewer restrictions on their activities. If you're travelling south, as we were, the chances are you won't be subject to any severe customs inspection until you get through the free zone into proper Mexico. There's a lot more I could say about the planning of this job, but even now, I would worry about implicating some of the high-level people who helped us. Take it from me. Money changed hands down the line.

Before we crossed into Mexico, I had to drive my truck to an address stateside where we could leave all our paperwork and warrants, ready for when we got back. Amongst the papers we had to have with us were tourist cards or FMTs – it stands for *Folleto De Migración Turistica*. Ramon warned us that each of us needed to keep our US passport with us at all times, as well as our driver's licence and a few other personal papers. Still, he drilled into us that we were not to be in possession of anything resembling an arrest warrant, which would immediately arouse the border guards' suspicions about our reasons for being in the country; nor in our possession any case notes or profiles of the skips. Anything we needed to know, we'd better remember it before we set off. And if we got caught, we were on our own.

Ramon planned that Hanson and I cross the border in my truck, leave it in the free zone, and switch to a local vehicle he had lined up. Our US insurance was of no use in Mexico. One more thing Ramon impressed on us was not to pick up any female hitch-hikers. 'You'll see 'em,' he said with a grin. 'Sexy, good-looking girls. Plenty of them. But keep away from them. This is work, not a vacation.'

Of course, he was right, but as I said to Hanson when we left the office, 'No reason why we shouldn't have a little fun along while we are there.' So we went to Walgreens and stocked up with a few packs of condoms. This was Hanson's idea. 'Quality American products,' he said, 'not those frigging re-treads they sell down in Mexico. I heard all I wanna know about those mothers.'

Back in my hotel room that night, I thought the whole thing over. We were well prepared. We needed to be. I didn't know I'd overlooked anything, and I'd considered all the dangers. The two skips we were going after were known drug addicts. They may be armed, and they wouldn't hesitate to open fire if they thought they were in danger of being re-captured. But I'd already been in that situation a few times, and so had Hanson. Hell, the guy had fought in Nam. Taking the skips wasn't the issue here. In that, we were confident. Getting them back across the border and into US custody that's what was bothering me. If officials caught us in Mexico with illegal firearms, we would be in trouble. But if the officials stopped the vehicle and they found these two guys hidden, handcuffed, and kidnapped, then any firearms rap would look like a speeding ticket in comparison. For kidnapping, we'd be looking at years, maybe decades in some dirty filthy slime-pit Mexican jail. I didn't even want to think about the company we'd be keeping.

So, why do it? Money was obviously a big draw, but even so, it was a crazy undertaking. When I thought over the possible outcomes, it was one nightmare scenario after another. As I sat in my motel room in Laredo, I realized that that was the whole point. The more dangerous it sounded, the more I wanted it, and I had to accept the risks – the consequences and, of course, the possibility of a shoot-out. It was a thrill thing. I wanted thrills, and I wanted excitement. I looked in the mirror, narrowed my eyes at my reflection. I knew that I was looking at a guy who was addicted to the danger. It's the thing that was always guaranteed to light me up and turn me into the resolute, unforgiving machine I liked to be.

I lay back on my bed and tried, just once, to see whether I could talk myself out of this. Supposing I did turn it down. What would that say about me? That I was scared? No, that wasn't the problem. I knew I was scared. Shit scared. The thought of doing time in some remote shithole prison somewhere in Mexico, with a fat leering jailer, a bed crawling with lice and roaches – yes, sure, that brought me out in a cold sweat. But there was another fear tightening its grip on my stomach. The fear of living out my days in the knowledge that I'd walked away from a challenge. That I'd turned down the chance of an action-adventure such as few men ever know.

I went to the fridge and got out a beer. Besides, I told myself as I held the chilled bottle in my hands and twisted the top off, whoever said this would end badly? Think positive. You can do it, man. If I was putting my reputation on the line, along with my freedom, I knew damned well what I was doing. I was building that reputation. Even at this early stage, a part of my mind had leaped ahead of me, imagining the thing unfolding. And that part of me couldn't wait to tell people about it one day. Already a part of me was writing the stories I'd be telling once it was over.

We had to wait until our bondsman was ready to go. It was only a couple of days but the time dragged on. Laredo isn't a bad place, but the temptation was to hang out in bars and chase women. So I was relieved when I got the call. I contacted Hanson, and together we drove down toward the border to meet Ramon. He picked us up outside the old Spanish cathedral. 'We're gonna take a look at the border,' he said. He drove us out of town. Pretty soon, we were on a bumpy track, ploughing through the long grass where we could see the old Rio Grande. It wasn't what I was expecting. It was mostly mud and scrubby trees and a few murky trickles of water – and in the *bosque*,[21] the chewed-up dirt where the border patrol had been doing their rounds in 4x4s. Beyond this so-called river was Mexico. I had no idea yet what that would be like; just a few ideas picked up off crummy westerns, cartoons, and the kind of crap people talk in bars. Ramon briefed us further, then led us back to town to the place

---

[21] See glossary

where we would store everything we didn't need until we got back. Then he wished us luck.

'Don't you fucking worry,' I said. 'We'll be okay. Just make sure you got your checkbook ready when we call by with your skips, eh?' Ramon had three manila envelopes, all sealed and marked with a set of initials. 'These are for the people we're paying off over there,' he said. 'This one's for the guide, this one for the weapons guy. And this,' he said, handing me the biggest of the three, 'this is for the border guard Jose Antonio, the password is, Goodbye and adios Jose.'

Ramon also told us to give the keys, any guns, and all the skips personnel documents to Rudy or Jamie before leaving the area. Some Biohazard clean-up team will go in after leaving to remove any vehicles and remove any prints, blood, and bodily fluids. There would be no evidence of anybody ever being there. We shook hands, got back in the truck, and drove into town. An hour later, Hanson and I were approaching the border crossing that would take us into Mexico.

We could see right away; this was going to take some time. There must have been eight, maybe ten lanes, plus the ones dedicated to the trucks. People were walking around, smoking, sipping cold drinks as they waited for the line to inch forward, one vehicle at a time.

'Why so goddam slow?' Hanson said. 'I mean, what they so worried about? It's the fuckers coming the other way they wanna be questioning.'

I had no idea. I just kept quiet.

When we got to the booth, the United States Border Patrol officer wanted to know all about us. She was a small, dark Irish woman with green eyes. I don't mean natural; these were bright, emerald green. She was wearing those tinted contacts, and it made her look kind of spooky. Her questions came thick and fast.

Why were we going to Mexico? How long would we be gone? What were we going to do down there? Were we related?

We were going for a week, maybe two, we told her. You sure? Depends on how long the money lasts, we said with a laugh. Hey, we're just two old buddies off on a vacation trip. Surely she could see that from our loud shirts and big grins and Disney hats? 'Are you carrying any guns?' she asked. 'Drugs?'

'No, sir – I mean ma'am,' I replied. It was quite a grilling like they suspected there was something a bit odd about us but couldn't nail it. We just sat there while she examined our passports and answered all her questions friendly and politely. Then she glanced around inside the truck and told us to go ahead. Even wished us a good time.

'Jesus, what the fuck happens on the other side? If I don't make it back, remember you are the one who talked me into coming. Can you live with that? Hanson said.

'Yes, of course, I will lose a night's sleep.' I said. But we needn't have worried. As we approached the barrier, the guy just raised it and waved us through, no questions asked.

It didn't take us very long to get to our first destination; we had our first name – Pedro – and an address in the country, just inside the free zone. It was maybe half an hour's drive. At first sight, it was just some little old adobe[22] place straight out of a comic strip. It had a flat roof with vigars[23] protruding along the top of the house. Strings of blood-red chilli peppers hung from a beam over the porch. There was even an old sombrero hanging from a nail at the door. To one side was a corral with a couple of horses stirring up the dust. We parked the truck, not knowing what to expect, and stepped out into the sunlight.

---

[22] See glossary
[23] See glossary

'Jesus, that's hot.' Hanson winced as he caught his forearm on the door. As we approached the house, the door creaked open, and a man stepped through the fly-screen. He had a large belly and a drooping black moustache. '*Hola,*' he said and gestured us inside.

It was cool in there, a large fan circling lazily under a low, white ceiling. It was nicer than I expected. Clean, with a basket of fresh peaches on a scrubbed pine table.

'*Sintese,*' the guy said. 'Seet down.' He placed two bottles of beer in front of us, each with a slice of lime wedged onto the neck. He clicked his fingers, and two gorgeous young women came in from a room out the back, carrying a plate of chips and a bowl of salsa.

'*Algo a comer?* You wan' eat?' our host asked. 'My daughters, they bring you something.'

'Sure,' I said. 'I'm kind of hungry.' I glanced at Hanson, who nodded. 'Me too,' he said.

The girls went out and returned with two trays of food, a proper meal: Carne asada, tortillas, tacos, and a big bowl of salsa and guacamole.

'*Mis hijas,*' he said. 'Yolande and Francesca.' Then he turned to them and spoke in Spanish. The only word I could make out was '*amigos.*'

'I tell them you ol' friends,' he said. 'From Texas.'

We all ate together, his wife too. She never said anything, just served the food and looked us over as we talked with her husband. After the meal, the girls brought us coffee and disappeared out the back with Mama.

Pedro's English wasn't the best, but he spoke slowly, and his message was simple enough. The place where the skips were hiding out was a fair way away, some town called Le Ferreria on the far side of Durango. It was maybe a day or two's drive. They were regularly staying separately at temporary places in the town, but they had a regular place they were staying at with all their gear stored, but nobody knew exactly where. But at least there were a few addresses we could try. Nobody was sure which one they'd be at when we got there. It wasn't going to be easy. Pedro added that he didn't think the skips would be expecting a visit. 'Those *cabrones*,' he said, 'they don' think' – and he gestured at us – 'They got no idea.' He meant that this would be the last thing on their mind. The idea of some guys coming all the way from the States and kidnapping them – why, would they even think of such a thing? It was good to hear that. We would have the surprise element. Besides, Pedro added, they were both addicts. Half the time, they'd be out of it. '*Loco*,' he said, tapping his forehead.

Pedro gave us a room for the night. The next day he made the calls and set up a rendezvous with our contact in Saltillo, which is on Monterrey's far side. Ramon had brought to us in a large holder. We sorted through all the gear Inside. There were photographs of the skips, and a whole load of gear, cuffs, bulletproof vests, a vintage car tracker, lock-picking tools, combat knives, four walkie-talkies, binoculars, two rolls of duct tape, and six black balaclavas – the type that covers your full face, with holes for your eyes, nose, and mouth. But no guns yet, which bugged me. We packed everything into a big canvas bag, loaded it onto Pedro's truck, and set off for the customs post at the point where the free zone ended. The guys at the barriers didn't delay us, not for a minute. They seemed to know Pedro. It was all smiles, a big wave, and off you go.

It was midsummer, and the sun was almost directly overhead. Jesus, it was hot. We had the AC full-on, but it was blowing out tepid air. When we asked Pedro what was wrong with it, he shrugged, gave it a whack, and opened the windows. So we sweated and slid about in the plastic seats, the rush of air from outside bringing in dust and the occasional insect, but precious little relief.

As we were driving, we started seeing many hitch-hikers, amongst them some pretty young hot-looking women. I nudged Hanson and pointed at them. Pedro saw me and held up his hand. 'They steal everythin',' he said. 'You find some nice *chiquitas* in Saltillo. Nice girls. *Muy linda.* Very cute.' He added that we needed to watch out for *Bandidos* along the highway. I didn't like the sound of that. Without a gun strapped to my side, I felt naked. Vulnerable too. Despite having Hanson and Pedro for company, I felt very alone. This was the first time I'd crossed into Latin America, and I was edgy. I think I was afraid, but not sure what of. Whatever we had to do, I wanted to get on with it and get it over.

In Saltillo, we met up with Pedro's contacts, Rudy and Jaime. I wasn't crazy about them, and neither was Hanson. 'They don' even speak English,' Hanson muttered when we were introduced. They did, but not too well. They seemed to be having some kind of disagreement and were shouting at each other in Spanish.

I asked Pedro, 'What the hell's going on with these guys?'

'We got us a leedle *problemo*,' he said. It seemed the guns hadn't arrived yet. 'We stay here tonight,' he said. I looked at Hanson, and he shrugged. 'SNAFU.[24] Just like the goddam movies,' was all he said. We didn't argue with Pedro. It was late. Hanson and I got a room apiece. After we had showered, we checked out our surroundings. There was a nice little *cantina* across the road. It looked busy, and there was loud music blaring out through the open doorway, with a bunch of Mexican girls lined up to go in. Pretty ones too. Hanson and I looked at each other, then back at the girls. He raised an eyebrow. 'Hell yeah,' I

---

[24] See glossary

said.

We were soon on our way, smelling sweet and all dressed up in our best shirts. Pedro and our two guides came with us. They seemed to have quit squabbling, and we're talking food. Inside, we left them to order, got a couple of beers, and checked the place out.

It was packed, and it was hard not to bump against people as we made our way back to our table. The place was a proper Mexican joint. They had every wall decorated with pictures of bullfights; they had cactuses in huge earthenware pots. Above us, sombreros hung from heavy wooden beams. Over by the stage, a Mexican mariachi band was belting out romantic songs. We spotted a couple of local girls giving us the once-over. They were dark-eyed and pretty, with bright red lips, and were dressed in short, short dresses with low-cut tops. They couldn't have been more than eighteen or nineteen years old. As we walked towards them, they grabbed a table and shoved a couple of spare chairs towards us.

'Looks promising,' I said; we asked the girls if we could join them. It wasn't as if they had anything else on their minds. They spoke enough English to get by. The girls explained the menu for us, helped us order; we got up and danced. My girl, Rosita, pressed her body close to mine. I ran my hands up and down her sides, over her voluptuous curves, letting my fingers rest on her sexy ass.

When we all sat down to eat, she shifted her chair up very close to mine, her warm thigh pressed against mine. She was one of those women who seem to radiate heat from between their legs. Later, when the band started to pack up, and people began to leave, we invited the girls back to our place for a nightcap. Not that the nightcap ever happened. As we approached our rooms, Rosita shoved her friend towards Hanson's door, grabbed my arm, and steered me towards mine.

Sometime in the night, somewhere between waking and sleeping, I felt her slip out of bed and go to the door. I wondered what the hell was going on. I reached for my gun, then realised I still didn't have one. But as the door opened, there was Hanson's girl exchanging a quiet word with Rosita. Next moment Josefina was worming her way across the bed towards me, reaching out to see whether she could get a response from my weary dick.

The next morning we took their contact details, said our farewells, and told the girls we'd be back in a day or two. Then it was down to business. Pedro had told us we were meeting up later that evening with Jaime and Rudy. We'd be leaving early the following morning to meet our guide.

While we were talking, the guy with the guns turned up. He called himself Jojo and was all smiles, especially when I reached into my pocket and pulled out his envelope.

'Let's see the merchandise first,' Hanson said. The guy had a pair of Smith & Wesson nine-millimeter pieces, both with a full clip of ammo for us, and there were three revolvers with bullets for the others. I'd felt edgy the past twenty-four hours without a weapon on my belt. Did this feel any better? Not a lot. It was as if I'd put on a pair of underpants and not much else. They were sorry-looking pieces, but after checking them, they seemed to function okay.

A little while later in the evening, our guide arrived and introduced himself. 'My name, *eet ees* Hondo,' he said.

Hanson laughed out loud. 'Jesus, I saw that movie,' he said. 'Big John Wayne.'

The little fellow just grinned and said, '*Si*. John Wayne,' and nodded at us all. We told Hondo he would get his cash when he led us to the skips' hide-out. He said we would start in the morning, first thing.

So now Hanson and I had another evening to kill. We called the girls; surprise, surprise, ladies. The boys are back in town. They both showed up at the motel within an hour. I told Rosita we'd be leaving at six the next morning, so if she wanted to play her swapping games, we'd better get the 'BOHICA'[25] started.

We were on the road early, as planned. We headed south-west, Hanson and me in Pedro's truck, the other guys leading the way in Hondo's car. It was a fair drive, even though we stuck to the main roads. We got into Durango in the early afternoon and put up at a motel.

The next morning we had breakfast, loaded the truck, and got to work. Again, we followed Hondo. When we arrived at our destination, we split up. Hanson, Hondo, and Jaime would try one address while I teamed up with Pedro and Rudy and drove out to another. It was a typical suburban bungalow, out on the edge of town. Even as we approached the place, it looked unlikely anyone was home. There was a mailbox on the gate with junk stuffed in it. The blinds were down, and trash was swirling around the front porch as a hot, dry wind blew in from the plains. Rudy drove around the block and asked a couple of guys if the place was empty. *Si*, they said, there had been a couple of guys living there, a *Negro* and a *Gringo*, but they'd moved out a week or so previously. We checked in with Hanson by phone. He wasn't having much luck either.

It was hot and thirsty work, and it was exhausting. Hanson and I decided we'd be better off leaving the guys to do the legwork for us. Not being able to speak the language, we weren't a lot of help. We got them to drop us off at a motel, us and Pedro, on the understanding that we'd be ready to move as soon as they found the skips.

---

[25] See glossary

We'd just got bedded down when Hondo called in, babbling away in broken English. When he'd calmed down, he told us that he and Jaime had seen our guys, in a bar, about thirty minutes' drive away.

'That's great,' I said, 'but we can't grab them in a public place. We'll follow them home when they leave.'

We drove way out to the edge of town. And beyond. The bar was down by a dry riverbed on a big sandy lot. It must have been three o'clock when we got there. We found no more than a handful of vehicles parked outside, and as we pulled in, two of them moved away with couples inside.

I called Hondo. No answer. Pedro went in and checked out the bar. He wasn't gone more than a minute or two. '*Ees* empty,' he said. 'Ten people, mebbe twelve.'

Hanson grunted. 'And no goddam fucking skips, right? Shit, SUSFU,' he said. 'Why's Hondo drag us all the fucking way out here then go AWOL? Dumb sonofabitch.'

'He probably got no signal,' Pedro said and shrugged. 'We in zee desert now. Someplace yes signal, other places no.'

'Why not try one of the other addresses you got?' I said. 'That's gotta be worth a shot.'

Pedro was happy to do that, but just as we were leaving, his phone went. It was Hondo. He'd got lucky. He'd been on the highway heading back to town when he spotted the skips' car and followed it.

'So where is this?' I said. Pedro was still talking to Hondo on the phone. He waited a moment, then said, 'I got the address, but one of these *hombres*, *hee hass* gone. Vamoosed.'

'What do you mean?' I said. 'They there or not?'
It took a bit of untangling, but the fact was one skip had got out at this address while the other had driven off with two females.

'Well, what the fuck?' I said to Hanson. 'One skip's better

than none. We going in?'

'Sure,' he said. 'Let's do it. Nail one sonofabitch – makes it easier to get his buddy.'

We headed out to the place Hondo had given us. It was a dirt road, more of a track that wound its way between tall cactuses. We drove with the lights out, going slow to keep the noise down. As we bumped around potholes, dodging rocks and kicking up a cloud of dust, a coyote streaked across the road in front of us.

The house was set well back from the trail under some little trees of some kind and encircled by a sagging wire fence, but well hidden from view. These guys had their shit together, not letting their girlfriends or anyone know where they were living; The skips had this well thought out; they would be ready for a quick getaway if they were rumbled, residing in the middle of no man's land. There was a light from the window; a car tucked away along the side. Just as we were debating whether to go right in, Hondo came on the phone. He told us the other skip had dropped one of the girls off at her house and seemed to be saying goodnight to the other one.

'Okay,' I said. 'You stick close to that mother. We're going to get his buddy sorted, now.'

We pulled off onto the dirt, got out, and crept towards the house, hiding behind the rocks. We all pulled on our balaclavas and checked our guns. The wind was still whipping up the dirt as we stumbled, eyes half-closed, towards the side of the house. The plan was for Hanson to stay out of sight while I tried to get a look inside. Pedro followed me, crouching low and creeping along the front until we reached the window. Through a crack in the blind, I saw one of the skips, the black guy, lying on the sofa. He was out cold. I felt my pulse quicken. This was the kind of break we needed.

I turned back to see Hanson looking at me from around the

end of the front fence. I motioned him to cover the back, and with my pistol in one hand, I reached up and tried the door handle. Jesus, I nearly whooped in celebration; the doors wasn't locked; that's how safe and secure these bastards felt down in old Mexico. With my pistol in one hand, I turned the front door handle while Pedro covered the target from the front window.

I was about to enter inside. Suddenly I felt a tap on my shoulder and almost crapped my pants there and then. It was Hanson; he had checked the rear of the house; there was no other window or door; if the guy wanted to run, he could only head our way. I could hear our guy snoring loudly inside.

'Okay, let's go,' I whispered.

We crept into the hallway. I made a final check that we were both ready, then launched myself at the door. As it flew open, I stood in the ready to fire position. 'Don't move! Federal agents!' I saw Hanson look at me and shrugged. As if this fucker would know who we were. 'Hands on your fucking head! Now!'

What happened next nearly threw me. From being fast asleep and snoring, this guy leaped from the couch and went for us. He caught me in the face with an elbow and tried to trip Hanson. I had the move covered and was all set to throw him over when Hanson got up and whacked him over the back of the head with his pistol. As he fell to the floor, I placed my knee on his throat while Hanson grabbed the holdall and pulled out the nylon cuffs.

'For fuck's sake,' I said, 'that wasn't necessary.' Next moment my heart nearly stopped as the window slid up. It was Pedro, climbing in to join us. 'Jesus,' I said, 'couldn't you use the fucking door?'

I turned to look at the black guy. Blood was running freely from the guy's head onto the carpeted floor. 'Did you have to do that?' I said.

Hanson shook his head. 'I panicked, wasn't thinking,' he

muttered.

'Not as if he's even armed,' I added. 'Just calm down, pal.'

I got my first aid kit and cleaned the wound, and put some butterfly stitches on it. Hanson tied his feet together and taped his mouth, then laid him on the sofa and covered him with a blanket. The phone vibrated in my pocket. It was Hondo. The white guy had finished his goodnight kiss and was heading back towards us, alone. He'd be with us in about fifteen minutes, maybe less. Hondo and Jamie were going to follow at a safe distance.

With buddy boy out cold on the sofa, we quickly tidied up the busted lamp, straightened the coffee table and various bits and pieces that had got scattered in the fight, then did our best to close the inner door, even though the hinges were slightly misaligned. Hanson hid at the back of the house while Pedro and I went to the kitchen, leaving the door open just a couple of inches so that we had a clear view of the hallway.

'Do not shoot to kill,' I told them both. 'Not unless he has a gun, and it's you or him. Got that?'

'Si,' Pedro said. Hanson nodded his head in agreement.

We didn't have long to wait before we heard a truck pull up outside. As the engine died, a single door slammed shut. I nudged Pedro and held up one finger. It seemed like the guy really was alone. The outer door opened, and he walked inside. I saw him throw his keys onto a little table and watched as he reached out to open the living-room door.

'Federal agents! Freeze, motherfucker!' I sprang out from the kitchen, pointing my gun at him. 'On the goddam floor!'

This one decided to run. It wasn't the right decision. Just as Hondo and Jamie were getting out of the truck, balaclava's on; the skip reached the outer door, they had their weapons drawn. Hanson, too appeared pistol at the ready. Give the skip his due; he had the sense to read the situation. The skip sank to his knees and lay across the threshold, face down with his hands behind his back. He knew the form, and he knew this way he wouldn't get hurt. Hanson cuffed and taped his legs together, and while Pedro went to get his truck, we called the other two in; they both had their balaclavas on; these guys were local and could easily be recognised.

We put the skips in the back of the truck, then returned to the house and collected all their clothes and personal stuff – drugs, money, the keys to their vehicle, the lot. I then handed Rudy and Jamie the necessary items, which Ramon told us to leave with them. After searching the skips, wearing latex gloves, and removing and checking their IDs, I realised that they were both false to get them across the borders. I showed them to Hanson; then I gave their false IDs to Rudy; the rest of the stuff we put into a couple of black plastic sack bags and threw them into the truck. Before we set off, we put balaclavas over their heads and taped over the eye-holes. Only then did we take ours off and wipe the sweat from our faces.

We headed back to our motel, collected all our personal belongings. By now, it was two-thirty in the morning, and Hanson and I decided we might as well get the job done. We would all head back to Saltillo, taking turns at the wheel. We didn't even stop for food or drink – just made do with the water we carried in bottles in the foot-well. When we took the tape off the skips' mouths to give them a drink, they started to ask us what the fuck was going on.

'We're delivering you to the feds, stateside,' I said.

'You think we'll let you take us back across the border without a fight?' the white guy said.

'I do,' I answered. 'In fact, I know I will. Believe me, my friend, I always get my man and bring him in. Dead or alive, It's all the same to me. I'll tell you something. Dead is a whole lot easier and less hassle. Fewer out-of-pocket expenses too, so it's your choice which you choose.' Hanson liked that. He cracked up. The skips never said another word, and we drove on in peace, sticking to the main roads. The way I figured it, a truck full of guys on a back road would be way more likely to attract bandits or the Federales' attention.[26] Not that we saw any that night.

It was late the next afternoon when we pulled up to the back of the house in Saltillo and carried our skips inside, cuffed and hooded. They were in pretty bad shape by now, having gone fifteen hours or more without a fix. 'Lucky for you, we brought your dope,' I said as Hanson injected them. They would soon be high as kites, so we locked them in a room. We paid Hondo, who kissed his envelope and gave us a big grin before shaking our hands. '*Hombre*, is good to do business with you,' he said. Then he got in his truck and drove off.

So far, so good. Pretty easy, too. All that remained now was the little matter of getting our captives across the border. Next morning the day didn't get off to the best of starts. When I went to shower, I found myself itching like a flea-bitten hound. I wrapped a towel around myself, went to Hanson's bed, and gave him a shake. 'How are your balls doing this morning?' I asked him.

He frowned and scratched around. 'Kinda real itchy,' he said. 'You don't think...?'

I nodded. 'Afraid so,' I said. 'We got fucking crabs off those *chiquitas*. Still, worse things happen at sea. You going to go to the pharmacy?'

Hanson grunted and threw some clothes on. Within half an hour, he was back with some kind of cream. We slathered it on nice and thick and prayed that that was the worst of our trouble.

---

[26] See glossary

We fed the skips breakfast and a fix of cocaine, then cuffed them and put them in the back of the truck with their faces covered. We made sure they wouldn't see any person or place on the way back. They didn't know what had hit them from the get-go; no idea who we really are and not the faintest idea of where they were, and that's the way we liked it.

We then headed back towards Pedro's place, as we got nearer towards the border. About ten miles out, Pedro had us pull over. The skips were awake now and gagging for a drink. I got out a bottle of water, but before I could pass it, Pedro pulled out a little brown phial, unscrewed the lid, and squeezed a few drops of something into their water. Twenty minutes later, the two of them were out cold once more.

'So what the fuck is that you doped 'em with?' Hanson asked.
Pedro explained it was liquid GHB. Plus a special little surprise he had added. He also showed us a bottle of chloroform he had brought along just in case we needed it. I explained to Hanson that it was a date-rape drug we gave the skips.

'Yeah, I heard about that shit,' Hanson said. 'Lasts about six hours, and after that, they can't trace it, right?'

'You got it,' I said. 'Just fucking disappears from your system.'

We then laid the skips into the back of Pedro's truck and covered them with blankets like they were asleep, and hoped that the border guards would not check them as we had no papers for them.

Getting into the free zone now was a matter of pulling up and letting Pedro strut his stuff. He chatted to the guards like he'd known them all his life. They laughed and joked and took out the tequila bottles he'd bought, especially with them in mind, then waved us through.

It was a short run back to Pedro's place, and he'd set things up nicely. His wife and daughters had gone to visit family way across in Chihuahua. When we arrived, we loaded the unconscious skips into a back room to sleep it off. The truck went into the garage, out of sight. Within an hour, Pedro had heated some rice and chilli beans his wife had left for us all. We woke the skips and fed them. By this time, they didn't even know what day it was, never mind where the hell they were. Soon as they'd eaten, we dosed them up with cocaine and put them back to bed.

We got up early the next morning and prepared for the final phase of the operation. 'Let's take things nice and easy,' I said to Hanson. 'We screw this part up, and we really are in the shit. We don't want to face a kidnap rap in fucking Mexico.'

The whole thing now hung on one final detail. As Pedro spelled it out, it was clear and straightforward. We had a friendly border guard, and we had to make contact with him. His name was –Jose Antonio. And his password would be 'Goodbye and adios Jose.' Why they chose that I'll never know, but all it needed to do was work.

The tension arose from the fact that until the guy got to work each day, he never knew which gate he'd be working at – and there was a whole line of gates at Nuevo Laredo, spread across a dozen lanes of traffic. The guy had a beeper (Pager), compatible with the one Pedro was now giving me. We'd beep him as we approached the crossing, and he'd get a message to us telling us which lane number to queue. He had details of our vehicle make and registration plate. What could go wrong? When we got to his border hut window, we would hand him the spondoolicks in another manila envelope. Simple enough, but I had a long history of seeing simple, straightforward plans go all to hell when the pressure was on.

We hadn't even left Pedro's place when the beeper went off. 'What's this?' I said, showing it to our man. 'Some kinda trial run?' Pedro had a look. '*Ees* good,' he said. 'Jose is working in the afternoon. Twelve to eight.'

I looked at my watch. Ten thirty. There was no great rush.

Later, Pedro gave the skips another drink laced with liquid ecstasy. Then we waited until the drugs took effect. It was now time to put the skips into the unique coffin bed we'd prepared for them. We eased them into the recessed compartment I'd constructed on the floor of the truck, closed the lid, and covered it with blankets and baggage. Then we threw around a few items of dirty clothing, bedding, a beat-up old volleyball, a couple of odd shoes, and squashed beer cans. It looked like two guys coming back off vacation. It seemed pretty convincing.

After we'd got the baggage all piled up on top, we handed all the guns over to our man, shook hands, and hugged him. He'd done his job well. We thanked him for his hospitality, got in the truck, and headed north. It was another scorcher, the horizon shimmering, the sun glaring at us from a deep blue sky.

We hit the border a little after noon and beeped our guy. I looked at the multiple lines of vehicles and said, 'Go on, Hanson, pick us a winner.' The beeper remained silent.

'Jesus,' he said, 'it's like picking the fast lane at the supermarket checkout. He pointed at a lane that showed some sign at least of moving. 'Try that first,' he said. We soon realised we'd backed a loser. We'd moved forward ten, maybe fifteen yards when the beeper went. It was Jose, telling us he was at Gate 2, way across the other side.

'Well, ain't that fucking beautiful?' Hanson said. 'We're fucking TARFU!'

I pulled up and stepped out into the broiling heat. I waved a couple of cars passed us and shouted up to Hanson, 'Hey, flip the hood open, will you?' We poked around in the engine for a minute or two, making it look like we had a problem. Then we got back

106

in, switched on the hazard lights, and eased our way towards the right, crossing a couple of lines, then a couple more.

We did the hazard lights again, farted about under the hood once more. I even pulled a pair of leads off and rammed them back on – just in case some nosy cop was watching us through binoculars. Then I got back in and slipped across to the last but one line.

As we approached the border booth, we saw there were two guards. 'So which one's our man?' Hanson said, stubbing out a cigarette and immediately lighting another.

'Relax,' I said. 'Whichever guard it is, he's got our licence plate number.'

One of the border guards was already approaching us. He had a clipboard in his hand. Hanson puffed nervously. I nudged him and winked. 'We'll be fine. Just need to stay cool.' I said. '*Papeles*[27]?' The guard had his hand out. We gave him our passports and papers. He leafed through them, went towards the back of the truck, then reappeared at the passenger side window. '*Abrir*,' he said, jerking his head towards the end of the truck. 'Open it.' I took the keys from the ignition and got out. He stood there while I unlocked the tailgate. Was this the guy? I glanced at his name badge. Rodriguez. Shit.

He rummaged through the contents, flicking aside the dirty clothing, opening one or two of the holdalls, and looking inside. I was sweating, and it wasn't just the heat. But he didn't look too interested.

'*Bueno*,' he said and gestured to me to close it. While I locked up, he wandered around the side and kicked at the tyres. I returned to my seat and shut the window, directing the AC full blast into my face. Hanson was lighting up again, the cigarette jiggling up

---

[27] See glossary

107

and down between his fingers. I wanted to shout at him to calm the fuck down. Instead, I murmured, 'Relax, buddy. It's all sorted.' The guard Rodriguez came to the window and tapped hard on it. I wound it down. He leaned in, still clutching the clipboard and looked around inside, and then said the magic words, 'Goodbye and adios Jose.'

Jesus H Christ. I don't know whether I spoke the words or what, but I could feel a load of tension slide off my shoulders. I wanted to kiss the ugly sonofabitch full on the lips. As I took the envelope from my inside pocket, he said, 'Put her *een* here,' and leaned forward casually. He had the top two buttons of his shirt undone, exposing his hairy chest and a little gold chain with some saint or other dangling off it. I popped it inside, and he passed me our documents. Then he waved to his buddy in the booth, and up went the barrier. I resisted the temptation to stamp my foot on the gas, just drove nice and steady away from Mexico and back into the good old US of A.

I guess things could still have got sticky on the American side, but not for us. This was our lucky day. The guy asked us to pull over and show our documents. Hanson barely had time to light another of his frigging cigarettes before there was a loud crunching sound as a car behind us ran smack into the rear end of another one, followed by a lot of shouting. The guard looked up, groaned, and handed us back our passports before going to sort it out. Stateside we drove maybe twenty miles, came off the freeway, and took the old highway towards Las Cruces. We found a shaded vacant lot surrounded by tall cottonwood trees, pulled up, and checked our skips. They were still out cold. We phoned the bondsman and told him we had a couple of packages for the delivery. Was he glad to hear from us? 'Didn't know if you boys could pull it off,' he said when we met up in a superstore parking lot about an hour later.

'Neither did we,' I told him, 'but it looks like you came to the right guys, eh? Hannibal and Murdock from the A-Team.'

'Yeah,' he said, 'more like Batman and Robin.' He wanted to know if we had gathered up the skips' belongings.

'Sure,' I said. 'Where d'you want us to put it?'

He gave us an address, an old deserted, abandoned house, the edge of town, and said we'd be okay to go there after it got dark. He handed us a box containing cocaine and a bunch of old used needles. Before taking them to jail, we were to inject the skips, but not until the date-rape dope was out of their systems. As for all the extra needles, we were to make sure the skips' fingerprints were all over them; then, we would scatter them all around the house with the rest of their belongings. We took my home-made coffin from the truck and left that with him. I told him he was welcome to it. It might come in useful again someday. He agreed to look after the skips in his garage while we did the business at the house.

When we finished, Hanson and I checked into a motel, then went and cooled off with a couple of beers and a Mexican combo platter apiece. 'Kinda makes ya tired,' Hanson said, 'all that excitement. Shit, I been in combat, and I don' think I've ever been so scared in all my life when that guard searched the back of the truck, and I saw Rodriguez on his badge.'

'Me too,' I said. 'But hey,' I said, 'it's payday, we did it, and we're back home. Relax. Tequila?' 'Same blood, bud,' I said as we bumped fists.

Early the next morning, we went and collected the skips from the bondsman's place and took them to the police, still drugged up and unconscious. We handed in our reports, which said we'd arrested them at an abandoned house, and gave the address. We told the cops we'd found them in this drugged-up state and that there was a whole lot of drugs and narcotic paraphernalia at the residence. And it needs to be searched.

After we got the warrants signed, we met up with the

bondsman and collected our bounty. We heard later that the skips told the police that we had kidnapped them from Mexico. They even got their lawyers on the case. That was as far as it went. The law knew damned well that nobody would ever dream of pulling a stunt like that. Goddam, junkies, they said, they're so full of shit. And in the end, the lawyers had to agree, there was no evidence in what they had told, and they backed off.

Later we found out that Mexicans sometimes use their mother and father's surname, so that was why the name was different on the border guards' badge.

A Man's Best Friend

W. C. Fields was the first credited with the immortal line, 'Never work with children or animals. Pity we can't all make a choice. Kids aren't often an issue in my line of work, but animals? They're a fact of life. When some pussy of a guy wants the world to think he's a genuine hard man, he can pull one of the cheapest tricks to get himself a dog. Start with a breed renowned for its aggression and tenacity, treat it mean, and pretty soon, you'll have a lethal weapon on your hands. A fighting breed is the lowlife criminal's accessory of choice, and boy, can they get ugly. Ask me to choose between facing down your average drug-crazed gunman and a wannabe tough guy with a maltreated dog, and I know which way I'd be heading.

In this particular case, I had a partner with me, an interested partner. I mean the actual owner, the bondsman, and that too presented problems. For Mikey, the fact that the guy had skipped bail made it personal for him. He decided he would ride shotgun with me. He insisted I needed him to ID the guy we were after. I questioned his decision. I had a picture of the guy. What else did I need?

'Nah, this is no good,' he said. We were looking at a photo of a stocky bald, clean-shaven guy, an ugly sonofabitch by any standard, with his hollow, staring, dark eyes.

'Why not?' I asked him.

'Cos he don't look like this no more.'

'So how's he changed?' I asked. I wasn't crazy about Mikey.

He was a little short-ass fucker, maybe five feet tall, and skinny. He had a podgy sort of face, soft hands, and a rat-a-tat voice that drilled straight into your inner ear. Think Ratso in *Midnight Cowboy*. Danny De Vito on crack.

'For one thing, the guy's grown his hair,' Mikey said. 'And he's got himself a crazy man's beard. You know the kind. Shaped like the goddam ace of spades.' He looked up at me and grinned. 'He's got an entirely new look – kinda Charlie Manson, you know what I mean? And he's gained weight.'

Looking at this character's photo – he had some Hispanic name, Trementino, if I remember right – he looked wild-eyed and pretty scary. Even so, on paper, this should be a piece of cake; Trementino had a long history of assault and drug-related offences. But nothing to get in a stew about. Nothing I didn't think I couldn't handle. But yeah, it might be useful to have someone alongside who could make a positive ID.

So I asked Mikey if he had a gun, and he said sure he had. 'I got two,' he told me, sticking his chest out. 'Couple of little beauties. A pump-action shotgun and an American version Walther PPK/S.' He failed to mention what I was to find out later, that he'd never fired either one of the frigging things. The guy was just full of crap. I should've left him in the office.

But as I said, this looked like easy meat. Our snitch's tip-off was that our man had rented some kind of old shack, way out of town, out in the boonies.[28] According to our source, Trementino was collecting a delivery of drugs the previous day.

So we got in the truck and set off, the three of us: me, Mikey, and his ever-yapping mouth. These backwoods trips weren't as easy then as they are now. There were no Sat Nav's in those days, and the likelihood of getting a signal on your phone was – well,

---

[28] See glossary

on a scale of one to ten, it was just above zero. Not that I was too worried. I always was a map guy. Remember maps? I mean large-scale local ones, which folded out the entire width of your truck cab and covered maybe fifteen miles of the country you were driving through. Or I'd have a book of maps for that particular state – like an A4 ring-binder with scores of pages, about three inches thick. Those are what I relied on – them and the good old-fashioned compass. Map-reading was an excellent skill to have. Still is. Sat Nav's are excellent until your battery goes flat and you can't find your charger. Then what are you supposed to do?

We drove for about 60 miles way out beyond the edge of town and into the backwoods. Pretty soon, we hit the dirt. It was late summer, the weather still very hot, and everywhere was parched. Mikey made it plain and simple; he didn't get out of town much. 'Jesus,' he said, looking around at the blackened hillsides, 'what the fuck happened here? I thought this was a beauty spot. Kinda place people go picnicking on July Fourth. Not me, I gotta tell ya. I prefer to stay home, watch a ball game. A fridge full of beer. I mean, where ya gonna get a beer out here for chrissake?'

I let him rattle on, then I told him. A massive forest fire had been a few weeks previously; we were driving through great swathes of the burned-out country, with the scorched stems of ponderosa pines, all tilted at crazy angles. It would still be burning now, I told him, if it hadn't been for that thunderstorm that passed through. There was an unpleasant smell in the air, and we were kicking up a mixture of yellow dust and dark ash that irritated my nose. I pulled over and checked the map; I still had a way to go yet. We entered a real wasteland, with burned-out trees and piles of dirt, where the bulldozers had been through trying to stop the fire from spreading.

We then crossed slowly over a railroad line, and Mikey

kicked off again. 'Hey, I never knew they had trains out here. Where's it go?' He didn't wait for an answer, just steamrollered ahead. 'You know, I've never been on a train in my life. Have you? My old man did, back in the day. He talked about it all the time. And his brother. Did I ever tell you about his brother? Yeah, he worked on the railroad as an engineer or something. I guess their old man did too, and that's how they got to ride when they were kids. So I always liked the idea of riding the train, but where the fuck do they go? That's the question.'

I explained it was a freight line that ran the west coast's length, from California all the way to Canada. That shut him up – for about ten seconds.

'Canada, huh? You ever been up there?'

'No,' I said.

'Me neither. I mean, why would ya? I dated a girl from Winnipeg one time, or was it Toronto? Somewhere up there. She wanted me to go live there, but her old man, boy he was —'

'Hey Mikey,' I said. 'Give it a rest, will you? Just you know, let me concentrate on where we're heading.' I brought the truck to a halt, looked at the map, and pointed at two-tracks that veered off up a hill to our right. About two hundred yards ahead, I could clearly make out a very low-pitched roof, a smokestack, and a window that glinted in the sunlight. 'Christ,' I said. 'If that's the place he's gonna see us when we walk up to the place, plain as day.'

'Yeah,' Mikey said. 'Guess you're right. So what we – whadda we do?'

'How about we stop yapping and think?' I said. I checked the map; there was a small town about 5 miles from where we were; I showed Mickey the map position. 'We'll go there to see if there's a cop shop, maybe pick up something to eat on the way back; you hungry?' I said.

'Yeh sounds good,' said Mikey.'

I drove slowly up the track to get a better view, then took out my binoculars. It was a single-storey shack with a blue sedan parked outside. The yard around it was full of junk – lengths of steel pipe, piles of rocks, lumber, a couple of rusting cars with their wheels missing, and their windows out. Around it, all ran a wire fence. There were no other houses nearby, just an old outbuilding and a defunct pump-jack. Jesus, it was one lonely spot. I drove on until we were within fifty yards or so, then stopped the truck and got out. I checked that Mikey had his bulletproof vest on, then said, 'Okay, you stay here. I'm gonna check this place over.'

'Hell no,' he said. 'I'm not staying here. I'm coming with you. That motherfucker burned me big-time. I'm gonna enjoy slamming his ass.' Mikey got out and patting his Walther in its holster like he'd known it all his life and reaching into the footwell for his shotgun. It was one of those black pieces with a pistol grip. Mikey was making me edgy. He was up for this. No doubt about it. No telling what he'd do if things got rough.

'Okay,' I said. 'Badges on display and – hey, leave the shotgun behind, will you? No point in frightening the guy to death.' Unless I knew that a skip was dangerous, I preferred to act businesslike because that was what it was when you think about it, a kind of business transaction. 'Dead-beat punk like this,' I said, 'he shouldn't give us too much trouble.'

Between us and the shack was a single stand of trees that the fire had missed. For the next few yards, we were out of sight, screened by their branches. Then we turned a corner, and the place was right there, a stone's throw away.

I advanced at a steady walk. Mikey followed a few feet behind me. I can't have been more than fifteen or twenty yards away when the door was flung open and out stepped our Manson lookalike, preceded by two snarling pit bull terriers, front feet pawing the air as they strained at their leashes. Leashes? No, Trementino had them each on a length of chain. Jesus, he was ugly. Filthy too, a rag of a shirt hanging off his tattooed shoulders, his hair tousled, a greasy baseball cap perched on his head, the lower half of his face covered with a tangled beard. He spat out a cigarette and shouted at us. 'Git your asses off my property, mothafuckas! Now!'

'Shit,' I murmured. I could hardly take my eyes off the dogs. 'They banned these bastards back home. If they get their teeth into you —'

'Hey, tell me about it.' Mikey had dropped off a few yards and looked back at the truck, its nose just visible through the trees. 'But that – that's the guy okay,' he said. 'That's our man.' He was still facing me but backing slowly away along the track.

'Yeah,' I said. 'I kinda figured that.' I called out to Trementino. 'Listen, we're bail enforcement agents.'

'Assholes is what you are, man. Now git.' He shook the chains and let the dogs haul him a couple of yards closer to us, then tugged them back. I could hear their wheezing as they fought for air. 'Git,' he said, 'or I'll sic the dogs on ya.'

I was desperately trying to work out a plan, any plan. Those dogs, Jesus, they had me rattled. One I could deal with, but two? 'Okay,' I said, trying to stay calm as I turned to tell Mikey what I had in mind, but the chicken-hearted bastard was in full retreat, scattering dirt as he ran stumbling towards the truck. 'Hey! Where you fucking going?' I called out. He turned to see me draw my 9mm Sig from its holster. 'Come on, man,' he gasped, 'let's get the fuck outa here.'

I turned away from him, aimed at each dog in turn, then pointed it at a spot right between Trementino's eyes. Trouble was if I shot him, I'd have the dogs on me. Would I have time to pick them off? One, maybe, but not both of them. That would be some shooting. It would call for a steady hand, and I could already hear my teeth chattering. Either one of those brutes could rip me to shreds in an instant.

'Okay, okay!' I shouted, stepping slowly backwards and holstering my pistol.

'Drop yer damned gun. On the fucking ground, ya dumbass motherfucker!' Trementino was jabbing his gun in my direction, still letting the dogs pull him towards me a step or two at a time.

'Okay, just cool it,' I shouted. 'We're going.' I held onto my gun. He wasn't going to have that. Behind me, I heard Mikey fire up the truck. I walked backwards towards him. No way was I going to turn my back on the skip, no way at all. Mikey swung the truck around in a tight circle and crunching the gears, showering me with dust and gravel. 'Fuck's sake,' I shouted. 'Just calm down, will you?'

I turned now and made the last few yards to the truck, somehow restraining myself from running. I had my hand on the passenger side door handle. Mikey was already on his phone, trying to get help, shouting 'No signal.' Trementino was laughing out loud and cackling like he was demented. 'Go on,' he called. 'Run, ya dickhead motherfuckers.'

Mikey was screaming at me. 'Get in, will ya! Let's get the fuck outa here. Let the cops deal with him.'

'Wait one minute, let me think,' I said.

I stood still and thought. The moment we disappeared from view, that slimeball would be heading out the other way, taking with him my chance of an eight-thousand dollar payday. Fuck waiting for the cops. Was I a professional, or what? I walked to the back of the truck, lifted the tail-gate, and pulled out my

Franchi SPAS-12[29] Combat shotgun. It's an assault weapon and an absolute beauty. You hardly have to aim it, just point it towards your target and let the thing do its worst. When I say, worst, we're talking a 900-millimeter spread at forty metres. That's three feet in English, and with a capacity of four shots per second, it gives you every chance of hitting your target, way more than any bullet from a handgun.

I checked the gun to make sure it was loaded—eight in the tube plus one in the barrel. I looped the strap over my head, and my right shoulder pulled out my other 9mm pistol, cocked that, and shoved it through my belt. Then I grabbed the SPAS and pressed the button on the foregrip, clicking it into semi-automatic position. Nine shells, two fully loaded 9mm semi-auto pistols, I was thinking, and three targets. Not bad odds.

I turned to Mikey. 'You gonna back me up, or what?'

His face seemed frozen in an expression of shock. Sweat beaded over his eyebrows. His tongue flickered across his lips, and his hands gripped the steering wheel. 'What? Are you fucking insane? You think I'm going back down there with that maniac on the loose and get ripped to fucking shreds? No way, Ted. No fucking way.'

The guy was clearly terrified. I was scared too, but I was used to that. Any sane man would be. But I'd taught myself to treat it as just another factor, like the sweat making your eyes sting. Something you have to deal with. 'Go,' I said. 'Go on now. Get the cops, but be gentle with my truck, hey?'

Before I could even close the tailgate, he sped off down the track. I took my mirrored shades out of my top pocket, wiped away the sweat from my face, then put them on. I was ready. Ready to rumble.

---

[29] See glossary

Trementino had obviously been watching us from the house. As soon as I started walking back down the hill, the door suddenly flew open again, and there he was. 'Didn't I just warn you, mothafucker?' he snarled, but I wasn't listening. In that state, I was part trance, part dream, my every movement playing out in slo-mo. I was concentrating on what I could control: my actions, not his.

I had both hands on the SPAS, aiming and holding it in front of my face. I was aware of my footsteps crunching on the loose gravel, my breath coming in out, in out through my open mouth. It sounded louder than it ought to. Likewise, my heartbeat was echoing in my ears as if I was underwater. My eyes were now firmly focussed on Trementino, standing there on his front porch, and the dogs letting out strangled growls as they lunged towards me, over and over, each time hauled back as he yanked on their chains.

Trementino let out a loud, weird cry, like the scream of a deranged man, and let them go. What I saw, what I focussed on along the gun's barrel, was the slobbery open jaws and jagged teeth as they hurtled towards me, gobbling up the space between us at an alarming rate, their chains dragging and stirring up dust clouds behind them.

I pulled the trigger and fired and missed, fired again, and again missed. Then I threw caution to the wind and rapid-fired, swinging the gun left and right, the seven remaining shots seeming to blur into one.

Both dogs went tumbling over, one minus his front legs, the other with his entire hip and rear right leg blasted away in a livid splash of blood and rendered flesh. Where the hell was Trementino? I was still pulling the trigger as I swept the landscape, left, right, and left again. But the gun was empty, and he was gone.

I dropped the shotgun, the strap tugging at my neck as it swung to my hip. I quickly pulled out my two pistols. Trementino had to be in the shack. There was little cover in the yard to hide, apart from the lengths of discarded pipe lying on the ground, and a couple of old tractor tyres. I slowly made my way towards the rickety porch. I had one pistol in my left hand pointing straight out, the other in my right hand across my chest; I stood very still for a moment watching the door and windows and concentrating on getting my breathing under control. You can't aim and shoot straight when you're gasping for air; I reminded myself. So if he's in there, I need to be ready for what's coming next.

One more deep breath. In, in, in, and hold it. Then I let it out, nice, slow, and steady. Yes. That's better. Now I'm ready. I'm standing about fifteen yards from the place. I hear footsteps and the torn screen door creak open, and there he is, a gun in each hand, holding the pistols sideways and screaming at the top of his voice like a wailing banshee as he opens fire with both guns.

I hear the bullets zip past me on either side of my head. I face him standing side-on; I hold steady, both guns aimed and raised, and I fire simultaneously. One bullet hits him in the forehead, the other in the chest. There's a ping sound as my bullet rips through him and hits something behind him.

He stumbles backwards; his gun manages to fire off a shot, shattering a window to his left side before hitting the floor, whump! Then a loud clattering sound as both his weapons went Skidding across the baseboards.

I advance slowly. I feel myself emerge from that other place, and now I am suddenly conscious of the two trembling dogs, whining and whimpering, one on each side of me. I check my stride, turn, and despatch the first with two bullets to the head, then repeat. None of this is their damned fault—no need for them to suffer. I lower the guns to my side and walk up to the door where Trementino lies quite still, the blood flowing from the bullet exit wound and creeping across the grimy floor of the shack, draining down a crack between the boards as the first fly lands on his blood-soaked shirt.

I step over his motionless body and enter the cabin; the place stinks. I can see a mess of abandoned takeaway food, beer cans, full ashtrays, cigarette ends, and bottles littering the floor and bowls full of dog food. Over by the window, the floor covered with bullets in among the broken glass. I find a bag of cocaine, a spoon, and scales on a table in the middle of the room.

I holster one gun and put the other in my trouser belt. There's the sound of sirens from the burned-out woods, and here comes the first car, bouncing over the rocks towards me with a cruiser behind it. I walk out of the shack to meet them. I've got my uniform on, of course, so they will see who I am. They still jump out of their cars and come towards me, three, four, five of them, all aiming their weapons at me, but I'm already lowering myself to the ground, face down before the order is out of their mouths. They pull my guns and SPAS from me, search me, then cuff me before a female officer reads me my rights.

'No offence,' she says. 'Just doing our job.'

'No offence taken,' I tell her. 'I was doing mine. Would you mind getting me some water? Please?'

She takes me to the patrol car and pulls out a bottle, and feeds it to me. Then we go to the cruiser. A door opens, and Mikey gets out. The guy's white as a sheet. 'Hey,' I tell him, 'don't forget my cheque, man—eight big ones. Oh, and get your ass downtown soon as you can, will you? Bail my ass out. Will you do that?'

He grins nervously. 'Sure thing, Ted. No problemo.' Then he looked at the ground and said, 'Yeah, and thanks.'

You get used to the procedures. When you've killed a man, you'll be charged – generally with murder. They read you your rights and formally arrest you. A judge will set bail pending a trial. Then you call your bondsman, and he gets you your lawyer. Generally, the judge will recognise it's a case of self-defence when he sees one. The charges will get dropped, and Like I say, it's procedures. Nothing more.

Living out a Boyhood Dream

One time, when I was a kid, I wanted to be a commando. I never was one, but I did get to act out a few commando-style scenarios. That's the great thing about this line of work. Some of the things you do it's like living out your childhood fantasies. Like the time I found myself walking along the top of a line of railroad wagons, gun in hand, ducking under trees as the train snaked its way through the Cascade mountains at forty miles an hour. 'A scene straight out of Hollywood.' But that's a story for later. When I think Commando, I think about a pair of skips who were holed up in a remote holiday home on a lake, out of State. It was way up in Minnesota. The land of ten thousand lakes, as it says on their licence plates. What it doesn't mention are the ten billion mosquitoes.

These were high-profile guys we were after. They had high prices on their heads. The word was that they were partying up there with their girlfriends. They were also heavily armed and known to be violent. They would undoubtedly resist arrest. If we were going to move in on them, we needed to have a clear idea of the terrain because your first concern is always approaching a place unseen. How do you work it to avoid casualties, how to hit them when they least expect it? You cannot under-estimate the value of taking your opponent by surprise.

Another of the issues you weigh up when you go after a skip is the expenses you'll incur. Gas, food, lodgings – those always figure. Car rental, too – because you rarely want to use your own vehicle. Anonymity is crucial. You would most likely go to Rent-a-Wreck and pick up something that goes well but looks like a pile of shit. So you can see how the outlays build up. You sometimes find yourself thinking, does this case warrant the extra money for that big truck, that fast car, that particular piece of equipment? In this case, I had no such questions. It was crucial to get the layout of the place I would be approaching. I wanted to have it clear in my head; I wanted to photograph and video it, and I also needed a sighting of the skips; I needed a positive confirmation that they were where my informant said they were. So studying a map wasn't going to cut the mustard.

I had a think and decided to go for it. I hired myself a pilot, packed my best camera equipment, and surveyed the target area in a two-seater Cessna. And then, after I'd got some shots of the cabin and videoed the area around it, I went back the next day by helicopter. It was a resort area, with backwoods cabins dotted around every lake. Nobody would give much thought to a plane or chopper, as tourists were always flying over, joyriding, or taking lessons. But no way would I consider going back with the same aircraft or helicopter, two or three times over the same area. So the preparation was expensive, but the way I saw it, if I got the skips, the bondsman would pick up the tab. Just get my man; that was the main thing. Otherwise, I was going to wake up to a great big hole in my bank account.

What I saw from the air confirmed what the maps told us. There was no road to the house. The only access appeared to be by water, and I got a good photo of the wooden jetty with a motorised dinghy tied up alongside it. The nearest a car would get to the location was about half a mile away, after which we would have to approach the place on foot, working our way through dense forest with no tracks – at least, none that we could see from the sky. Difficult in daylight, much more so in the dark. So this needed a bit of thought. I chewed it over for some time, and I came up with a plan, and in order to execute that plan, I required a team.

I got hold of an old oppo[30] of mine, Jake. He was a guy I trusted and liked. I had him recruit four more good agents and arranged a meeting – well, a briefing session would be correct because this was going to be like a military operation. We would approach the place on two fronts and launch a co-ordinated strike – four coming in by land and two of us, Jake and me, by water. When I told Jake what I had in mind, he thought for a moment, then said, 'What kind of boats were we going to use? I mean, if we go sailing in there, even in the middle of the night, they're gonna see us, aren't they?'

'Let me explain,' I said. 'The plan is to get so far across the lake on a dinghy, then swim the rest of the way.'

'Swim?' Jake said. 'What, are you insane? You ever watched me swim, man? I'm like a pregnant fucking duck. Splish splash. They'd see me a fucking mile off if I didn't drown first.'

After I'd stopped laughing, I spelled it out for him. 'Relax my friend. We're going in wearing frogman gear. Wetsuits, flippers, and swim inside camouflaged inner tubes, we have a spare guy that will paddle out with us part of the way in the dinghy, then once we are inside the tubes, he will paddle the dinghy back to shore.'

'Yeah,' he said, 'but you still gotta swim. I'm telling you, I'm no good at that. Never have been.'

'Listen,' I said, 'we will have large inflated inner tubes with dark ropes tied around them, you will be tied to my tube in case you get into problems, and I will be at your side as we cross the lake. We have watertight bags with our guns and radios in. We

[30] See glossary

push them in front of us and get inside the ring, guns forward with our night vision goggles on, and camouflaged with bushes and branches on the front. All you got to do is grab hold of your tube and wiggle your flippers. Piece of piss.'

'And this is what, you and me doing a frontal assault on our own?'

'No, as I said, the rest of the team – these four guys we've recruited – they do the hard part, creeping up from the woods behind the house with their night-vision goggles. We're in touch with them by radio, and we all go together.'

Jake thought about it a while, then said, 'Yeah, workable. I guess.' He didn't sound convinced.

'Workable?' I said. 'Course it is.' I had trained in this kind of operation some time previously. I was sure it would work. 'This'll be the best crack you ever had,' I told him. 'We'll be living fucking legends when we pull this one off.' I sometimes think that was the difference between a lot of bounty hunters and me. I tended to see these capers as just that – adventures. Sure, it was dangerous work with high stakes. But to the little boy inside me, it was a game, a game of cops and robbers. But at the end of it, the reward would be 20% commission for me, which adds up to $100.000 plus expenses fewer overheads.

Next day we went back to the airport and chartered another plane. I wanted to have one final look, to make sure that our skips were still enjoying their vacation. They were all sprawled out on the little sandy beach with their girlfriends, all four of them stark bloody naked. It was time to get to work.

First, I had to show Jake how to put on the frogman gear and swim with the tubes. Then we worked on the hand signals – for when we approached the beach. The only real worry for me was the fact that we could not wear bulletproof vests. They would be way too heavy. 'So,' I explained, 'we do our best not to get shot.

Right?' He didn't laugh. Didn't even answer.

That same afternoon we met up to brief the rest of the team. We drove out to the far side of the lake, where Jake and I unloaded our inflatable dinghy and cut a few bits of foliage to camouflage it. When darkness fell, we sent the rest of the boys out to drive around the far side and approach the house through the forest. They were relieved to be on the move. I think they had an idea they could escape those damned mosquitoes. We agreed that they would get to within fifty yards of the beach house, then await contact from us. We'd look to launch the assault around midnight. My thinking was that our skips would still be partying, and not at their sharpest.

After we'd seen the land crew take off, Jake and I went over our plan once more. I had a good feeling about this one from the get-go. Everything seemed in our favour: it was a dark night, no moon, and the water was flat calm. Despite that, though, I felt my body shiver as we gave ourselves a final dose of insect repellent, slipped on our night goggles, as our man paddled us out in the dinghy. The snub nose of the craft was bobbing its way out into the lake before I realised Jake was in the bottom, lying on his back cursing to himself, having got one of his flippers tangled up in the netting and camouflage. I hoped That neither of us would snag it when it came time to get into the water.

It was a vast lake. The recent storm had littered the surface with branches and twigs. At times they slowed us down, but on the plus side, they helped camouflage us. It was good to be out on the water and away from the worst of the bugs. We paddled the dingy very softly and quietly. Then suddenly, a few hundred yards in front of us, we could see a yellow light flickering on the far shore. I nudged Jake. 'Looks like they got a fire going,' I said.

He nodded. 'Party time,' he said, 'except they got some uninvited guests gonna come calling.'

I called the land party. They reported that they were all set and were in position and were standing by. I reminded them to keep the camcorder zoomed in and recording the skips. I put the radio away, then slowly and quietly, we both slipped into the water and got in the middle of our tubes, camouflaged with netting and foliage; the spare guy passed us all our equipment and gave me the thumbs up, then quietly paddled the dinghy back to the shore. We then both concentrated on working our flippers. It was harder than I'd expected. There were currents in the lake threatening to push us off course, and the water was surprisingly cold.

Soon we could hear music playing and voices. I could even see the skips and their girls, dancing and kissing by the fire, their half-naked forms lit up by the flickering flames. As we paddled closer, I could make out two rifles leaning against a tree just behind them. One of the guys had a pistol. He looked weird, barefoot and wearing shorts, swaying to and fro with an arm around his girl and a holster on his hip. I realised that we had to think this through. No way could we just open fire and risk killing the females.

I radioed the land crew. I told them to wait until they heard us firing, and I gave them the order to – Fire! Fire! Fire! – on the radio, then open up themselves – but to shoot wide into the ground around them, not at them, they also needed to keep the camcorder recording, because if the skips fired at us, it was shoot to kill, and we will need evidence they fired first. All I wanted them to do was stir up a racket to frighten the girls and distract the skips. That ought to make it easy for us to get ashore and make the arrests. I wanted to take the skips alive, although I was prepared to shoot to kill if our lives were at risk. We all understood that.

We were within twenty feet of the shoreline. I stopped

paddling, and my feet immediately hit the ground. I signalled to Jake to stop. We kicked the flippers off, knelt inside our inner tubes, and raised our rifles. Then we executed our carefully choreographed plan. At my signal, Jake took a couple of shots at their dinghy, opening up two long gashes in the yellow rubber. 'FUBAR[31],' he shouted. The explosion of escaping air was drowned out as I put the loudhailer to my lips and called, 'Federal agents! Hands up, or you all die! Now!' Then I raised my rifle and squeezed the trigger, aiming in the direction of their rifles against the tree while giving the firing order to our land crew. At the precise same moment, the land crew responded. You could almost feel sorry for the skips and their girls as they stood there around the fire, hands aloft, jumping up and down on the spot, girls screaming at the top of their voices, guns going off all around them but unable to see their assailants in person.

We stood up and walked towards the party through the shallow water, skeins of slimy weed wrapped around my legs. I shouted at them to get to the ground. They obeyed instantly, the men silent, the girls whimpering and quaking.

I shouted into the walkie-talkie, ordering the backup team to move in fast. Christ knows what the skips made of it, two frogmen in black with night vision goggles emerging from the lake, slimy weeds hanging from our dripping wet suits, guns blazing, and all lit up by the flames of a log fire, but I wasn't thinking about them. I was feeling on top of the world. A well thought out plan coming to fruition without a glitch? For deep satisfaction, I'd put it up there with a bout of good, raunchy sex.

We tied up the four of them. Then I sent Jake to check the house and gather any guns, drugs, or other incriminating articles. When the skips heard me radio the cops, they started kicking up

---

[31] See glossary

129

a fuss. They realised a gang of bounty hunters had routed them, and boy did they start bellyaching. 'Oh, man! fucking bounty hunters. You serious? Thought you were the feds.' That made me feel even better. That was one slick operation we'd executed. The feds would've been proud to pull it off.

The Stripper

A skip is a skip. It could be old, or young, white or black. Could be calm, might be crazy. Some will come in like little lambs; others will come at you all guns blazing, willing to fight you to the death. When you go after a skip, you have no way of knowing how they're going to behave.

For a lot of them, it's a new experience, facing up to a mean-looking sonofabitch in a black uniform, wielding a gun and a badge, exploding into their home at three in the morning. I remember the time I was creeping along a dimly lit corridor to make an arrest and spotting this apparition of a mean-looking sonofabitch coming towards me with a gun. We aimed at each other precisely at the same time. Scared the living crap out of me, I nearly opened fire on him until I realised it was my own reflection in a mirror. Jesus, I looked frightening. So how would you react? You'd better hope you never have to find out. Of course, the enforcer always has the advantage of surprise. And experience. He's done this before. He has control over the way he conducts himself. And when you're bringing in a female – which accounts for ten percent of cases, maybe a little more – boy, do you need that control.

The girl in question was Laurie Gonzalez. She'd been working as a Pole dancing stripper, although she would have called herself an exotic dancer. Either way, Laurie was always showing off what she had – and to be fair, when they showed me a semi-clothed photograph, well, I couldn't fail to notice that she had plenty. She was a real beauty. Dark hair, Hispanic features, beautiful figure, and a good sassy look about her. Self-confident and intelligent, which, to my mind, is a big turn-on. If I'd spotted her in some bar, I would have made a beeline for her. You bet your ass I would.

Laurie worked at one of those joints where the girls gyrate on a pole, on stage, then go round the tables performing for individuals or groups. They charge maybe twenty, twenty-five bucks for a few minutes. They dance topless, fully naked if you pay extra. These girls do okay. They can make over a thousand bucks a day in tips. And the club does well too. They charge an entrance fee and jack up the price of the drinks. Sky-high. Everybody wins – except maybe the punter.

I have been in a few of those clubs. Not because that's my thing, but there are times when you follow a lead and end up in some strange places. And, yes, I did have a few female friends who were into it as a way of topping up their income. So, when one of them asked me to drop in and see her in action, it would have been rude not to. It was a weird feeling, having a friend strip naked for me, gyrating on my lap. Confusing – but very enjoyable.

A lot of these places are no more than a front for prostitution. Even so, the rules are strict. If you want a private dance at your table or in your booth, you pay upfront. The girls will take all their clothes off, and they'll be there, right in your face, almost touching you. You can feel the heat, smell the scent, and I'd be lying if I said it's not a turn-on. It's supposed to be. And that's how it works. You get a guy with a rampant hard-on, and he won't think twice about slapping an extra twenty-dollar bill onto the table. Or a fifty, or maybe a hundred. But that's as far as you ever go. You touch the girl, just once, and the management will be down on you like flies on shit. When I say management, of course, I mean the heavies. And if you're damned fool enough to try it a second time – well, that's one quick way to find out what the sidewalk tastes like—seasoned with a little blood.

All of that doesn't mean you can't cozy up to the girls. They'll come and sit down with you; sure they will – at the cost of a round of drinks. And if they're that kind, they might enter into negotiations about extras. In some clubs you go in, you'll see those same services being administered in the dim light of a corner booth. Sure, it's tacky, but it keeps crime off the streets. And the staff clean up.

So back to Laurie. As I understood it, she'd skipped bail, and Tony, who worked in the bonding company office, had called to tell me that it was the manager of some club where she performed who'd put up the bond for her. So naturally, the guy was pissed off and would doubtless offer me any assistance in tracking her down. Tony had met Laurie when the bond was written and offered to come out with me too. It was an unusual offer, but I didn't think much of it at the time. As he explained it to me, he would be able to identify her – with or without her clothes.

The club was in Washington State. When I called the owner, he agreed to meet us to discuss arrangements for the arrest. Understandably, he didn't want us collaring the girl on club premises. He wanted us to meet at his home in the suburbs. Tony and I drove out there.

It was a very posh address and a very fancy house. It was all on one floor, a prominent place that stood alone, in the middle of a large lawned area, with tall trees marking the perimeter. The windows, I noticed, were barred. As both the electric gates opened, we drove up the drive; we could see the surveillance cameras turning to track our progress. This guy was doing all right. At the main front door, a flunkey of some kind directed us towards a garage whose twin doors parted to let us in. We parked alongside a couple of black stretch limos. As we got out of the car, the flunkey re-appeared from a side door and led us into the house. In a large entrance hall, we were met by a small, podgy man, about fifty. I saw a big oval bed with one of those fancy carved wooden headboards through an open door behind him. Two girls in skimpy panties and nothing else were lounging across it, one of them painting the other's toenails.

Our man had receding hair, dyed black and tied in a ponytail. He had silver rings on his fingers, gold in his ears, and a chunky wrist-watch studded with gemstones. If you were dreaming up a pimp or a porn magnate, he would be your man. A freshly ironed shirt covered his paunch. He had on neatly pressed grey slacks and on his feet a pair of flip-flops – like he'd just got out of the pool or something. Behind him was a much larger man. Muscle, I guessed – and maybe a butler on the side. When Shorty snapped his fingers, the gorilla went to the fridge and took out a few beers, which he placed on a large, glass-topped table. I took a seat and noted the camera pointing right at me from a fake beam on the ceiling.

'Okay,' our host began, 'we're here to talk about Laurie.' He drummed his fingers on the table and said, 'I don't like people running off with my money.'

'Who does?' I said, taking a sip of beer.

He ignored the remark. Went on to say he was prepared to show us the house where Laurie lived with her friends.

'Boyfriends?' I asked.

He shook his head. 'Nah. Just a couple of girls. Dancers. They're all dancers. I got a whole bunch of them.'

'What about guns?' I said. 'They armed?'

He seemed surprised by the question. 'Guns?' He shook his head. 'No, not to my knowledge.' Then he said, 'So I'm good to go, soon as you are. Relax, enjoy your beer, and then we'll take off. I'll show you the place, but I don't want you making any arrests until I'm out of the neighbourhood.'

'No problem,' I said. This guy wanted this girl out of circulation as quickly as possible, and that suited me fine. It was a case of, let's get it done and pocket the money.

Half an hour later, we were following him in his none descript car past a new modest, two-storey corner house on the outskirts of town. He pointed out of the window to it. The place looked neat and well maintained – even the yard, which had a manicured front lawn and a row of tidy shrubs. After I'd taken in the surrounding detail, I looked around for Shorty's car. He'd already taken off.

The road itself was pretty quiet. But then it was that quiet time, early afternoon. It was a chilly, late winter day. Nobody much was out, just the mailman cruising by and some motor mechanic working on a car on the front-drive a few houses away. Even as I noticed him, I could see his breath coming in clouds. We parked on the corner, right across the road from Laurie's place.

'That was all bullshit,' I said, as Tony looked at me, wondering what my next move would be.

'Oh yeah?' He questioned me with his eyes.

'All that about her jumping bail. Look, I've got the documents right here. She ain't due in court for another month yet.'

'Yeah, I know that,' Tony snapped.

'What do you think – I don't read the fucking paperwork? He's just decided to come off the bond, that's all.' I said.

I laughed. 'Yeah, while the bastard was screwing her, he put the bond money up, right? Now he's got a new squeeze, and it's goodnight Irene. Bastard. He'll be back home now, hoping we're kicking the door down and scaring the living shit out of her.' I looked around at the nice suburban street, but there's no need for that. What this neighbourhood needs is a bit of market research. Old style.'

I started up the car, drove around the block, and parked next to the side of the house. There was a tall wooden fence there that hid us from view. I leaned over to the rear seat and picked up a clipboard. 'And I'm not going to the door in uniform. Neither are you.' I got out, opened the trunk, and picked up a nice blazer for me and a jacket for Tony. I kept all kinds of clothes in there. You never knew when they'd come in useful. I then walked around the corner, Tony following behind me, approached the house's front door and gave it a couple of sharp knocks. While I stood and waited, I flicked through the papers on the clipboard.

Out of the corner of my eye, I could see the drapes part. I just caught a glimpse of someone with long dark hair, and she was gone. A moment later, the door opened a few inches – only as far as the chain lock allowed it.

I looked up, and there was Laurie. I recognised her right away, even before Tony dug his fingers in my back and said, 'That's her.'

'Can I help you?' She seemed calm and in control, but this wasn't a time to start a conversation. In situations like these, you have one significant asset, surprise. And you'd better take advantage of it. I took a step back, then charged the door with my shoulder. My weight and the speed of movement ripped the chain from its anchor point. The door flew open, and I landed inside the house, knocking Laurie over and landing in a heap on top of her. She was wearing nothing but a pair of panties and a skimpy T-shirt that rode up to her shoulders as she fell, exposing her breasts. A lot of things flash through your mind in a situation like that. You learn to shove them aside. I grabbed one of her wrists, twisted it behind her back, and had one cuff on before she could register her shock.

She started to wrestle, her hair getting all tangled across her face. I tightened my grip and got the second cuff on. 'Hold still,' I said. 'I'm a bail enforcer.' As I pulled my badge out from inside my T-shirt, I gave her the name of the company and added, 'I got a warrant for your arrest.'

As I pulled her upright, she spat a strand of hair out of her mouth. 'For Christ's sake, I'm not due in court till next month,' she said. At that moment, I heard Tony come into the house behind me. I was about to explain the situation to her when I heard a door open upstairs and footsteps along the landing. Then a voice.

'What the fuck's going on, Laurie? You okay?'

I looked up to see two men, both in jockey shorts and nothing else, except that one of them held a baseball bat and made his way towards me. I pulled out my gun. I didn't aim it at the guys, but at the floor. 'I'm enforcing a warrant,' I said, reaching for my badge. 'Now, put down the bat before someone gets seriously hurt. And all of you get your hands up.'

For a moment, it looked like he was going to try his luck. Then I heard the guy behind him say, 'Do it, Eddie.' His buddy dropped the bat and held up his hands, palms outwards.

Laurie was now crying. 'This ain't right,' she was saying. 'It ain't fair either. I was going to court next month. Ask my boss at the club. I already booked the day off. What gives you the right to come in here and —?'

'Listen,' I said, 'I'm just here to execute an arrest warrant; I don't care if you were going to court or not; at this moment in time, my job is to take you in. Now, let me do my job.'

I started to pull her towards the door, but she dug her heels in the carpet. 'Christ's sake, can't I get dressed? What are you, animals?'

'Yeah, sure,' I said. 'Excuse my manners.' I turned to Tony. 'Take these fellers into the lounge there, will you?' As he edged past me, I whispered, 'One hand behind your back like you have a gun, okay?' I knew he wasn't carrying, but as far as the boys were concerned, he had a gun in his waistband, same as me. I called up to them on the stairs. 'You follow my partner here, and let me tell you he's under orders. Any fancy shit, and he'll shoot you.' They were both staring at me, still maybe weighing up their chances. 'In the kneecaps,' I added. 'Unless he misses, of course. In that case, I'd advise you to place your hands over your balls.' I turned to Laurie. 'Okay, anyone else in the house?'

She nodded towards the stairs as two young women poked their heads around the corner. They were both wrapped in man-sized towelling robes.

'Okay, down here! Hands above your head!' They came slowly down, hugging the wall as if they thought I was about to shoot. Still holding on to Laurie, I put my gun in my belt and ran my right hand over them. They were clean. 'In there.' I pointed to the living room where Tony had rounded up the two guys. I turned to Laurie and led her to the foot of the stairs. 'Okay, you can get dressed now.'

She looked at me and said, 'And what, you gonna stand and watch me? Is that what you want?'

'Sure,' I said. 'Someone has to.'

Upstairs I checked each room in turn, under the beds, in the closets, the en suites, I'd heard about guys getting blown away by some fucker hiding in a wardrobe. It happened to a friend of mine one time. We went to her bedroom. 'Okay,' I said, 'tell me what you want – and where it is, and I'll get it for you.'

She realised now I was serious. She pointed to a tall closet. 'Get me some jeans,' she said, 'and those red sneakers.' She glanced out the window at a bare tree tossed by the wind. 'Better have that sweater too,' she said.

I picked the various items up and took her to the bathroom. First, I checked it for scissors or anything else she might try and attack me with. I picked up a glass tumbler and threw it on the bed, then removed her cuffs and left her to it, the door half-open, my gun at the ready.

As she washed her face and got dressed, I looked around the room. Like the whole of the rest of the place, it was luxuriously furnished. Laurie had very expensive taste. Lacy curtains, a deep-pile carpet, and a king-size water-bed. The bedside table had a heavy marble top with an ornate clock and a Tiffany lamp. There were mirrors everywhere with heavy frames. She was doing okay for herself. I wondered why she'd gone and done a dumb thing like taking a car without the owner's permission. But that was most likely our pimp friend, dumping on her. There was a DWI charge too, and assaulting a cop. Whatever had happened, she'd let it spiral out of control.

Laurie was dressed now. She'd even put a bit of make-up on. There was no denying the fact: she was gorgeous. I put the cuffs back on her, hands in front this time. We had a long drive ahead, I had Tony with me, and there was no need for her to be uncomfortable. I searched her again and took her downstairs. She didn't say a word. It seemed she was resigned to what was happening—or may be thinking.

'When we book you in, all you need to do is call another bonding up and get someone else to bail you out again; you haven't jumped bail so that it won't be a problem,' I explained to Laurie.

'Okay.' I addressed the others. 'You lot will stay in the house until we've gone.' I looked at the girls and nodded at the guys. 'And don't do anything I wouldn't do, eh?'

Tony and I took Laurie out to the car. Tony got in the back

with her. Laurie's warrant had come from another jurisdiction, which meant we had about an eighty-mile drive ahead of us. For the first ten minutes or so, we drove pretty much in silence. Then Laurie started. It was like she'd been brewing this up for some time.

'Okay, fellows, let's talk this through, yeah? Like, what does it take for you to let me go? You guys want cash or...?' I glanced over my shoulder and saw her reaching her cuffed hands across to Tony's right knee. 'I mean, I can make it worth your while,' she said. 'Anal, head. It's your call.' She gave a little laugh and said, 'I mean guys pay extra for cuffs, and hey, look at me – all tied up and helpless.' In the rear-view mirror, I saw her hold her hands up and flash a kittenish grin at me.

'Just shut the fuck up,' I said. 'You're going to jail, lady, so save your tricks for those nice lady guards they have down there.'

She didn't take any notice, just carried right on. 'Look, I'm good. I'm a thousand bucks a night girl – plus extras. C'mon, I can show you a real good time—both of you. Say the word, and I'll call one of the girls from the house. Which one do you want? I can get both of them. We could party like there's no tomorrow.'

I didn't answer. I was looking at Tony in the mirror. All this time, he'd been keeping shtum. When he spoke, it was to ask me to pull in at a gas station. 'I need something to drink. Can I get you anything?'

'Nah.' We stopped at a Seven-Eleven. As soon as he was out the door, Laurie started up again. 'Come on, babe. Lighten up, won't you? You seen my body. I can give you a real good time. And what does it cost you?'

'It would cost me something you don't understand,' I said. I was getting pretty well pissed off with Laurie by now.

'Like what?'

'Try self-esteem,' I said. 'You heard of that? Now do me a

140

favour, will you, and shut your goddam mouth – or do you want me to tape it shut?'

'Hey, whatever turns you on,' she replied. 'I met plenty of guys who dig that shit.'

I was all set to get out the duct-tape when Tony returned. He handed her a can of soda through the window, then came tapping at my side.

I wound the window down. 'Yeah, what's up?' I said.

He jerked his head to one side and spoke in a low voice. 'Let's you and me talk,' he said. 'Outside.' I had a feeling I knew what was coming, and I was right. Standing there in the cold and wind, he put it to me. 'Look, man, we can have us a bit of fun here. Why not just— you know, check into a motel room for a couple of hours?'

'Tony, no.' I looked him right in the eye and repeated the word. 'The answer is… no.'

'Listen,' he said, 'you ain't been sitting there next to her for forty fucking miles. I'm telling you she's giving me a boner like I ain't had in months.' He grabbed my arm. 'I'm telling you, man, this babe is hot.'

'I can see that,' I told him. 'What do you think? Am I fucking blind? But that isn't the way I work. And this is work, remember? You know law enforcement?' I pulled away from him and reached for the car door. 'The answer's no. And if this is why you were so fucking eager come on this ride with me, tough shit. This woman's going where she belongs in jail. She will not pass go, and she will not collect two hundred bucks.'

We drove off in silence. And then, just a few miles further on, I looked in the mirror, and what did I see? I saw the sonofabitch sliding his hands up her sweater, groping her tits.

'Jesus Christ, man!' I swung the car off the road and slammed on the brakes. They both lurched forward. As Tony protested, I jumped out, opened his door, and dragged him onto the shoulder. I had my hands on his jacket collar, and I was shouting right into this dumb-fuck's face. 'Do you want to keep your fucking job? D'you wanna keep drawing your salary cheque every month? Yeah? So's you can pay your fucking mortgage and keep a fucking roof over your fucking family's head? Your wife and that kid of yours – remember them? So keep your fucking hands off my prisoner, you hear me? And your fucking dick in your pants.'

Tony wasn't having it. He was under a spell and had one thing on his mind, and he couldn't shake it off. 'Screw you!' he shouted and turned to get back in the car. 'This is pussy on a plate – for both of us, and I'm gonna get me some. You play the boy scout if you want. I'll take your cookies. Guy gets quite a fucking appetite, y'know, when you've been married fifteen years.'

There was only one way out of this now. I drew back my right fist and landed one on him, smack on the jaw. Nearly broke my knuckles, but I laid him out cold.

He came round soon enough. 'Jesus,' he said. 'That wasn't called for, man. All I wanted was a bit of fun.' But I wasn't listening. I'd made up my mind. He was toast. I threw him his coat, then spelled it out for him, just in case the dumb fuck hadn't got the message. 'Think about it, Tony. Let's say you get to screw her. Yeah, she'll give you a fucking good time, but what's the first thing she does when we get to town? Huh? I'll tell you what she does. She tells the cops we raped her, the pair of us. And they'll have her examined. And what are you gonna tell them? Oh, so sorry, officer, but she said it was okay?' I turned to get back in the car, then paused. 'My prisoners,' I said, 'are delivered in one piece. Safe and unharmed. Every fucking time.' I gunned the engine. 'Enjoy your walk back to town.'

I slammed the door and took off. Laurie never said a word

the entire rest of the journey, and that suited me fine. I took her to the sheriff's, got my warrant signed, then headed back to the office to collect my fee. I told them what had happened and laid it on the line. I wasn't going to entertain another co-rider unless I had good reason to – and unless it was someone I knew I could trust. Meanwhile, maybe they could talk to their people about a professional code of ethics.

After I left there, my mood lightened. Tucking a cheque for $4,000 inside your wallet soothes away a lot of bad feelings. I headed home for a shower and a change of clothes. Unsurprisingly, I had women on my mind. That Laurie – sure she was hot, and I dare say I would've been turned on if that had been me in the back seat. The difference is, I can control my dick— most of the time.

I went out that night with the deliberate intention of scoring. And I wasn't going to be fussy. It was all about need, and I was going to satisfy it. The bar I chose was downtown. It was a place I knew I'd feel safe. I'd never had reason to work there; in fact, I'd never visited it before, but it had a reputation as a classy sort of place with good food and mellow sounds.

It was early evening when I showed up. It was still cold, but the wind had dropped, and I was comfortable enough, walking across the parking lot in my lightweight suit. I like to look smart when I go out looking for a woman. I expect her to look good for me, so it's only right that I put my best foot forward too. It was an attractive place with a bar in the centre and tables running along each sidewall. Smartly dressed waitresses worked the tables, while three or four athletic-looking guys in black polo shirts tended the bar. Music was playing; just loud enough drown out the conversation at the next table, soft enough that you could hear what was being said on your own. Not that I had anyone to talk to just yet. I chose a seat with my back to the wall, where I

143

could see the whole place. It's a sort of habit you get into in my line of work, for most security professionals; it's always a priority to position yourself correctly for survival. That's because when it comes to public places such as restaurants, bars, waiting rooms, we still want to remain aware of our surroundings and the small choices we can make to help maintain our situational awareness. Remember that the career criminal will exhibit tell-tale signs, like soaking in everything around them and pausing too long at certain places. You've seen it before; you either paid attention to it or ignored it. That's the goal here, stop ignoring things that are out of place. It's the first sign you'll get before something even worse occurs. Something that will give you a leg up in your reconnaissance of the building and more advance notice of impending threats is to sit facing the door. Be that as it may, I know many folks who don't think about choosing where to sit or stand in a restaurant, bar, store, school, or anywhere else, for that matter.

Not only should the right location give you a vantage point overlooking the entire restaurant, but it will also let you observe the foot traffic through the primary entrance. Ideally, take a seat with your back against a wall and as close to a secondary exit as possible. You are also looking around for makeshift weapons to use if a threat occurs.

Realizing that danger is coming and possibly even *seeing* it coming may provide you with life-sparing seconds that you wouldn't have had if your back was to the threat. It all starts with forming that habit. I challenge you all to begin picking out the best place to sit or stand (and the best way to leave) every time you enter a new space. Whether it's a restaurant, business, or even another person's home, I hope you all begin taking these actions to improve your situational awareness at all times.

But even on a night out, it has its uses. I was scanning the bar for talent.

I'd just finished my avocado and prawns when I spotted her. She caught my eye right away. She was a beauty, was alone, and walked in like she owned the damned place. She had the same colouring as the dancing girl – well, that may have had something to do with it, although she had one thing Laurie Gonzalez lacked. Class. Oodles of it. She wore a pale blue dress, beautifully cut so that the hem caressed her bare, tanned legs just above the knee and tailored to hint at the curves of her body rather than put them all in the shop window. I would've said she was twenty-eight, maybe thirty.

The waitress arrived and took my plate, pausing to follow my stare and nod approvingly. 'I wish I could afford dresses like that.'

I laughed. 'I bet you do, sweetheart.'

'But hey,' she said, 'when you own the store…'

'Pretty young to own her own place,' I said, but the girl had gone.

I didn't rush it. I finished my food, keeping an eye on her. She seemed well known at the bar, trading jokes with the staff, chatting with one or two regulars. I wiped my mouth on a napkin, stood up and brushed a couple of crumbs off my shirt front, then walked over and took a seat beside her.

Her name was Melodie. She had the most beautiful voice – deep, slow, seductive with a distinct Southern accent. 'Why yes,' she said, when I asked her if it was right that she owned a dress shop, 'it's my own business, although my daddy owns the property. I was always into fashion, growing up in New Orleans.' Then she looked at me and asked, 'So what do you do?'

I told her I was in covert security, then added, 'Tell you the truth, I'm not supposed to talk about it to people I meet in bars.'

She laughed and didn't pursue it – which I appreciated. A lot of people see it as a challenge. Oh, you're doing secret stuff. Let me see if I can worm it out of you. But Melodie was happy to talk about her own work, and I was delighted to listen. That voice, man. I was already fantasising about hearing her tell me what she wanted as we made love, calling out my name as she hit the high spots. When I asked her whether she'd like to dance, she smiled and said, 'Why, it'd be a pleasure, honey.'

She was a brilliant dancer. She moved quickly in my embrace but never got in too close. Just let her dress slide across my pants' leg, allowing her hair to drift tantalisingly close to my cheek. After a couple of numbers, I asked her to join me at my table, where I still had half a bottle of Nuits St Georges. 'Sure,' she said and checked her watch. She told me she was expecting a friend to show up – sometime. She wasn't sure when.

We emptied the bottle, ordered coffee, and I started to speculate. Would Melodie he invite me to her place, or would we go back to my hotel? In my mind, I was racing ahead. I'd got her into bed, was undressing her slowly, caressing her silky-smooth skin and firm young body. I thought I'd get the ball rolling by asking whether I could take her home.

'That won't be necessary,' she said, and her voice had a slightly cooler edge to it. 'I think that's my friend arriving now.' She stood up to greet him. Yeah, him. Her friend was a guy – young, well built, handsome, and wearing the kind of suit you'd re-mortgage your home to buy.

He walked up to our table with his arms out and a big wide grin on his face. Yeah, I thought, me too if I had a woman like this waiting for me. 'Hi sweetheart,' I heard him say, 'sorry I'm late, but I had to check the brief for tomorrow's case. You know what these mega-corp clients are like.'

'Why, that's quite all right, honey.' Her voice was as smooth as the dark, creamy coffee she was pushing to one side. 'I've been talking to Ted here. He's in covert security. For the Government.

Except it's so secret, he couldn't tell me anything about it.'

The guy held out his hand to me. 'That sounds real interesting,' he said, with all the sincerity of a politician on the stump. Then he checked his watch. 'Well,' he said, 'our table should be ready. Good to meet you.'

It was a let-down, sure it was. But one thing I learned as a single man is, there's always another opportunity – just so long as you aren't too particular. Within an hour of Melodie's departure, I was sitting at the bar with Claire and Marcia, a couple of legal secretaries. They told me they worked together and liked to play together with each other. I took the hint – you bet I did – and we ended the night in a big round bed in Marcia's apartment, the three of us, glasses of Champagne, strawberries, and cream; it turned out to be a regular threesome. Who was it who said, as one door shuts, another opens?

Did He Have a Gun or Didn't He?

I had only been doing this job less than a couple of years; I decided I wanted more of the federal cases coming my way from time to time, fewer of the nickel and dime jobs. So I decided to launch a campaign. It wasn't that I was fussy. To me, work was work, and I always took whatever came along. Many of these were routine jobs – bringing in people for small-time offences, like failing to appear in court for, driving without a licence, making menaces, domestic violence, harassment, that kind of thing. Mostly, these people were easy to track down. They didn't take off and hide in the woods. They didn't come at you armed to the teeth. And even though I was only getting my 10% ($500) from a $5000 bail bond. The fact that I could sometimes round up eight or ten skips in a single day kept the pot boiling nicely. I needed that for my overheads.

I was working out of Phoenix, Arizona. Not my favourite place – mostly because it's so damned hot. Back in the day, they'll tell you; it was a desert climate. Hot but dry, and cooling off some at night. Then came the population boom, the spread of vast suburbs, where everybody thought they needed a lawn out front. And the grass needs water. So every mother's son has a sprinkler system, and what do you have then? Moisture in the atmosphere, and a nasty, sticky heat. In the summertime, it can be 110 and up to 115, with added humidity. People get cranky.

I was after a small-time crook, who was facing charges of assault with a deadly weapon. Well, two deadly weapons, a knife, and a baseball bat. The defendant had been bailed and had absconded. When I checked his files, I saw that this was no kid who'd gone astray one time. No, he had a string of previous offences, mostly VUCSA (Violation of the Uniform Controlled Substance Act).

On top of that, there were several assaults too. Desmond Alderton was a guy to approach with care. When I read his rap sheet, I saw he was six foot three inches tall and built like the proverbial brick shit-house. A guy like me, five-eight, he could knock me down any time he felt like it. There was another thing about this guy. Looking at his previous rap sheet, it had a weapon warning flagged up.

One thing that's always on your mind as a bounty hunter is a fear of causing injury or death to a suspect when it's not demonstrably justifiable. The only time when it's within the law to use your weapon is if the person you go to arrest is armed and you have reason to believe your life – or someone else's – is in danger. Unfortunately, there's no way of knowing for sure what a person's response will be when you come knocking on their door.

I decided, in this case, I could do with backup. I called an old buddy of mine from DC, a guy called Rob. I used to meet up with Rob from time to time, sink a few cold ones, and of course, he knew what I did for a living. He had a job on a production line, a three-shift system, and he was bored out of his skull. He said he wanted some excitement. Maybe he'd get into my line of work, he'd say. It sounded like easy money. 'Okay,' I told him, 'let's see what we can do for you.'

Rob was a keen hunter, so I knew he could handle a gun, also that he had one characteristic that is so crucial in my line of work. I'm talking about patience – the understanding and acceptance of the fact that you cannot predict people's movements, that you will spend long hours, whole days and nights even, in places that are always too hot or too cold, waiting for your skip to show – or to make his move. Rob knew all about that. His wife was a cop in the city, so he understood the risk factor. And another thing: he was a big, athletic guy—lots of muscle and quick on his feet.

It was cloudy in Phoenix, with the threat of thunder in the air. They were forecasting a cooler-than-usual July day. A modest ninety-eight degrees. I was doing the rounds of Alderton's known hang-outs and getting nowhere – just stinking hot and listless.

I decided I needed a break. I took refuge in a bar where Alderton was supposed to be known. Just my luck: I'd already bought my soda-water and chips when they told me the AC was down, and all we had was a warm breeze coming through the doorway. The place was almost empty, just a bunch of diehards playing pool. After a while, I decided to hang around, and they asked me if I wanted a game. I got chatting. It turned out one of these guys was owed money by Alderton – and he was pissed off because he knew the guy was in a position to pay him. I asked him what he meant, and he told me he was back dealing with drugs. 'D'you know that for sure?' I asked.

He laughed. 'Sure I do; my buddy just bought some fucking dope off him.'

'So where is he? Where can I find him?'

He gave me an address. I knew the area he meant: low-income housing, plenty of gang activity. I gave him a down payment and agreed on a bonus if I got Alderton into custody. Soon as I left the bar, I called Rob. 'How you fixed for tomorrow?' I asked him. 'I got a little job on. Could do with some muscle beside me.'

'I'll call work,' he said. 'Tell 'em I'm sick.' He thought for a moment, then added, 'And that's no lie. I am sick. Sick of that fucking graveyard shift.'

I told him to stand by for a second call. Before I made any

plans, I needed to check that this address was for real.

It wasn't hard to locate the house. As I drove past the place, I caught a glimpse of my skip, right there on the sidewalk, doing a deal with a couple of teenagers, probably high school kids. I drove on maybe fifty yards, then pulled over, and watched in the mirror as he strolled nonchalantly back into the house.

I'd rented a beat-up old Dodge for this job. It had a hanging rear fender, a cracked windscreen, and a frayed rag-top.[32] It was just the kind of car you'd expect to find in these lowlife neighbourhoods. So long as it had functioning AC and a motor with a bit of oomph in it, I was happy enough.

I sat there for a while, trying to figure out the best way to tackle this. The neighbourhood was only one stage away from being derelict. Alderton's house hadn't seen a lick of paint in an age. The windows were all boarded up – had sheets tacked up in place of blinds. You would've mistaken it for an abandoned home were it not for a skinny girl in purple hot pants, squatting on the front porch, eating an ice-cream cone. Eighteen years old, maybe less. The houses on either side had gone. The one on my side had burned down. You could still see the charred remnants of sheet-rock walls and molten plastic window frames, one or two blackened spars of timber. The one on the far side, I guessed, had been demolished and removed, leaving a plot of wasteland dotted with all kinds of trash and a few tall weeds.

I had an idea of how this one would play, and having seen the skip; I decided not to hang about. I called Rob back. 'It's on,' I said. 'Now.'

'You mean— like, now - Now?'

'You got it, bud. I need you to get your ass over here pronto.'

'Can't it wait?'

---

[32] See glossary

'Rob,' I said, 'you wanted action. I'm offering a chance to—' In the background, I could hear some woman bellyaching, then a door slamming.

'Okay, okay. I'm on my way. Just tell me where.'

I gave him the address and explained the situation. 'I'm driving a big old Dodge sedan,' I told him. 'Mostly rust with patches of silver.' I gave him the licence-plate number. 'When you get here, pull up behind me as near as you can, but stay in your car. Wait for my signal. Got that?'

'Sure,' he said. 'I got it.'

I had a sense of unease about this one. Usually, I would try to go early in the day to get a skip. First, in a place like Phoenix, you're going to be relaxed and fresh. Second, at that time of day, your skip is likely to be still in bed, often in a drug-induced stupor. In early mornings, there are fewer people around on the streets to get in the way if anything goes wrong. So why was I doing this in the heat of the day? Because I'd seen the sonofabitch, that's why. I needed to nail this guy, and this was too good an opportunity to miss.

Rob showed up barely twenty minutes after my call. He pulled up behind me, as instructed. There was just one guy on the street, some old-timer picking up empty beer cans with a sharpened stick, but he soon shuffled on by with his plastic sack over his shoulder. The girl with the ice-cream cone, a car had come by, and she'd ridden off with a couple of young dudes. I signalled to Rob and he got in the car with me.

'Everything cool?' he asked.

'Yeah,' I said. 'It's quiet just now. But I've seen our man. He did a deal right out the front there. With any luck, he'll be inside chilling with a big fat one.' I reached forward, switched on the ignition.

'Where we going?' Rob asked.

'I'm going around the back in case he runs out that way. You're gonna cover the front. Here, take this.' I handed him a walkie-talkie. He got out, and I drove up to the STOP sign, turned right and right again. Before I got out of the car, my set crackled into life. '*In position.*'

'I read you. I'm going in right now. Stand by.'

Before I made my move, I looked up and down the street. Empty, this was a day for sitting still in a cool dark place. I got out of the car and walked towards the back door. There was a mess of chicken bones on the path, burger wrappers, a smear of dog crap. With my gun in my hand, I tried the handle; unlocked. Jesus, this could be a piece of cake. I pushed against it, really steady. There was a scuffing sound as it dragged one of those pizza flyers across a dirty tiled floor. I had it halfway open when it smashed back in my face, hurling me across the porch. I bounced off the rail and launched myself at the door, my right foot raised.

'Recovery agents!' I shouted, kicking the door open and stepping inside, my gun raised. 'Down on the floor!' I was in a kitchen. There was nobody there, just a frying pan, abandoned on the stove, flames licking around it, smoke rising in the air.

There was a door to one side that led into an empty passageway. I pressed the talk button on the two-way. 'Rob, is he coming your way out front?'

There was no reply, just a shout and then two loud gunshots from the other side of the house. I dashed down the passageway to the door and opened it. Rob was lying on the ground, eyes open but stunned. In his right hand, he held his gun. Out of the corner of my eye, I could see Alderton running across the vacant lot, stumbling as he turned to look back at the house. 'I'm okay,' Rob gasped. 'Fucker took a couple of shots at me.'

'You hit?'

He shook his head. 'Nah. Just fell.' Then he looked at me and asked, 'You?'

He was looking at the blood that was trickling down my upper lip. 'Nothing,' I said, 'just banged my nose.'

I pulled out my warrant and gave it to him. 'Okay, you call the cops, and soon as they show up, you be sure to give 'em this.' Then I set off after my man. He was no greyhound. Way too big. He was still trying to get over the wire boundary fence and into the street. 'Stop!' I shouted. 'Get your hands up.'

He was wobbling, half on the fence, half of it. To my surprise, he stopped and turned. I only saw that he had a gun in his hand and was loading a fresh clip.

'Drop it,' I shouted. 'Drop the gun right now, or I'll fire!'

You don't have time to think in these situations. What you see is a guy loading a gun. And you look around and see you're the only possible target. There was nobody behind him, nobody in the line of fire. I loosed one shot off; I didn't aim properly. The fact was, it was a shit or bust situation. I fired four, maybe five shots; as I dived on the ground, I heard his bullets zip past me.

I ducked my head, pressing my face into the dust. A final bullet pinged off an abandoned washing machine right beside me. Then there was silence, just the cicadas in the trees and a distant voice going, 'Fuck, man. Wass going down?'

I looked up and saw Alderton on his knees, head down, slumping to the ground.

Shit, surely I hadn't killed him? I got to my feet and wiped more blood off my lips. I walked forward, crouching, pausing every step to look around. I heard a screen door swing shut from across the road as someone came outside to take a look. In another house, a window slid open. A car turned into the street and stopped abruptly with a squeal of tyres.

I flipped open my phone, dialled 911, and summoned police

and ambulance. People were now coming out from the houses and walking – some towards me, one or two approaching the fallen man.

I was frantically trying to remember how many rounds I'd loosed off. I realised I must have panicked – and that's no excuse whatsoever, especially in a court of law. The thought ran through my head that this was not the first time I'd shot a man in action and killed him. I heard myself let out a weary 'Shit.'

As I approached Alderton's prone body, I saw nothing but blood. It was all over his shirt, shoes, and baseball cap, which lay in the dirt beside him. Oh fuck. And now his neighbours were pressing in. There was a big, tall man about forty. 'You white mothafucka!' he shouted. 'What you done, boy?'

I heard another voice and looked around to see a younger guy, broad-shouldered, and naked to the waist. 'You fuckin' murdered him, plain as day. I seen ya, ya honky white shit.'

'Back!' I screamed, turning to level the gun at them each in turn. Others were coming, slowly, from all sides, mostly male, all black. I raised my gun and fired off a couple of rounds into the air. Someone screamed. Three or four of them backed off. The first guy said, 'You in big trouble, white boy. We witnessed the whole damned thing. You gonna fry for what you done, boy.'

Bam! I let another off. I couldn't think of what else to do. 'Who's next?' I shouted. A woman, short, heavily built, her mouth twisted in rage, was screaming at me. 'He never had no gun. You nothin' but a cold-blooded killer, damn your rotten soul.'

'He fired first,' I said. 'I saw a gun.' I turned to look at Alderton's body. Oh fuck. Where was it? Where was the fucking gun? Both his hands were empty. I was going to be on a murder rap if someone else had fire that gun. I stepped closer to take another look. Blood was flowing from his right hand. He had two

155

of his fingers missing, which I had shot off.

I looked up at the crowd, slowly encircling me. Where the hell were the cops? Where was my backup? I was just about to fire off another shot when I heard Rob's voice. 'Okay, get back! Stand back, now!' I saw the crowd parting as he made his way through to me, gun raised. Then the welcome sound of police sirens, maybe two streets away.

Suddenly the crowd was backing away. A couple of young guys took off down the street like startled rabbits. The squad cars were coming along the road from both directions and squealing to a halt – one, two, three, four. Cops were spilling out onto the sidewalk.

As they surrounded me, I dropped my gun and lowered myself to the ground. Rob's voice seemed remote and faint as he explained the situation to them. I looked up and saw that one of the cops was his wife. Another cop came across and checked my ID. 'Okay,' he said, 'on your feet.' He pointed to where someone was bending over Alderton. 'That the guy?' he asked.

'Yeah,' I said as I glanced down; he lay on his back, motionless, eyes open. He looked pretty dead to me. The cop was searching around the weeds. When I saw him bend down, I felt the relief flood through my veins. He'd found the gun except that it wasn't a gun. It was a piece of iron. 'Oh, fuck me,' I said as he tossed it aside.

It wasn't the first time I'd been cuffed and taken downtown from such a scene. It's standard practice if the cops aren't sure who's who or what happened. All the evidence pointed to me having shot dead an unarmed man. All I could do was insist that Alderton fired first, a small-caliber pistol, but where it had gone, I had no idea.

As I sat in the holding area at the cop station, the doubts set in. I kept seeing the angry faces around me, accusing me. Did he fire at me? Could I have fired a warning shot first? Was it someone else, someone I hadn't seen, that fired at me? Rob couldn't help. By his admission, he was too far away, and in any case, also shaken up. The only thing was, he was standing firm in his accusation that Alderton had discharged a gun at him and that he'd fired back at him when he was on the back porch. Surely the cops would find a stray bullet in the woodwork or someplace?

The cops kept us apart in separate cells. We gave our statements in different rooms. I was all too familiar with what followed. I spent a couple of hours locked in a cell, waiting for the bonding company to come and bail me out. I kept going over and over the details in my head. The cops had confirmed that Alderton was dead, so there was no question about the charge if I was wrong. It would be a homicide, and I'd be pleading extenuating circumstances.

They offered me food, but I had no appetite. I could only imagine what life would be like for a white bounty hunter on the inside if I have made an error.

A cop came in to interview, and I nearly gagged; he was finishing off a giant slice of pizza. A minute later, I could've kissed the ugly bastard full on the lips, mozzarella grease and all. He told me they'd searched the waste ground where the incident took place, found two bullet holes, retrieved the slugs and an ammunition clip from a Walther PPK 9mm. I asked him whether they'd found the guy's prints on it. 'Prints?' he laughed out loud, between mouthfuls of Margherita. 'That's a good one. You blew the guy's fingers clean off.' Then he said, 'Yeah, sure, we'll be checking that. Still no gun, though.'

The bonding company posted bail my bail. It was dark by now but still horribly warm. Thunder rumbled around the sky, but the rain we'd hoped for refused to come. I got home and took a cool shower, cracked open a beer, and watched mindless crap on

TV until, finally, I felt sleep beckoning.

My worst fears didn't come to fruition, thank Christ. The next morning I learned through my attorney that the cops had now found two witnesses who stated that Alderton had a gun and that he'd fired first. Better still, they'd seen an unknown bystander pick it up and run the scene with it. Welcome news, of course, but I still wasn't in the clear. It wouldn't be until the court decision.

The next day I was still uptight. I needed to unwind. I called Rob, and we went for a beer and something to eat. Pizza Margherita. It must've been on my mind. I talked through my worries, then listened to him as he told me about the difficulties of being married to a female cop, how it affected the kids, and the anxieties that came with it. The more he talked, the more I realised how happy he and his wife were together, not free from problems, but comfortable. I decided I wouldn't put him at risk again. The guy Alderton could have taken him out, and how would I have felt then?

As apparent as it was, I had no case to answer; I still had to make my appearance in court and go through the formalities. But by then, Phoenix had had its storm. The streets were washed clean, the skies were blue, the air fresh, and suddenly everybody seemed more relaxed.

Mother's Boy

When you go after someone who's skipped bail, you're entering an uncertain world populated by unpredictable characters. You never know how your skip is going to react when you try to place him under arrest. Neither does he, come to that. Why should he? It doesn't happen to him every day; maybe never has. It doesn't matter whether you've walked up to him in a parking lot and placed a hand on his shoulder or kicked his door down and bust in on him screwing his girlfriend. The fact is you've caught him off guard, maybe embarrassed him. And he's going to react spontaneously, and sometimes with instincts he didn't know he possessed. But it's not always that way. Just once in a while, you get the chance to get into someone's head and figure out what makes them tick. Then, if you're lucky, you can psyche them out.

James Lietiner was no big-time crook, but he had a string of convictions, most of them drug-related. When the bonding company told me to bring him and his car in, I called the police station and asked the case officer to send the details to our office. Usually, the police file will have a bit of background information on the guy and maybe a few addresses, the names of contacts, family, a girlfriend – perhaps a list of his favourite hangouts, a recent photo. It can save you a lot of time. It gives you a chance to try and assess his character. Lietiner's file came with – the 'pink'[33] that gives the vehicle owner's details. However, my problem was with the current address. I'd recently arrested a guy

[33] See glossary

on that same street, a dealer, and he'd sworn he was going to have my head on a spike, blow me away, all the usual bullshit threats. I wouldn't usually have been worried, but I had heard that he was trying to make a name for himself in a local gang, a street gang with a reputation for revenge attacks. Even as I was handing him over to the cops downtown, he was threatening to set them onto me. I had further reason to be wary of them: this guy I'd collared was their supplier, and they were seriously pissed off that he'd been taken out of action. So I didn't want to be bumping into those guys on a dark night when I was on my own.

But back to James Lietiner. He was thirty-five years old, unmarried. He weighed 200 pounds – most of it fat rather than muscle. Maybe that's why he was still single. He'd always lived in the same area, until recently with his mother, although it had changed somewhat since he was a kid. What used to be a decent blue-collar neighbourhood had gone down the toilet—big time. Most of the houses were decrepit; some boarded up. Trees were growing out of front porches; gutters were hanging loose. The streets were full of trash – much of it of the human variety – and lined with the sort of vehicles you'd look at, and you couldn't tell whether they were abandoned or not. And then, as if you couldn't see what was staring you in the face – that this was dealer central you were driving through – there was the giveaway. In amongst all the cars with missing wheels and smashed windscreens, the blue sedans with a single red door, the ones with the hood up and the engine burned out. You'd suddenly spot a Cadillac, a fancy convertible, a Lincoln. Not new ones, but still nice old cars fixed up with gold trim, tinted glass, and customised licence plates. Dealer cars.

I had an address for Lietiner that the police claimed was current. I figured I'd cruise around in daylight before I tried hauling the guy into custody. DC is one of those so segregated towns; a white guy stands out like a whore in a convent. Besides, first things first, I planned to repossess his car, a white Caddy that the bonding company had as surety. While I was at it, I could check out the place he was supposed to live, always conscious that I had enemies in these parts.

I was navigating the area by street-maps, looking for the car. At every street corner, I was crawling along, checking each building in turn. It was a cloudy, grey November afternoon, and it was hard to make out the numbers. I glanced up at a lousy, run-down apartment block, a crumbling redbrick place set back from the road behind the remains of a wall. Stone steps led up to a heavy wooden door. Three or four youths were lounging around there. Their eyes followed me as I drove on by, resisting the urge to put my foot on the gas. It was a mean neighbourhood, and I was getting a bad vibe.

According to the information I had, Lietiner never had a regular job. He had always been in trouble with the law – mostly minor league stuff, but invariably involving drugs. He'd served time once or twice but still went back home to his mom. He might have been any one of hundreds, maybe thousands of men his age that you'd meet on the streets of DC. Most of his neighbours fell into two categories: there were those who were too old, feeble, or lazy to get the hell out, and then those who used the area as a base for drug-dealing and associated activities.

I found the car, finally, parked up against the curb next to a vacant lot. I slowed down and took a look at it. I needed to check that it was worth repossessing. In an area like that, you always feel vulnerable when you show up with a tow truck. It's easy to attract a crowd, and then anything can happen. I wasn't going to go through a lot of hassle for some worthless piece of junk. But to my surprise, it looked to be in pretty good shape. I went around the block, pulled up next to it, and got out to take a closer look. It was late afternoon now, and it was icy cold. Even so, I waited a while before calling the tow-truck company. I wanted to time it so that the light would be fading by the time they showed up, so it would be less chance of aggravation from the locals. When it started to snow, I felt myself relax. The shuffling bums and old men who had been on the streets earlier just melted away.

The tow truck guys showed up pretty soon and got to work. Like me, they didn't want to hang around. It didn't take long to fix a hook under the Cadillac's fender, and when they set off, I followed them to our compound. On the way, I put a call into the Police Department, giving them the car's registration number and identifying myself as the repo man. If someone called in and reported it stolen, the cops would have an answer ready. By the time I'd completed the necessary paperwork and collected my $250 fee, I was ready to eat. I decided I would take my time, wait until eight or nine when everyone was indoors and watching the TV or whatever they did at night. The element of surprise: it's your greatest ally in these situations. By the time I set off to check out Lietiner's supposed to be address, it was snowing heavily; and the streets were completely deserted.

I was surprised by what I found. Lietiner's place was a halfway decent-looking apartment block. It stood out like a beacon in those ugly surroundings. No abandoned refrigerators in the yard, no boarded-up windows; they had new metal bars on them and shiny new padlocks, fancy drapes, and all. Having surveyed the front, I decided to look around the back to see what possible access there was. I drove around the corner and turned into the alleyway, which I noted was only wide enough for one car. Again, the place looked pretty clean, not what I'd expected at all.

I completed the circuit of the block and parked within sight of the front of the building. Then I pulled out my phone. I might as well try the number we had on file. See whether the skip was in or not.

'Hello?' It was a woman's voice answering.

I answered in my best English accent. That always got people guessing; it puts them on the back foot. 'Hello,' I said, 'would it be possible to speak to James? I'm guessing you must be his mum. Is that right?'

'Yeah, that's me. Who is this?'

'Just a friend of his, from England. You're Elena, am I right?'

She laughed. 'Oh, he told you that?'

'Oh, he told me a lot of things,' I said. 'I was passing through town and wondered whether he might be home. I'd like to have a word with him. We have a lot to catch up on.'

'Well, he's out right now.' There was a pause. 'And you say you're from England?'

'That's right. Tell him it's Mark. He'll know who it is.'

'Well, if you can tell me how he can get back to you...'

'Of course.' I gave her my cell phone number and wished her well. I'd baited the hook, and she seemed keen to bite.

An hour or so later, a couple of guys emerged from the main doors; they just stood there, shoulders hunched, hoods up over their heads, looking up and down the street and stamping their feet. But It was clear they were waiting for someone. Might it by my fat friend? I sank low in my seat, turned up my coat collar, and pulled my dark beanie hat low over my forehead. After a few minutes, a car pulled up in front of me, and a tall black dude got out. Certainly not Fatso, he went across to the entrance and stood talking to the other guys on the porch for a minute or two. As they spoke, one of them kept looking around; for a moment, he seemed to be staring right at me. Soon they all disappeared inside.

I started up the car, then slowly drove around the back, 'Oh, fuck!' I was just turning into the alleyway when I caught sight of a pickup with the same three men standing around it. Seeing them caught in my headlights, I knew right away who they were: members of that gang. The ones who were pissed off because I'd collared their candy-man.[34] Even as I slung my car into reverse, I saw one of them point at me and shout. How I got out of that alleyway without ripping the side off my car, I'll never know. I swerved out onto the road, hit the gas, and tore down the street, one eye watching out for any pedestrians, the other glued to the rear-view mirror. The bastards were hard on my tail, lights on high beam.

I did two rights and a left turn, and I was away from the hood and onto a stretch of a divided highway; there was very little traffic on the roads, and the surface had recently salted. I checked the thermometer on the dash. Twenty-eight degrees. I took the Uzi out of my bag, which was sitting on the passenger seat, and laid it on my lap. Who knew what the fuckers might try? I was up to eighty miles an hour, and they were hard on my tail. I reached up and twisted the rear-view to one side to save my eyes. I needed to take the initiative; otherwise, I just a sitting duck. I saw a turning up ahead, braked late and hard, and swung the car into it. It was a narrow track, unpaved, rutted, with frozen puddles and furrows of thick mud. A sign said it was a dead-end leading down to the riverbank. In other words, a dead-end. If ever the words 'time to shit or get off the pot' were called for, this was it. I slowed down, then sharply swung sideways, grabbed the gun, and threw my door open. The guy behind braked hard and skidded towards me. Their vehicle stopped, no more than ten yards short of mine. As I got out, I slid out of my coat, exposing my full uniform. In the moment that my pursuers hesitated, trying to figure out whether this was the cops they'd been chasing or what, I opened

---

[34] See glossary

fire with my Uzi sub-machine gun. I hit both front lights, which made their minds up for them. They were in reverse, spinning around and spraying me with icy slush, before skidding their way back toward the highway.

I got back in the car and raced after them. I had no intention of giving chase; I just wanted them to them think I was; it got them rattled, and, on the run, I liked it that way. I watched as they turned right and sped off towards the city. I composed myself and took out my phone. I still had work to do and didn't see why I should let a little thing like a car chase and a shoot-out stand between me and a decent payday. I called Lietiner's mother again. Whether she'd been in touch with her boy or whether she'd had a long think about our previous conversation and realised how unlikely it was that he would be hanging out with an English guy, who knows? The fact is she tried to bullshit me. 'No, you got the wrong number,' she said. 'I was confused before.'

'Okay,' I said. 'Listen up. What I am is a fugitive recovery agent—a bounty hunter in your language. Your boy has violated the terms of his bail. I've already repossessed his car, and now I want his ass in jail. Are you aware of what security you signed away for the bail bond?'

There was a silence that lasted ten, maybe fifteen seconds.

'Well, are you?' I said.

Then I heard her sigh. 'Yeah,' she said. 'Kinda.'

'Let me remind you, lady,' I said. 'There were several other properties, including your home secured on the bond. If James has not surrendered to the bonding company and fast. I mean by tomorrow before noon, you're going to be living on the street, without your furniture. Now I'm not a hard man. I'm going to give you a bit of time to talk him into doing the right thing. You got that?'

She'd got it all right. I rang off and then called the bonding company. 'Okay,' I told them. 'Prepare yourself. Your boy Lietiner?'

'Yeah, wassup? You gonna bring him in?'

'No need. James should be turning himself in, most likely in the morning, but it could be tonight. So why don't you make his bed up for him and put his electric blanket on? He's gonna need all the sleep he can get.'

'You're giving me a load of bullshit. You seriously think that mother's gonna hand himself over?' the bondsman added.

I was out on a limb here, and I knew it, but after talking with Lietiner's old lady, I just had that feeling. Like many of these dudes, he was more scared of his mother than he was of the cops. 'Sure,' I said. 'Just wait and see. Have I ever let you down?'

'Ah, you're talking out your limey ass, pal. Care to put your money where your mouth is?'

I laughed. 'Lucky for you, I'm not a gambling man,' I said. 'Otherwise, I'd take you for everything you got, you sorry bastards.'

I went home then and crashed. It was past midnight.

I slept like a dead man, and the phone ringing suddenly woke me. It was Ryan at the bonding company. 'What are you, Oliver? fucking psychic? Or did you put a hex on this fucker?'

I looked at the alarm clock. It was a little before seven. 'This Lietiner you're talking about?'

'Damned right it is. Son of a bitch showed up six-thirty, in his mom's car.'

'There you go, my man. I told you he would.'

'Okay, so get your ass down here and collect your fee.'

'Get the donuts and coffee on, dude. I'll be there by the time it's brewed.'

Maybe Lietiner decided to turn himself in to keep a roof over his mother's head. Perhaps he had something going there that he

166

didn't want me to find out about, should I have to bust into his mom's apartment. Something like a little drug-retailing enterprise, maybe. I never found out. The only regret I have about that case is, I wish I'd broken the habit of a lifetime and taken on that bet.

Sha'Dawg

I wasn't sure why I kept going after Sha'Dawg. On his file, he was just another deadbeat gangbanger, embroiled in all the usual crimes that you'd expect of a young, inner-city guy. He was a high-school dropout with a liking for pharmaceutical kicks who'd never done an honest day's work in his life. And, like all those kind of guys, he'd adopted a fancy rap-style name, as if he thought it made him some sort of character on the street. Maybe it did – if you were his twelve-year-old kid brother – but to me, looking at his details, he was just another loser. But I do remember that the price in his head was $200,000. So maybe that's one reason why I'd been on his trail, doggedly, for five or six weeks already. Perhaps too, it was just that – the fact that I had put in so many hours and failed to bring him in. I guess that niggled me more than the money. I take a considerable amount of pride in my work and my record of bringing in nine out of every ten skips I go after.

Many of my fellow bounty hunters would have forgotten all about a case like this and would have just written it off. They'd have shrugged and said, 'Hey, you can't win 'em all.' Well, that's true enough. You can't, and you don't. But any time I fail at something I've set my sights on, it gnaws at me. It keeps me awake. I hate it with a passion. So I kept after this lowlife. And of course, as so often happens, the time when he was furthest from my mind, that's when I came across him, by pure chance. The fact that I was in his neighbourhood was coincidental. I'd been checking on another guy altogether. I'd spent a long hot day, middle of summer, sitting in my car watching the front entrance of a bar-cum-pool-hall, hoping that my skip would show up. And now, late in the evening, dog tired, desperate for some grub and a cool shower, I was on my way home. I'd just called in at a Seven-Eleven to get a cold drink. I remember strolling back to my car and holding the bottle to the back of my neck to try and cool off. Next to me was a vacant site where some of the locals had parked their cars haphazardly.

All I heard was the sound of footsteps on gravel. I don't even know why I bothered to look, but I did. Naturally curious, that's me. Plus, it was starting to get dark, and the sound made me edgy. I glanced across, instinctively, and there he was, the man himself, a big lump of lard with his pants hanging off his ass and his midriff spilling over the top of his underpants. I acted without thinking. Before I even had time to weigh the situation up in my mind, I dropped my drink and ran towards him, dancing around the cars that stood between us. He turned to look over his shoulder and started to run. But this was one big fat sonofabitch, with no acceleration at all. I was within feet of him when I went for it. I took off and got him with a 'Yoko Tobi Geri' (flying karate sidekick), smack in the centre of his back. He hit the ground with an almighty thud, face to the dirt, and I was jumping on his back.

'Federal bail agent!' I gasped, reaching for the cuffs that hung on my belt. 'You're under arrest.' But there was a lot of Mister Dawg. And boy, could he wriggle. Even though I was perched on top of him and had a cuff snapped onto his right wrist, he managed to roll like a frigging whale and throw me off, then punched me hard in the chest. We were between two cars, and as I landed, my head cracked against a fender, drawing blood.

Right fuck it, I thought. You asked for it, you piece of shit. I went for my gun; I was on my back now, trying to sit up but struggling to breathe. Sha'Dawg was slowly getting to his feet and grunting like a hog.

Damn, why couldn't I catch my breath? I put a hand to my chest, and that's when I felt it, then saw the knife sticking out of my chest. That's when it hit me; what felt like a punch to my chest was a knife, and now I was fucked.

It's at moments like these that you realise why you get into good habits. Like always, make sure you're armed in these neighbourhoods. And still – even on a steamy July night like this – making sure you don't hit the streets without putting your undershirt 'Kevlar' vest on. A bulletproof vest will stop most bullets, depending on the grade, but most will not stop a sharp blade. And part of the edge will penetrate through.

Blood was seeping through the Kevlar. I had no idea how far the knife had penetrated. All I knew was my heart was pounding, my breath was coming in a series of shallow gaps, and Sha'Dawg was now on his feet. And all of the above was happening in slow motion. I don't know whether I said it out loud, but I know the words ran through my head. I'm gonna die. Fuck it; I'm finished, and so are you, Mister Dawg.

As I lay there, wondering how long I had, I watched the fat bastard shuffling away from me. I drew my pistol from its holster. I squirmed my way back a foot or so to prop myself up against the front wheel of a car. Then he stopped; reaching into his pants, he turned around and raised his right hand. I was now about to be looking down the short ugly barrel of a snub-nose pistol.

I was already controlling my breathing and aiming my 9mm Sig Sauer directly at him. He wasn't going to miss from there. But neither was I. All I had to do was squeeze the trigger before he did.

I fired off two rounds. One caught him on the right shoulder, the other in his chest. He fired off a shot into the air as he staggered backwards and fell, hitting the ground hard, letting out a gurgling scream as he fell on the dirt. Then he struggled to lift himself on his good arm staring at me, his eyes wide as if he couldn't believe what had happened.

Again he tried to reach for his gun, this time with his left hand. I aimed, both hands on my gun. If I was going to die, I was taking this fucker with me. I fired off three, maybe four rounds. One hit him in the left eye, another in his mouth. It blew the back of his head out like a bursting balloon, showering blood and flesh over the vehicles behind him, blood pouring from his eye onto the dusty ground like a bottle of knocked over claret wine. It was not a pretty sight, but he still had his hand on the gun, so I waited and watched as the blood flowed from his body.

Once he was still, I pulled out my cell phone and dialled 911. I asked for police and a trauma unit to be sent to my location. They wanted to know if I was sure it was necessary. 'Fucking right it is.' I rasped out the words. 'I got one dead, and I'll be joining him on the other side soon if you don't get here fast. I'm a Federal bail agent, and I've been stabbed in the chest and bleeding badly.'

'Okay, hold tight. We'll have someone with you just as soon as we can.'

I eased my grip on the phone, and it dropped to the ground. I picked up my pistol and checked it for ammo. In an area like this, the sound of shooting might bring all kinds of lowlifes out of the woodwork. I reached for my ankle holster and pulled out my .38. If any of Sha'Dawg's buddies wanted to come to see what had happened to their bro, let them come. I was prepared and ready to fight to the end.

I was now starting to feel pain from the knife wound. My instinct was to pull it out and relieve the pressure. My training and good sense told me to leave it where it was, plugging the wound. At least I was breathing normally now, and my heart rate had dropped to a moderate level, but I knew I had lost a lot of blood.

I'll never know how long I lay there. It felt like hours. In reality, I guess it was less than twenty minutes. Twice I heard sirens, and twice they faded away. DC is that kind of city. There's always something kicking off. Finally, they showed up in full force. The cops followed a minute or two later by the paramedics. I barely had the strength to get to my feet. I felt myself wobble and leaned against the hood of a car. Christ knows what I looked like, swaying like a drunk with my warrant in one hand, the other resting on my gut, blood soaking through my white uniform shirt, just below the knife – which moved in and out, in and out, as I breathed.

The cops weren't taking any chances. They grabbed me, kicked my gun away, and I fell backward, hitting the ground a second time. The blow all but knocked me out. I was sure I could feel the life draining out of me. I didn't realize I was lapsing into unconsciousness.

I came to in the hospital. And I had visitors, two of them, perched on my bed: an old cop and a young cop. At first, I couldn't focus on them. As I breathed, I felt an ache in my chest, nothing too bad. I looked down and saw where they had stitched me, a neat wound about an inch long. Soon as the cops had a statement from me, they left. It didn't take long.

When one of the medics came by, I learned that the knife had been heading right towards my heart. If I hadn't had the bulletproof vest on, it would have sliced into it and killed me.

They let me sip some water, and then the bail bondsman came in to see me. 'You okay?' he asked.

'Yeah,' I said. 'I'm okay. You got a cheque for me?'

He ignored the question. 'Jesus,' he said, 'that was one hell of a job you did there on your own.'

'Routine,' I said. 'It's what I do.'

'Yeah, but— going into that neighbourhood with no backup? Takes some balls, or have you got some kinda death wish?'

'Don't talk fucking crap,' I said. 'I was doing my job. As far as I'm concerned, that's one more lowlife cockroach off the streets for good.' Then I asked him the question that was on my mind. 'You think I'll be charged? I shot him about six times'

He shook his head. 'It was self-defence. They all know that. The guy had a rap sheet longer than a bog roll.'

'Yeah? Like what?'

'Off the top of my head, drive-by shootings, pimping, drug-dealing, and a list of VUCSAs.[35] That enough?' He waited for me to answer, and when I didn't, he added, 'Plus rape and murder.'

'Right,' I said, 'Now I see why he didn't want to come quietly.'

'And he violated his bail condition. I mean carrying a gun. You got nothing to worry about, Teddy boy. Just how to spend your reward cheque.'

I'm not too fond of post mortems. To me, my job was done; case closed. I changed the subject and said, "as soon as I get these drip-feeds out and get discharged, it's back to work – maybe the next day or so. Time is money," I said.

'You're shitting me,' he said. 'You're going to take a long vacation, surely? A break at least?'

'No,' I told him. 'Not me. I'm fine. They've fixed me up, pumped new blood into me, and I'm alive and kicking; I'm good to go' ready to take on the scum of the world.

I was back at work in a couple of days – well, sort of. I had what I call an admin day. First to the bank to pay in my fee. Then to the cop station to recover my gear. The desk sergeant handed

[35] See glossary

me my guns and cell phone in a plastic evidence bag. He reminded me not to load the weapons until I'd left the precinct. Then he said, 'Helluva job you did there – for a Limey. You shoulda been a cop.'

'A cop?' I said. 'No way, Jose. I'm not too fond of rules, taking orders, and I don't want to have to report to some guy behind a desk at the end of the day. What I do suits me fine.' I left him chewing on that and went shopping. I needed a new Kevlar undervest, as once they are damaged, it needs replacing.

You May Run, but You Can't Fly

Until I met Superman, I thought I'd seen and done it all. I'd been shot at, attacked with knives, chased by dogs, hit with a frying pan, punched and clobbered with the occasional length of two-by-four. I have been menaced with golf clubs, tyre-levers, hammers, and axes, and a complete auto exhaust system on one memorable occasion. I'd hunted down the drunk, the drugged, the deluded, and the paranoid. I'd tackled the old and the young; seven-stone weaklings and muscle-bound bikers, male and female – and let me tell you, I'd choose the male of that species any time. But up until that moment, I'd yet to meet a guy who could fly, or rather a guy who thought he could.

He wasn't called Superman, of course, but that's how I'll always think of him. Whatever his real name was, I forgot that as soon as I met him, even though it was there on the warrant in capital letters. Let's call him Clark. I remember the case in detail, in particular, the circumstances under which we met and the way events unfolded. That will always stick in my mind, not just because of how bizarre it was, but because this was the one after the dust had settled and I'd got the stitches out of my head, this was the one when I first uttered the words, 'Y'know, I reckon I should write a book one day.'

Clark was no superstar criminal; he wasn't even a minor league. He was a genuine nobody. In fact, I'd hesitate to call him a criminal at all. What he turned out to be was a habitual transgressor, a repeat offender. He wasn't even a bad person, as far as I knew. He didn't go around abusing people. I'm not sure that he didn't ever hurt anybody – not intentionally. You might say that anybody who deals in drugs – and that's what our superhero did – is hurting someone. And in principle, I would agree with that. He is at least complicit in the pain they suffer, but what you have to remember is that most of those people are lining up with cash in their hands, waiting for their man to show. As the old saying goes, it takes two to tango.

So that's what he did for a living, selling drugs. And he did okay at it. Sure, he lived in a dump of an apartment in a shitty neighbourhood, but that's where most of his clients lived. He ran a decent enough vehicle, and he liked to party. Oh yes, he sure liked to party. Naturally enough, the time came when he was arrested, charged with dealing, and bailed pending a court appearance. And the evidence against him was such that he knew a custodial sentence would follow and as sure as night follows day. So he did what plenty of others would have done in the circumstances. He went to ground, and who could blame him? The fact that I picked up his papers and was assigned to find him was bad news for both of us: for him because I had a ninety percent success rate in bringing my skips home; for me, because the job involved a long drive to Colorado during a record-breaking heatwave. I had a few other jobs in the area, so it made sense to pack up the truck and make a sweep through there. The idea on a long trip like that is always to make it pay.

I like Colorado. When I get the time, I go skiing or out on my jet-ski there. It's a beautiful, young, energetic state with great swathes of wilderness. You get out in the mountains there, and you can forget everything you know about humanity's dirty under-belly, which in my case is plenty. You meet Nature face to face, and you feel restored. Unfortunately, this was no backwood trip. I had been tracking Clark. I had ended up in Denver, a thriving modern-day city but still home to some dilapidated derelict houses, run-down neighbourhoods, boarded-up shops, and fly-by-night businesses.

This particular day I was just driving through the area when I happened to spot one of Clark's known associates, a guy who'd been seen with him at least twice over the previous few weeks. If I'd been on foot, I might have grabbed the guy. As it happened, I was in my car, sweating like a pig. It was mid-afternoon. I had a chilled can of soda in one hand, a burrito in the other, my first bite of food since the previous night. I didn't recognise the guy straight away. I was watching as he got into a light brown Chevy sedan right in front of me. As he turned his head to check the road was clear before pulling out, that's when I realised who he was; I dumped the remains of the food in the footwell of the car, but in my hurry knocked the soda can, spilling the contents all over my pants, Fuck. When I looked up, the guy was gone, leaving a cloud of black smoke that was already drifting in through my open side window.

There was no point trying to give chase. He'd swung left into a maze of back alleys, and my exit blocked by a UPS truck that had pulled up right beside me, slap bang in the middle of the road. What the hell? I had the plate number. That would do me. I ran the licence plate and got an address a little more than a mile away. Even so, the drive took me a good thirty minutes, such as the chaos on the roads. Construction vehicles, mostly. It seemed like every lot around me was being demolished and re-developed. I put the radio on to drown out the fucking noise of pneumatic drills, pile-drivers, and snarling trucks, and this damned DJ was reading out the weather report. 'Ninety-six degrees downtown and peaking at a ninety-eight,' he was saying. 'Could get close to a record high for July thirty-first. That was a scorching one hundred degrees back in 1889.'

I leaned forward, my T-shirt parting from the car seat with a sound like Velcro being ripped apart, as I turned the radio switch off. All right for you, I was thinking, sitting in your air-conditioned radio studio on a fat salary. Here's me, my pants all wet and sticking to my legs.

I found the address without a problem, and at first glance, the house looked abandoned, built in the late fifties and already condemned. The house was but a hundred yards from a busy commercial street lined with shops and cafés. A single block in the other direction, a tall crane, lowered long steel sections onto a construction site. I parked the car under a big old Mexican bean tree and sat for a while, listening to the cicadas chirruping.

Was the guy in the house? There was no sign of his car. I checked the address once more. Yup, this was the place okay. It was looking as though I faced another long, hot wait, and a thirsty one. The nearest grocery was back on the main drag. All I had now was a bottle half full of tepid, two-day-old water tainted with the taste of warm plastic. I was just starting to wonder whether to risk a trip to the store when I saw, in my rear-view mirror, the brown Chevy coming around the corner.

Even as the guy cruised past me and pulled in outside the house, I was preparing myself to follow him inside. I wanted to get this over, go home, get out of these pants. Jesus, it was uncomfortable. But this shouldn't take long, I told myself. I had the element of surprise. As far as I knew, the guy had no outstanding charges against him, so the last thing on his mind would have been a visit from an enforcer. Usually, I would have put on my uniform jacket, both for ID purposes and to conceal my gun. But today, in this heat? No way. All I had on was a loose black T-shirt and my ID badge on a chain around my neck. I tucked the Sig Sauer into my waistband and untucked the T-shirt to cover it.

I watched the guy walk around the side of the house. That figured as the front door boarded up – three or four lengths of wood and a square of plywood haphazardly nailed across it. One arm wrapped around a brown paper sack of groceries, the other arm a pack of Budweizer beer a giant bag of corn chips.

It could be, he was having a night off at home. It could also be he had company—only one way to find out. I took my time now. If you're going to bust in on someone, it's always better that they're chilling out. On the sofa, watching TV or in bed is great, even better if they've consumed a few beers first. One place you don't want them is in the kitchen. Too many sharp objects are available to attack you.

I pulled on my fingerless black leather gloves, just in case I had to punch my way through a pane of glass; I got out of the car and approached the house. I sneaked in through the broken gate and up the path to the front porch. Two large windows looked out onto it. The frames were bare and grey.

One of the windows was next to the door without any glass, just a screen with a long rip in the lower right-hand corner and behind it a faded yellow drape. I stood there listening, carefully. There was no sound coming from inside. I gave it twenty or thirty seconds, then grabbed hold of the torn screen, bent it back, and squeezed through the gap.

I was in a hallway, a sort of corridor no more than four or five feet wide. As I stepped forward, gun raised, I tripped on a torn patch of rotten carpet and stumbled against a pile of old newspapers, kicking up a cloud of dust. I stood very still, waiting. Jesus, it was hot. The blood throbbed through my temples. There were three doors off the corridor; all of them closed. I moved slowly forward, stopping at each one to listen, but the faint sound I was now hearing was coming from above me.

At the foot of a flight of stairs, I could hear it more distinctly.

Voices and laughter. More of a giggle. The sweat was dripping off me, and the air was stale. Something somewhere was rotting—a kind of garbage smell. I made my way slowly up the stairs, bracing myself at every step for that one loud creak that might give me away. But the conversation continued. And the laughter. I could also hear music playing. Somebody was having fun up there. Well, I thought, party on. The more noise they made, the better it suited me.

At the top of the stairs, I saw three more doors leading off a tight little landing. Two were wide open, the third almost closed. That was where the action was. I distinctly heard the hiss of a canned drink open, and someone said, 'Man, was she for real?'

I moved slowly across the landing and checked at each of the open doors. Both rooms were empty – apart from rickety beds piled high with dirty linen. At the third door, I pulled out my badge hanging around my neck, raised my gun to eye level, and peered through the crack on the hinged side. At a plastic-topped table piled high with beer cans were two guys, both about twenty-five. One was the driver of the brown Chevy, the other my skip. They were sitting on plastic garden seats that might have been white back in the day.

I swung the door open and walked in, gun raised. I'd got no further than, 'Put your hands in the air!' when Clark, my skip, grabbed a can and hurled it at me. It caught me smack on the forehead, just above my right eye. It was full, and it knocked me backwards through the doorway.

I almost blacked out. I struggled to hold onto my gun and get to my feet, but every time I pushed against the floor with my left hand, it slipped on something wet and sticky. My blood. Christ, the sonofabitch had split my head open.

I was on my feet, stumbling through the doorway, wiping my eye. Where the fuck was everyone? The room was empty. I checked behind me, went to the head of the stairs. Surely not. I would've seen them go by, wouldn't I?

Back in the room, I went to the open window. I leaned out and took a deep breath. In the corrugated metal roof below the window was a large dent. I wiped my eye once more, and there they were, jumping off the top of the wooden fence that surrounded the house and heading into the alleyway. I aimed, then decided against it. Even with a fugitive, you're going to have a hard time justifying a shot in the back. Instead, I watched until they disappeared around a corner.

I uncocked the gun, shoved it back in my waistband, and looked around for the bathroom. I needed to wash this cut and stop the bleeding. I went to the basin. There were several roaches in there, most of them dead. I tried one faucet, then the other. Neither one worked.

Back in the room where the guys had been playing cards, I ripped the top off a can of chilled beer, leaned forward, and let it flow over my wounded head, down my face, and onto the floor. It was a delicious sensation, instantly soothing. I tugged at my black T-shirt and used it to mop myself dry. Then I picked up another beer, cracked that, and drank a few mouthfuls. I then looked around the place and eventually picked up an old tea towel from behind a wooden box and held it against my wound to stop the bleeding.

I went downstairs and slipped out through the back door. Walking to my car, I realised that the wound was still bleeding freely. I drove to the Emergency Room, where they put in some stitches. Then I went home, took some painkillers, and got in the shower before collapsing onto my bed.

I took the next day off. A thunderstorm broke the heatwave and put out half the traffic lights. It was a good time not to be cruising the slums looking for deadbeats. I doubt that I was properly fit, I knew I wasn't, but I went back into battle the following day. This guy had got under my skin; I wanted him. And I wanted him badly.

I started at the Chevy guy's house. I even went inside again, but there was no sign of anyone having been back. On the floor, my blood had made a dark stain, with drips all the way across the landing. I returned to the car and started a systematic search of the neighbourhood.

It took me four days to find that Chevy, found It parked outside a beer-shack outside of town, huddled in a dark space between an overpass and a railroad freight siding. I parked right behind it, got out, and entered the bar. I guess I could've waited outside for my man to emerge, but I wanted a drink, and I needed to make quite sure this was the guy I was after, Clark's buddy.

It was him, okay. He was sitting on a high stool, leaning on the bar and trying to catch the girl's attention. The bar was only small, but they had it in a kind of horseshoe shape. I walked around to the far side so that I was opposite him. I sat down and ordered a glass of mineral water.

Some woman came and took the stool next to mine. She tried out a few questions. I haven't seen you in here before – you new to the neighbourhood? That kind of thing. She wasn't bad looking, and I fed her enough answers to keep her interest. I wanted to hear what was being said on the far side of the bar, without it being obvious that I was listening. I learned that my guy was called John. Once or twice I caught him looking at me, but I had no worries he'd ID me. There was no way I looked like the guy in the black T-shirt, baseball cap, and shades his pal had hurled that beer can at. Even the wound was barely visible now in the dim light, covered as it was with a flesh-coloured sticking plaster and a red baseball cap on my head to hide it. All this time, John was drinking beer. Sooner or later, he'd head for home, and when he did so, he wasn't going to be at his sharpest.

He left quite suddenly, checking his watch as if he'd remembered an appointment. I put a ten-dollar bill on the bar, said goodbye to the girl, and followed him. He was just pulling his key from his pocket when I reached out and shoved him in the small of the back, flattening him against the car door.

I flashed my badge in front of him. 'Put both your hands on the roof where I can see them and don't move,' I said. I searched him for weapons, removed his Motorola flip cell phone, and put it in my pocket, but otherwise, he was clean. 'You're over the drink limit for driving,' I said. 'Now put your hands down and get in the back seat of my car. I need to talk to you about your friend Clark.' He had no reason to think that I was anything but a cop. He obeyed meekly.

I cuffed him in my car and secured him to the leg cuffs, which were welded to the car floor. I pointed to my head. 'Your buddy did this,' I said. 'You remember when he threw that beer can?'

'Oh shit,' he said.

'Oh shit indeed,' I said. 'I have a warrant for his arrest and another one for you. You were with him, which makes you an accessory.'

'C'mon man, that can't be right. What the fuck did I do? Accessory to what?' The guy was suddenly on the counter-attack.

'What you did, was assist in the flight of a fugitive and be an accessory to an assault on a Federal officer. So don't even think about arguing. It'll be my word against yours. It could cost you five years in the slammer. Think about that for a moment.'

That calmed him down. I could see him checking out my truck, taking in the two-way radio on the dash, the nightstick holder and the gun rack in the centre holding my locked shotgun. 'Now listen carefully, John.' I spoke quietly, edging closer to him. He seemed surprised that I knew his name. 'I'm prepared to overlook the fact that you assisted a fugitive, was an accessory to an assault on a Federal officer, and even though I've watched you drink five beers, or was it six, you know what? I'm going to let you drive home. The only thing is, as your side of the deal, you're going to take me to your buddy's place. Right now.'

He looked at me like he didn't quite follow.

'You drive, and I'll follow. You got that?' He didn't answer, just nodded. 'Now let me spell it out to you. You try and lose me, John, and I'll have every cop in the area on your ass within minutes. DWI. You got that? You, my friend, are driving while intoxicated. So no funny stuff.'

'Sure,' he said. 'I'll do what you say.' I told him I am now going to search his car. I came back and told him I would ignore the baggies of white powder hidden under the driver's seat, and I have left his cell phone in his car less the battery, in case he calls his pal to warn him. I undid his cuffs.

He got in his Chevy and drove off, going real steady. I could see him checking his mirror periodically to see that I was following. Within five minutes, we were pulling into a small parking lot adjacent to an apartment block. I got out of my car and approached him. He told me my man was on the fourth floor, most likely with his girlfriend, probably doing coke.

'Does he carry a gun?' I said.

'Sometimes.'

'What about his girl?'

'I don't know.'

'Okay, John. Get home now. But remember, I have your address. If you're shitting me, you're in trouble – and I will come for you. You got that?'

'Look, I only meant to…' I ignored what he had to say and turned away. I didn't want to hear his bullshit story. The guy disgusted me.

184

I went into the apartment block and took the elevator to the fourth floor. I knocked on several doors on either side of Clark's place. It wasn't long before an old lady stuck her head out from an apartment further along the landing and asked me what I wanted. 'Number 47,' I said. 'D'you know if anyone's home?'

'Oh, they're home okay,' she answered. 'Been playing that damned music all morning. If you can, call it music.'

I showed her a Polaroid photograph of Clark. 'That him?' I asked.

She took a good look, then said, 'That's him. Yes, that's the one. Are you gonna tell him about the music? It's a public nuisance, that's what it is.'

'Of course,' I said. 'I'll make a point of that. But you're sure the guy is in right now?'

'Oh, yes. The noise only stopped a short while ago, and I haven't heard anybody use the elevator.' It occurred to me to ask her why she would hear it. Then she gave me a sort of wink and said, 'I leave my door open, just a few inches. Nobody comes or goes without me seeing them.'

'You're doing a great job,' I said, and took the elevator back to the ground floor and went to my car. I kitted myself up, then pulled out my mobile phone. I dialled 911 and asked for police assistance. I told them I was enforcing a bail bond warrant and gave them the details. 'You'll find him,' I said. 'He's in the system.' Then I added, 'While we're on the subject, I got a DWI for you, and check the small baggies under his seat. Just left here in a brown Chevy.' I gave them the guy John's name and registration number. Fuck him, I thought, driving around Denver dealing drugs with a belly full of beer. Who did he think he was? Kids were walking and playing in the streets.

I got to work fast. The police would be with me any moment, and I wanted to make the arrest immediately. I took the stairs to the fourth floor and crept along the landing to number 47. Approaching it, I pulled the pistol from my waistband and leaned against the door, listening. I couldn't hear a sound. Maybe he was in bed. I switched the gun to my left hand, wiped the sweat off my right hand on my pants leg, and took a long deep breath. I was ready now on a count of seven.

One two three four five six seven, all good bounty hunters go to heaven. BAM! I leaned back and kicked out, giving it everything. I saw the lock snap, but the damned chain held. I leaned back again and gave it a second whack. It flew open.

'Nobody move!' I was inside. In front of me was a large bed. Clark lay on it, on his back, naked apart from a pair of jockey shorts. He had a huge erection sticking out. A girl was kneeling beside him, hands on the bed, her head hovering over his dick, her breasts dangling. She had a black leather dog collar around her neck, with studs on it. Standing over them both was a girl with a shock of crimson hair, wearing nothing but a black leather corset and a matching G-string, and her tits were out. She had pierced nipples with gold-coloured rings in them. In her hand, she had a leather whip.

It was my own dumb mistake. In the second or two that I stood there gawping at the scene before me, the corseted girl leaped across the bed and dived at me. All I saw was her polished nails coming toward my eyes. I threw her to the floor, turning to point the gun at her. 'Don't shoot!' she screamed. 'Don't fucking move!' I shouted back. Then I turned towards the bed and saw my skip dash across the room to the balcony. As I aimed my pistol, he swung his legs over the little railing and vaulted it.

'Jesus Christ!' I ran to the railing, the girls following me. I leaned over the edge and looked down to the ground. It wasn't grass, it was blacktop – and the guy was lying there face down, arms and legs spread out like a goddam starfish.

'Oh shit.' I looked at the girls; their faces were frozen in shock. Already I was thinking about my own skin. All these two had to do was tell the cops I'd pushed him—two words against one. Jesus, I dashed out onto the landing and ran down the stairs outside, yelling into my cell phone for an ambulance.

I looked around, so where was the sonofabitch? Confused, I then dashed around to the back of the building. I must have got my directions wrong. But there was nothing that way either. Then a woman came running across from the entrance. She was pointing up the road. 'He went that way,' she gasped.

I looked at her. Went? What was she, crazy? The guy had plummeted from the fourth floor, landed flat on the ground. And he went? Did he run? Get out of here.

The sound of police sirens split the air, echoing off the tall buildings. A patrol car screeched to a halt a few yards from me, and an officer got out, hand on his gun, drawing it from his holster. Instinctively I held up my arms, let him frisk me, and remove my weapon. I told him who I was and showed him the warrant.

The ambulance arrived. I was so stunned that I became confused. I tapped my head and said, 'I'm okay. I don't need that. Did this a couple of days back.'

He looked blank. 'The ambulance is not for you, sir. It's for the guy that we ran down.'

'What guy?' I asked.

He explained that they were speeding to the scene when they hit him. 'Crazy bastard ran out right out in front of his police cruiser, wearing only his underpants, with his arms held out in front like he was trying to fly.'

I walked up to the ambulance, and there he was, my man Clark, lying on a stretcher-bed his face bruised with blood around his nose, which looked kind of flattened. He was out cold. For a moment, I thought he was dead. The paramedics stated that they thought he had broken or fractured every bone in his body.

'Jesus,' I said. 'That's my guy.' I still had the warrant in my hand. I showed it to the cop. 'See? That's the guy who jumped out of there.' I pointed up to the fourth-floor balcony.

The cop looked at him, then at me, then at the balcony, and closed the ambulance door. 'Well,' he said, 'he's one lucky sonofabitch, wouldn't you say?'

'Yep!' I said. 'Don't try to fly unless you got wings.'

They took Clark away. I hung around while the cops interviewed the girls. They didn't know a damned thing about Clark. They were just a pair of local (hookers) prostitutes. They said he was high on drugs – they thought PCP[36]. 'That makes sense,' I said. 'When I burst in, he panicked. Thought I was the law.'

I was more at ease now. I was starting to feel my kind of ecstasy, the kind that comes when you nail down a case. A few neighbours had come out and were standing around in groups. When the cops decided it was time to wind things up, they melted away. I made my way to my car and drove slowly back to the motel. In the morning, I began the long drive back to the north-west. I was heading north along the I-25 freeway when I found myself wondering what I would say to that guy Clark if I ever met up with him again. It was a while before it came to me, but I started to laugh out loud when it did. 'Yeah, Superman.'

'You may run, but you can't fly.'

---

[36] See glossary

Wipe Your Own Damned Ass!

The stories you read make it sound like my work was one long, non-stop, enjoyable fairground ride in this book. But what you are reading are the edited versions, the thrills, all the boring stuff taken out, like the days, weeks, months of surveillance, plowing through hundreds of phone numbers, having to visit many family members' addresses and known associates of the defendant. What I'm serving up here are the choice cuts, the selected highlights. You wouldn't want to hear about the rest of what I do. There wouldn't be enough hours in the day for you to read it – if you could stay awake that long. And not all of the jobs I got were on my doorstep. They involved travel over long distances. That might sound like fun, but it wasn't. More likely, it was just a pain in the ass – arduous and complicated.

Mostly in those early years, I'd been working around the Seattle area. Still, as my reputation slowly spread, I found I regularly communicated with bonding companies in other parts of the country. I got a call from Chicago, some outfit who had a long list of outstanding warrants with a lot of money at stake. It sounded to me like they were hiring too many fucking cowboys. One particular skip they wanted help with was a guy called Moody Darnell. He'd been charged with second-degree homicide, bailed for $250,000, and disappeared three weeks before he was due in court. To a Brit, that sort of thing seems crazy. The defendants suspected of murder, and there he is on the loose? Sure, there are restrictions on his freedoms – like checking in daily, being required to answer the phone whenever the bonding office calls, not being allowed to be out of their house after nine at night. Of course, they cannot leave the area – or the State – without the bondsman's permission. All of which means that if the guy wants to skip, he'll skip.

Neither his friends nor his family knew where Moody had gone. Or if they did, they weren't saying. However, as so often happens, it was the one relative who stood to lose out the most that came forward. He had an aunt, and she had put up her house as security on the bond. A lot of collateral had already been repossessed when he failed to report, but not enough to cover the full value of the bond. So now her house was in danger of being repossessed. You could understand her point of view: if her nephew didn't show up for his date in court, she would be living on the streets. She got in touch with me, said she wanted to arrange a meeting. Maybe she could help me track the guy down. She asked me to meet her out of town, at some diner. Her family was very clannish, and she knew she'd be in big trouble if anyone suspected that she'd spilled the beans on Moody. She was his mom's sister, so she knew many of the people he would be hanging out with; as it happens, several family members had already moved down to the Arizona-California border area, just handy for Mexico. She was pretty sure he was with a cousin of theirs in Yuma.

Yuma from Seattle is close to 1,500 miles – not a journey you'd generally do by road, but the fact was I needed to have all my equipment and guns with me. Given that I had to take the skip back to Chicago, and in those days, you weren't allowed to handcuff a prisoner and bring him onto a plane, I was in for two long drives. But I was okay with that. I can enjoy a road trip – and the outward part would be relaxing enough. Driving back 2,000 miles with a prisoner would be the hard part; that wouldn't be much fun, but maybe I could get help.

I decided to go in my truck; it was well equipped and had all the necessary equipment fitted inside; There were also eye bolts welded to the floor and sides to secure a prisoner in handcuffs or chains. I made the journey south in two legs, stopping overnight at Sacramento, then heading to LA before taking Interstate 10 eastward to the Arizona line. When I got to Yuma, I found myself a hotel room, then set about tracking my skip. I'd not been to that exact area before, although the time I'd spent in Phoenix should have prepared me. But no, I'd managed to forget just how hot it could be. There's an old joke the cowboys like to tell about a bad man who plied his trade around Yuma. When he died, the badman went straight to Hell – and the first thing he did when he got there was to telegraph his buddies to send him an overcoat.

I didn't rush. I checked a few of the addresses Moody's aunt had given me but made sure I took it easy. There's only so much of that you can do when the temperature's 105 and 110, dropping to the low eighties around dawn. On the plus side, at least there was no humidity. I did the usual round of bars and clubs Moody frequented in the evening. Nada. I never even got a sniff of him and was starting to wonder whether I was wasting my time. But one of the things I'd learned was that the most useful quality for a guy in my line – as it is for a gumshoe – is tenacity. Stick at it, and you'll get results. It isn't glamorous, it isn't fun, but in the end, it's what differentiates you from a run-of-the-mill operator, and when I say run-of-the-mill, I'm talking eighty to ninety percent of them.

It was evening time. I was eating a plate of tacos in some mom-and-pop joint when I talked to a Mexican guy who rented out apartments in the neighbourhood. He took me for a cop and was real keen to help me. When I showed him a photo of my man, he said he knew him and gave me an address. He insisted that the guy was living there. Rather than go straight round, I decided I'd wait until morning. I mean early morning, just before sunrise. One, the skip would most likely be in bed, and two, I could just about tolerate the temperatures at that time of day. Thirdly, the address I had was on a busy road down by the railroad tracks, and the last thing I wanted after I'd made my arrest was to get caught up in traffic. With luck, I'd be in there and out again before the morning build-up.

The place was a single-storey apartment, mock adobe with a rusting air-conditioning unit on the roof and shaded by a big old cottonwood. It hadn't seen a lick of paint in God knows how long. I parked right across the road and sat there for a minute or two, checking my equipment. It was a beautiful morning, the very best time of day. The sun was lighting up the treetops, and already the air was ringing with the sound of cicadas. I felt confident as I got out of the truck and approached the door. I slid my hand into my pocket and pulled out one of my favourite gizmos, a reverse tactical peephole viewer. Imagine a little pair of binoculars – like opera glasses, maybe smaller, but just the one barrel. You offer it up to a door peephole and get a 180-degree view inside the room you're about to bust into. Whoever invented that little beauty, I hope he took out a patent and retired to the Bahamas. He earned it if you ask me.

These apartments were poky little places, more like motel rooms, and the street door opened directly into the living room. Squinting through the eyepiece, I could see Moody asleep on a couch. He was fully dressed and surrounded by empty pizza boxes and crushed beer cans. I couldn't see a gun – not that that meant anything, but you don't like to see them tucked into a guy's pants or in a shoulder-holster. This guy looked pretty relaxed. He must have figured he was perfectly safe, a couple of thousand miles from home and barely half an hour from the Mexican border. Well, he had a surprise coming. I did a final check of my equipment, then stood facing the door. It was a flimsy little lock, and one good kick destroyed it. The door burst open, and by the time the guy had opened his eyes, he was staring down the barrel of my Sig Sauer 9mm.

'On the floor, asshole! Now, or I'll shoot you. I'm a bail recovery agent, and you're under arrest.' He did precisely as ordered. When he found his tongue, the first thing he said was, 'I thought you mothers woulda given up on me.'

'No way,' I said. 'Not this soldier. Giving up is never an option for me. There's only one choice for me to make now. Are you coming back with me dead or alive?' I've used that line more than once to pursue my duties, and it tends to quieten them down – not that this guy looked as though he was going to cause me any problems.

After I'd cuffed him, I led him out to the truck. There were already quite a few people on the street. There were half a dozen standing in line at a bus stop, watching me. I wondered whether anybody would call the cops. I hoped not, because although I was legit, they would have taken a couple of hours, maybe more, to check the warrants. And I was in a hurry. But then I did have my black uniform on, and the vest, the black cap, my guns and badge on display, so maybe the onlookers thought I was the police, arresting a felon.

I got my man into the rear passenger seat, looped a long chain through his cuffs, and tethered him to two separate anchor-points in the rear. He said he was hungry and wanted to know when he could eat. I told him I had plenty of bottled water in there, but food would have to wait until I filled up with gas, which would be most likely be the other side of the Sonoran Desert unless we passed a fast-food drive-in on the way.

We were soon out of town and onto Interstate 8. I put my foot down and held a steady eighty miles an hour. We stopped for gas at Gila Bend and picked up a few snacks to keep us going, reaching Tucson a little afternoon. Jesus, it was hot out there. I was watching the temperature, and it had hit 100 before the clock reached eight. As the drab desert scenery flashed by, Moody slept.

We entered New Mexico in the early afternoon and stopped for a proper meal. I aimed to get to Las Cruces by evening, put in two or three hours northward on I-25, and find a room somewhere south of Albuquerque. I figured that would put us within two days of the Windy City. We made good progress, and I decided I could make it as far as Socorro. I wasn't looking forward to the next part of the journey. What do you do at night when you're ferrying a prisoner on your own? The short answer is, you don't take chances. Moody was still asleep when I pulled off the freeway, down the business loop, and into the motel driveway. I left him alone while I went into the office. I got us a ground-floor room, on the corner at the end of the block, then drove across the highway to an all-night burger place for some food.

Back at the motel, I pulled up close to the room window, mounting the kerb until I was barely six inches away. The idea was to be so close that Moody couldn't open his door, just in case he wanted to try his luck. But he seemed docile enough, just took his grub and thanked me for it. Some enforcers are stern on their prisoners. They resent spending a few bucks on a burger and fries, even though they're going to reclaim every penny via the expenses sheet. They figure these people are lowlife criminals and don't deserve to be treated decently. The way I see it, they're going to spend the next few years in the pen[37] , so what does it cost you to treat them like a human being on their last day of freedom?

---

[37] See glossary

The room had two single beds. I brought Moody inside, put the leg irons on him, and cuffed his hands in front. Then I secured him to the chain, which I ran through one window and back in the other.

'What do I do when I wanna go to the john?' he asked.

'You wake me,' I said. 'And in case you get any ideas, let me tell you this, my friend. You try and get free or attack me, and I'm within my rights to shoot you dead.'

He looked at me, kind of scared, and it occurred to me that he was only a kid really, nineteen years old, and may never have been through this process before. Even so, I added the thing I usually say to a prisoner in such circumstances. 'Believe me; I won't hesitate to do that.' I put him on one bed, moved the other round so that it was at right angles to his, and sat down on it. I took the gun from my side holster and tucked it into the front of my pants, unbuckling my utility belt and leaving that on my left-hand side, away from Moody. I would spend the night sitting up, facing him.

You never sleep well in these circumstances, but you grab enough in snatches to last you through the next day. All through the night, every time he moved, the chains rattled like Jacob Marley's ghost, and I automatically went for the gun. Then about three in the morning, he decided he needed a dump. You have no choice but to accompany your prisoner to the can. You accept that you have to undo their pants and pull them down, but I draw the line at wiping their asses.

'Now, what the fuck do I do?' he asked. He was standing there with his pants around his ankles, his T-shirt too short to cover his privates.

I ripped off a few sheets of paper and handed them to him. 'You do your best, son.'

'Do I get to shower or what?'

I nodded my head. 'Sure, you do – soon as I get you to Chicago.'

We took off around five-thirty the next morning. I wanted to get through Albuquerque before the rush-hour traffic built up. The weather was a lot cooler now. We were a mile above sea level, and you couldn't half tell the difference. When we finally hit I-40, I got a thrill from seeing the signs they had along the side of the freeway, 'Old Route 66'. That was my favourite TV show when I was a kid. It planted the idea in my head that America was the place to be. As one of the signs flashed by, I started to sing that old Chuck Berry number, *Get your kicks on Route 66*. I turned to see if Moody was awake. 'D'you ever see that show?' I asked him. 'Route 66?' He opened his eyes, blinked at me, and frowned. 'Ah, guess you were too young,' I said. 'Used to be on the TV. Back in black-and-white TV days. But you're way too young to remember them.'

Despite the cooler air, I constantly felt like I might fall asleep at the wheel. That's why a lot of guys take amphetamines. Not me. I stick to greasy food and caffeine. We pulled off the freeway at Santa Rosa and had a huge Mexican platter apiece. After going into a drive-through and eating it on our laps, in the truck. Then I locked Moody in the truck while I called a few bounty hunters I knew in Texas. I needed help, and I needed it asap. I got hold of Hank, an amiable guy I'd worked with on a few occasions – and partied with once or twice. He was more than happy to take five grand for a couple of days' work – plus whatever time it took to get himself back to Texas when done. We agreed to meet in Amarillo early that afternoon.

Hank was a reliable kind of guy. When he said he'd be at a specific place at a certain time, you knew he'd show. I picked him up at a truck stop, we had a quick coffee-break, and I introduced him to Moody. Then we hit the road again, and suddenly the whole trip was a breeze. I slept for three hours straight, waking up just as we rolled through Oklahoma City. By the time we stopped for the night, we were in Springfield, Missouri, leaving us a nice five hundred miles to do on the final day. Making an early start, we were able to deliver our man to the office in Chicago around mid-afternoon and collect the money.

We found a nice hotel along the lakeshore, went out for an Italian meal and a few beers, then had an early night. We had a leisurely two-day drive ahead of us, and along the way, we chatted about some of the jobs we'd done together. It was a little like a vacation. I ended up extending my stay. Barely a couple of hours after I'd dropped Hank off in Amarillo, I met a little Irish waitress in a steakhouse. She invited me back to her place for what I thought would be the typical one-night stand but turned out to be a four-day epic. Well, I had a long lonely drive ahead of me, all the way back to Seattle, and it would help if I had a few memories to keep me smiling.

Sure, I'll Do You a Favour

Choosing to be a bounty hunter – well, you don't do that if you want a quiet life, do you? And even amongst that motley assortment of characters, which do the police's dirty work for them, I seemed to attract more trouble than anybody else. The strange thing is, it was often the most straightforward cases that throw up the most significant problems.

On and off between my bail bond cases, I was still helping out my old employer with the odd bit of simple investigatory work. Sandy (Sandra) Taylor ran her own business out of Tacoma – Taylor Investigations – and it was she who had hired me when I first came to the States. We got along well, even after I'd turned to bounty hunting. On the face of it, this was a goodwill thing, but of course, there was something in it for me. In return for my willingness to help her out when she was over-stretched, she was always there when I needed to run a car licence plate or a background check through her computer. Most of the work she threw my way was simple enough – no more than running an errand, in many cases. So when she rang one day to ask if I was free and could go out to collect a tracking device that someone had left on a truck, I didn't think twice. She explained that the reason for asking me was that vehicle in question was parked up at a ranch not so far from my place. 'Maybe go fetch it Sunday afternoon,' Sandy said. 'It'll be a nice run out in the boonies. You'll be there in thirty minutes.'

She was actually bullshitting me, and we both knew it.

Encroaching onto private land at any time is a dangerous business in the US of A, where a property owner has the right to shoot a trespasser. Most of Sandy's operatives were female; she must have realised that this was a job for a man – and I was just the kind whose dumb male pride wouldn't let him say no.

It was later after she'd given me the address of the place, and a few details about the people who lived out there, plus a description of the truck, that she thought to add a word about the dogs.

'Dogs?' I said.

There were, she told me, four or five of them. 'But it's okay,' she added. 'They're locked in a compound at night.'

Private property, out in the boondocks, guarded by dogs, and I needed to go in under cover of darkness. All for a goddam tracking device – although Sandy insisted it was a top-of-the-range job and worth recovering. Yes, I thought, but was it worth risking your life for? The longer I looked at this supposedly straightforward assignment, the more it took on the shape of an episode of *The A-Team*. Still, it wasn't far from home; I might as well take a look at the place in daylight and see what I was up against.

I drove out the next morning. I stopped about two hundred yards short of the house. It stood at the end of a long, straight drive, lined with trees. It was more like a ranch. To either side of it were broad stretches of tall grass, with trees scattered here and there. I would've preferred to have better visibility, but on the other hand, there would be plenty of cover for me. I took out my binoculars. After a few sweeps, I spotted a red Dodge pickup, as described by Sandy, parked at the front of the house but maybe twenty yards from it, only its windscreen visible from where I was. If they left it there overnight, it shouldn't be too difficult a job. I could make out the fenced dog pound, which was to the opposite side of the house from where the truck was. With any luck, I'd be in and out without disturbing anybody at all. It didn't seem to be a working ranch. There wasn't so much as a single corral or outbuilding, peace of piss. I'd seen enough. I drove home.

I decided to do the job the next morning, before dawn. I set off about four. I was dressed all in black, with my face blacked up as well. I was only lightly armed, having my 9mm Sig pistol in a hip holster and my combat knife on my belt – plus a pepper spray for the dogs and my Taser. I drove my black, Bronco truck slowly up to near the end of the drive, switched off the lights, and made sure it was well hidden.

As I cut the engine, a full moon appeared from behind the clouds, a coyote started yowling on a nearby hillside, and a bat swooped across the windscreen. If it had been a movie, there would've been double basses playing, just to add a little more atmosphere.

I sat there, waiting until the moon went back behind the clouds, then got out of the truck and started to make my way up the drive. I moved slowly from tree to tree, crouching down to take advantage of the long grass. It was all tranquil, just the occasional hushing sound as a light breeze bent the foliage. I had heard a single short bark from one of the dogs and gripped my pistol. I fully expected them all to join in – and if they did, I was ready to abort the mission immediately. There would be other opportunities to collect the damned tracker. But my luck was in. They settled back down, and I was able to approach the truck without any further alarms.

I covered the last twenty yards or so, crawling on my hands and knees, moving with slow deliberation as the grass rustled, and I strained my ears to hear any reaction from the dogs. I remember wondering whether I should've sprayed myself with bug repellent. It wouldn't be the first time I'd got home and found ticks all over my legs. I reached the truck, worming my way underneath it and taking out my mini Maglite. I switched it on and searched the underside from front to back. When I found the tracker, it was the work of a moment to remove it and slip it into my pocket.

There's a point in any operation like that when you start to relax. You know you shouldn't. It isn't over till it's over and all that, but sometimes you just do. Your brain is sending out the message, mission accomplished. I wriggled out from under the truck, turned over into a crouching crawling position, and started to head back towards the drive. I tried to move with the same slow deliberation as on the way up to the truck. If I was tense, then it was that tension that feared an explosion of barking from the guard dogs, or the shout from the front porch or the crack of a rifle shot.

The last thing on my mind was light, but here I was, bathed in it, dazzled by it, illuminated from head to toe by a searing white that burned into my eyes and scared the living shit out of me. Whatever kind of security system these people had, I could only guess they'd bought it at auction from a decommissioned POW camp in North Korea.

Even as I half turned to see where it was coming from – and it seemed to come from every damned where at once – I heard all the noises I'd been fearing: the house door unbolting, a shout, the dogs breaking out, and then the blast of a shotgun, which ripped a flurry of leaves off the trees beside me.

I ran. I ran like hell, zigzagging down the drive, tripping and stumbling through the long grass, in the hope that whoever had the gun would be unable to keep me in his sights. A couple more shots rang out; a few more leaves fell; I just kept going. Jesus, I was moving fast, but I could've sworn the sonofabitch was gaining on me. Whether he was or not, I never found out. I had eyes on one thing, and one thing only, my truck, now barely fifteen yards from me, I was moving like a wide receiver[38] on speed. I skidded on the gravel, flung the door open, and dived into the driver's seat.

Thank Christ I'd had the good sense to leave the keys in the ignition. It started the first time. I jammed my foot on the accelerator, swung the wheel, and took off like a dragster kicking up dirt. The pinging on the rear windscreen might have been gravel or buckshot. What did I care? Within seconds I knew I was out of range. A glance in the rear-view told me there was nobody on my tail – not yet, at any rate – and it was safe to turn on my lights. I guess when you're doing seventy mph in the half-light, with your foot on the floor, a little illumination's not a bad idea.

Or was it? I was sure the track ahead of me was straight, but my headlights told me otherwise. It curved, and I just had time to note that a line of tamarisk bushes bounded it before I crashed through them. The thought crossed my mind that it might be a quarry – and immediately my mind went into *Thelma and Louise* mode, except that when they took off over that canyon, the music played, the credits rolled. They wiped off their make-up, then went and pocketed a fat check for their performances. If I was heading over the edge of a quarry, it was going to be one hell of a bumpy landing, probably involving a fireball before the lights went out for good.

I had the sense to realise that the ground below me had disappeared. Oh fuck. It's a precipice,[39] and I've sailed over it. But then I realised that I'd travelled this same road the previous day, and I was sure I couldn't recall any cliffs.

---

[38] See glossary
[39] See glossary

There's nothing like the impact of a fast-moving truck on a hard surface to kick such fantasies out of your mind. I landed with an almighty crash and the sound of something breaking behind me. My head hit the roof, the window beside me shattered, and then everything was wonderfully quiet, just an intermittent hiss from under the hood and the sound of the dirt, as it trickled down the windscreen and gathered in the jagged crack that now split it from side to side.

As far as I could tell, I'd broken no bones; my mouth tasted of blood, and one front tooth was chipped, I thought I might have dislodged another, and my head hurt like hell. But reaching up, I could feel no blood on my scalp. I'd live.

I tried to open the door. I had to lean against it, and even then, it only creaked open reluctantly. I got out to see where the hell I was and immediately had to grab the handle to stop myself sliding down a steep embankment. When I checked, I could see my truck was perched on the edge of a drainage ditch. I'd almost cleared it, but not quite. I'd landed on the far side – or rather the front wheels had. The rear wheels were halfway down the bank, the truck's nose pointing up at the night sky. I reached inside and knocked the lights off. Despite the impact, the engine was still running smoothly enough. I turned that off too. What if the guy with the shot-gun was still after me with those damned hounds?

The highway was but a few hundred yards away across a level stretch of wasteland. It was unfenced. If I could get the truck started, I ought to be able to make it across there. I got back in, carefully. The truck rocked gently, and something creaked ominously from below me. I fired it up, put it in drive, and tried to ease the truck forward.

There was a sound of metal grinding on metal that set my teeth on edge. I'm a truck lover, and I don't like to inflict pain on a sick beast. 'Relax,' I said aloud. 'It's all in a good cause, babe.'

The truck responded, moving slowly forward, the drive wheels spinning as they sought traction on the earthen bank.

Up on level ground, I pressed my foot on the gas pedal. Again, it responded, but boy did it complain. Something was grating. There was a noise that sounded suspiciously like a death rattle. I looked out towards the highway and saw a cluster of lights and a blue sign in the distance. A gas station? Let's hope so. I pressed my foot on the gas pedal once more.

It wasn't to be. The noise was now so bad I had to get out and see what the true extent of the damage was. I flashed the mini Maglite over the underside. Oh, Christ, the rear leaf spring was broken – so much so that the truck's entire weight sat on the wheel. Even the gas station was too far for this ailing beast if that was what it was. It was FUBAR*.

I took out my MA1 bomber jacket[40], slipped it on, and started walking. I now realised I'd hurt my right leg. It was bleeding, and it wasn't the sort of injury you could walk off. I hobbled across that field as the daylight spread across the sky, revealing a bank of ominous dark clouds. It can't have been much more than half a mile to the highway, but the ground was rough and stony with gopher holes everywhere. With frequent stops to ease the pain, it took me the better part of an hour to cross it. It wasn't until I was within a hundred yards or so that I saw it was indeed a gas station and, glory be, it was open twenty-four hours.

I went to the toilet and looked at myself in the mirror—ugly as ever, but not much visible damage. I bared my teeth and saw that, yep, I'd snapped off an incisor and chipped two teeth, and that had made my lip bleed—nothing to get excited about. Then I rolled up my pants leg and saw a livid, swollen bruise on my upper shin and a bleeding gash on my knee. I washed up, then

---

[40] See glossary * FUBAR is also in glossary of terms.

went into the store, poured myself a hot coffee, grabbed a corn dog and a Hershey bar. When you're all shook up, there's nothing better than fat, caffeine, and sugar – as much as you can lay your hands on. I sat for a while and started to feel better. All the time, I watched the comings and goings in and out of the station forecourt, half expecting the guy with the dogs to come sniffing around looking for me. After the second cup of coffee, I started to feel less groggy. I went to the counter and got the gal there to order up a tow truck. She also gave me some band-aids (plasters) and bandages from her first aid kit.

I decided I'd better call Sandy. She ought to be in the office by now. She was generally there around seven. I felt for my cell phone. Not in my pockets. Not in any damned place. Had I dropped it in my hurry to get away from those dogs? If so, I'd need to go back for it. Or it might be in the truck. What the hell, there was a payphone out front. Just my luck that the rain started as I hobbled across to it. I mean, tropical rain. Stair rods. Shoes were squelching at every damned step kind of rain.

Sandy didn't answer right away. I was just starting to leave her a voice message when she picked up. I told her I'd got her damned tracker. I never mentioned what had happened. It's not the sort of thing you to talk about if you've any sense. Tell people the dogs chased you or some damned sod-buster with a shotgun, and they start seeing cartoons in their heads. They think it's funny. A few weeks later, I might have laughed along with them, but right now, I was weary, bruised, soaked to the skin. All this for a fucking gizmo she could have replaced with a cheaper version from Radio Shack. So I told her my truck was fucked, that I'd had a little accident. No details, just 'Get me outa here quickly.'

'Oh,' she said, 'you need a ride?' There was a pause; then, she gave a little laugh. 'Well, it looks like you got damn lucky.

Debbi's just arriving. You want her to come by and collect you?'
She put her hand over the mouthpiece, and I didn't hear the next
bit. Then she said, 'Yeah, Debbi says she would love to give you
a ride.'

'Debbi?' I said. I was all ears now. Debbi was a stunner, a
blonde hillbilly with a high sex drive who always wore sexy tight-
fitting clothes. I'd worked with her a few times, and more than
once, we'd ended up in the sack together. She had a regular
boyfriend, but for some reason, the dumb schmuck was always
too tired to rock – or so she said. Well, fuck him. Or, in this case,
fuck her. So we had this thing going – absolutely no strings, just
the occasional bout of incredibly raunchy sex.

'Yeah,' I said. 'Tell Debbi I'd appreciate a ride.' There was a
long pause. I could've sworn I heard a giggle in the background.
Then Sandy said with a smile in her voice, 'A ride you want?
Well, it looks like it's a ride you got.'

Freight Train, Freight Train, Goin' so Fast.

The way my life was playing out, I seemed to be living out all the dreams I'd had as a kid. The excitement was like a drug; I was hooked on it; there's no doubt about it. Sometimes it almost seemed as if I was starring in my own personal action-adventure movie. It felt like an ongoing series of movies, as if I'd signed up for a franchise. There was always another bad guy – the world is never short of them – and anyway, when the job was done, another girl.

There's one problem with living life as a movie, however, and that is that you don't write your own scripts. Situations of extreme danger and high excitement just happen out of the blue. The simplest case can explode into violence at any moment, and the only decision you're free to make is how you respond. Life, as they say, is full of surprises. But there are certain times when you just know, in your guts, that you're walking into danger. The day I went to work with a man called Travis, I knew before I even left the office that things were likely to turn crazy.

I don't make a lot of friends. I'm choosy that way. When I do take a shine to someone, I'm loyal – loyal to a fault, you might say. There was a bonding company in Portland that I had done a lot of work for in the past. They'd always treated me fair and square, so I never turned down an assignment from them. This one, though, I knew I should have refused, it stank from the get-go, not because of the set-up, but the guy they lined up to work with me. They told me the job was worth forty grand, so of course, I was interested. Trouble was the guy I would be working with was a worthless piece of shit. God knows why they'd hired him. From the moment I met him, I smelled trouble.

You get a lot of suspicious characters taking up bounty hunting. The truth is, it attracts a fair number of cowards, bullies, macho men, and downright crooks. I know plenty of decent, straightforward men and women, who act as a professional bounty hunter should, who treat their skips like human beings and just get on with the job in a sober, no-nonsense manner. And then I've met people who really shouldn't be in the position. Guys who want to prove to the world how tough they are, who want to take out their frustrations on their captives, steal their drugs—people who want to exercise power over others because it makes them feel important. The trouble with our line of work is that we have a lot of licence. We have more power than the police. We are entitled to arrest people, to defend ourselves with firearms, to break into private homes without a search warrant if we have reason to believe that a wanted individual is in there. It's a little like being a cop, but with less paperwork and far fewer rules about the procedure. You can see how that would appeal to certain people—especially a dumb inadequate like my man Travis.

That's how he struck me the moment I set eyes on him. He had long blond hair – bleached blond – and he dressed in black leather with fancy metal studs on his vest, and looked just like an older Mickey Rourke with a facelift; he had tattoos on his arms, torso, and even his head – right down to a set of teardrops hanging from his eyes at the side of his cheekbone. He looked what he was, a real slime ball. Tell the truth, if you'd seen him on the street, you would've figured him for a gang member. You'd look at him and think, yeah, he's been in the joint and got mixed up with the Aryan Brotherhood, crazy fuckers like that.

Okay, enough said. You get the picture, but there was one other thing that set me against Travis, and that was his claim to be ex-military. He boasted that he'd been in the Green Berets, a notoriously hard-nosed outfit. Now that branded him as a damned liar in my estimation. Nearly everyone I've ever met who's been in the Marines, the Commandos or the Green Berets tends to be modest, almost secretive about their past. Sure, they'd have that don't-mess-with-me look about them, but if you wanted to hear about their history, you had to be close to them. It was like a secret they would only share with a close friend. This guy wanted to tell the whole damned world what a great warrior he was and how many slant-eyed fuckers he'd blown away. I was convinced it was pure fantasy. So I marked his card as an 'A' for asshole, possibly a criminal. I couldn't have known that he was also a danger to everyone around him, including me.

We were after a pair of skips, a man and a woman. We had seven days before the bond got forfeited, so the pressure was mounting. Hence, the bounty was big 40,000 bucks. I wasn't convinced that this had to be a two-person job, but it turned out Travis had been assigned it initially, then the bondsman decided he could do with backup and roped me in.

The skips had hopped aboard a freight train, and our brief was to track them, board the train if necessary and bring them in. Our bondsman told us that the female skip – we'll call her Donna – had put the squeeze on her mother to put up collateral. The old lady had done just what her daughter asked, putting her entire life savings and her house secured against the bond. We had information that someone had said they had boarded a train, and a friend had driven them to get on the train. When Donna told the friend that she and her lover, Craig, were now going to disappear off the face of the earth, she fully realised what their intentions were. The friend was horrified at the thought of the old lady losing everything she had, all the money she'd saved over her lifetime. So the friend decided to cooperate with the bonding company, telling them what train the skips were on. She explained where they'd boarded it. Even though the whole operation seemed a bit like an episode from a superhero comic, we were well briefed.

As I said, I took an instant dislike to Travis. He seemed to think he would be in charge of this gig, and I wasn't having that. I smelled further trouble when we started looking over the skips' files. The woman Donna had been a high-class hooker, and from her photos, she looked seriously hot and well worth the $1000 a night charge. The first thing Travis said when he saw them was how much he'd like to fuck her. It was the sort of remark any guy might have made, casually. Yeah, sure, you could fancy her. Any guy would. But when there's a job to be done, you forget about that. It's a skip, not some woman on a dating site. But the thing with Travis was, he kept talking about it, like it was really on his mind, even down to what he was going to do to her when he found her, as if I gave a shit about his dirty little fantasies.

The first thing we tried was to get the train company, the Burlington Northern, to stop the train at an agreed point and let us aboard. They turned us down flat. They had a railroad to run and no legal obligation to assist us. We weren't the police, DEA, or the FBI, so they flipped us off. However, they did tell us that the train would make individual stops to change crew and refuel. That looked hopeful until they explained that there was no schedule, a lot of potential for delay, so no guarantees as to the timing. All they could give us was the changeover points. The train in question was on a great long loop, along the Union Pacific tracks down to southern California, then across to Texas, on to New Orleans and back up the Mississippi to Chicago, about 5,000 miles in all. We had no idea where or when our skips planned to drop off – and maybe they didn't, either.

We also got from the train company a series of updates on its present position, which, as we prepared to set off after it, was over in Idaho, east of Coeur d'Alene and heading towards Spokane, Washington. There was only one thing to do as far as I could see, and that was to try and catch it at its next stop. We planned to board the train dressed like hobos, carrying our badges, guns, and other equipment in backpacks. Hard to believe it, but people do still ride freight trains, sometimes for fun. Check them out on YouTube.

As soon as we got an update from the railroad company giving us the next refuelling point, we studied the maps. If we set off right away and drove like hell, we ought to be able to be there in time to board the train illegally while it was stationary. I'd heard too much about hobos dying or losing a leg, even to think about leaping onto a moving train; before departing, I contacted my old buddy Hanson. I knew he was active in these parts and I needed a helping hand with this one.

'Got a nice little earner for you,' I told him. 'If you're interested.'

'Might be,' he said, 'if you'd explain what the fuck a nice little earner is. You Limeys talk a lot of shit, ya know that?'

'Payday,' I said. 'Spondoolicks. Money for old rope.' I told him I needed a pickup man, trackside, for whenever we got off the train – with or without our skips. 'Could be way out in the boonies,' I added. He hesitated until I named the sum involved, then agreed.

All this would have been easy on my own. But Travis took an issue with everything I suggested. First, he wanted us to make the trip in his vehicle. I took one look at it and refused. The tyres were worn, belched smoke, and the seats looked like a pet bear had chewed them up. Plus, the footwells were full of old

Kleenexes, empty beer cans, and a bunch of other shit.

I somehow persuaded the lazy bastard to get his gear together and into my new Dodge truck, but I can't say I was too happy when he leaned back in the passenger seat and put his grubby sneakers on the dash; I slapped his legs, and said, 'Keep your fucking legs off my fucking dash.' Then he wanted to smoke, and I had to explain to him it was against the law. 'What fucking law?' he asked. 'Who says a guy can't have a cigarette in a truck?'

'I do,' I told him. 'My vehicle, my law, my dash, my fucking rules. Or get the fuck out of my truck. Okay?' I won that one but then had to put up with him chewing tobacco and winding the window every mile or two to spit a gob of brown juice out of his mouth. That at least got rid of the stink of his deodorant for a few minutes. It smelled like candy. While he chewed, Travis yapped, mostly about his heroic exploits in the Army, and all the women he'd fucked and all the nasty, sexually depraved things he had done to them. In the end, I put the radio on, loud, and he fell asleep.

I drove fast, and I drank coffee—lots of it. No way was I going to hand over the wheel to this dirty scummy bastard. I completed the 300-mile drive in less than four hours.

We reached the switching yard bang on schedule. We left the truck behind an old grain elevator, collected our gear, and set off to look for the train. The informant woman had given us a description – two orange BNSF locos and a string of ten empty livestock wagons at the front end followed by some of those Chinese container wagons – about fifty cars in all, so a short train by American standards. We soon spotted it: it was the only entirely made up train in the yard, and we could hear the locos thrumming as soon as we got out of the truck. All we had to do now was get on board without being seen. The weather was grey and windy, with spots of rain falling. There didn't seem to be anybody around. We ducked behind a string of stationary wagons and made our way slowly along with it, keeping an eye on our train through the gaps between the cars. We'd talked it over and decided to get on the rearmost wagon, then make our way forwards, one at a time, searching as we went. If the skips were on board, we would find them.

It was far from plain sailing. Just as we ducked between the stationary wagons and out onto a stretch of open ground, we heard the loco horn and saw our train starting to move. If we'd stood there and waited for the last wagon to pass us, there was every chance it would have been going too fast, so we ran towards it and just managed to grab a stanchion before hauling ourselves aboard.

I got myself onto the frame of the wagon and watched the track-bed flicking by as I sat there, getting my breath back. Travis stood there, rocking with the movement of the wagon. Then he pulled out his gun and said, 'Okay, let's go, get lover boy and that hot bitch of his.'

'Just hold it,' I said. 'We need a plan here.' I could see he was itching to get started. 'We're going to check each wagon – see if it's locked or unlocked, right? And who's inside.'

'Yeah yeah yeah,' he said. He was already climbing the iron ladder.

'Okay,' I shouted, 'so let's say you check the first ten. I'll overtake you and start at car number eleven, and so on, each takes ten wagons.'

It sounded easy enough, but I wasn't prepared for the bucking of the wagons as they bumped over the uneven track, the swaying as they made the tight curves that climbed away from the yard and the little town that surrounded it, out into the mountains. Crawling along the top of a boxcar or a steel container would be no problem when stationary, but at thirty or forty miles

213

an hour with light rain falling, it scared the living shit out of me – and then we came to a tunnel. Thank Christ it was only a couple of hundred yards long, or I honestly would have crapped my pants. Then came the business of climbing down to check the doors; some were locked, but one or two were open, and in each of these, I found a hobo, sometimes two or three, either sleeping or sitting cross-legged with their baggage and a pint of cheap booze. One guy had lit a fire on the floor and was cooking up a can of stew. I wished him well and went on my way.

I didn't have to go too far. I'd checked maybe eight or nine cars when I heard the walkie-talkie crackle. I pulled it out of my pocket. 'Yeah, reading you. Come in.'

The noise almost drowned his voice as the train rattled along. Even so, I could hear the sneering in his voice. 'Hey, hey hey,' he said, 'I got them motherfuckers. Like rats in a trap. No rush, buddy-boy, no rush at all. They ain't going nowhere.' And then he let out a crazy sort of cackle.

'Okay,' I said, 'so where the fuck are you?'

There was a pause. I thought I heard a woman scream, but it could have been the wind. 'Yeah, uh…' I heard him grunt and what sounded like a door sliding. 'Right, uh, make it car number eight from the back end. Bright orange. A lot of bullshit Chinese lettering on it. You'll see her easy enough. Just come right in. The door's open, and the woman's hot. Pity we don't have a few bottles of whiskey to share around. Over and out, good buddy.'

Relieved as I was that we'd found them, all my fears about this guy were proving to be well-founded. He was pure trash. I needed rest and a drink of water, my clothes were wet from the rain, and I was out of breath and tired from the slipping and sliding, jumping from one wagon to the other, thank Christ I had on my high Doctor Martin boots on and not trainers. I slowly and carefully made my way back towards the rear of the train as fast as I could, but it was travelling downhill now, through a dense forest, and gathering speed. Fifty, maybe

, sixty miles an hour. Less rocking and rolling but Jesus, the way that scenery whipped past. One slip, and I'd be headfirst onto a mess of jagged rocks or impaled on a broken tree.

I soon picked out the orange wagon and started to prepare myself, mentally, for what might lie ahead. I had no illusions about Travis. I'd had him figured for a criminal all along. Now it was looking like he was a psycho too. As I carefully clambered down from the wet roof, gripping the damp iron handrail, preparing myself for what I would find, as I slid off the wagon top and in through the door of that box-car, hit me like a lightning bolt.

Travis was standing, legs wide apart, pistol in one hand, the other stroking his crotch. He was pointing it at the guy Craig, who lay slumped in a corner, blood all over the side of his face. A few feet away sat Donna. She wore a white blouse that had been ripped open, completely exposing her breasts. Her jeans were unzipped, showing a pair of red silk panties.

'What the fuck happened?' I asked, stumbling towards her, reaching out to steady myself as the wagon lurched on a tight bend.

Travis pointed the gun in Craig's direction. 'Goddam, if this sorry fucker didn't jump me,' he said.

The female screamed her denial. 'No, he didn't, you lying sonofabitch!' She jabbed her finger towards Travis. 'He came in and punched him, then—' she hesitated, and started tugging at the zipper of her jeans '— then he started groping me, the goddam pervert.'

Travis looked at me and laughed. 'Do a lot more 'n grope the bitch once we've dumped her boyfriend off,' he said. He looked me right in the eye. 'But me first, right?'

215

'Just shut the fuck up,' I said. I was on my knees now, opening my backpack to find the first aid kit. This guy Craig was bleeding profusely. He was barely conscious, and looking like he would pass out at any moment. I looked at the girl. 'Don't you worry,' I said, 'there ain't any screwing going to take place on this train? Not while I'm in charge.'

That did it for Travis. He jabbed his gun in my ribs, snatched my pistol from my belt, and bellowed, 'Hands up and Sit on the floor, you Limey cocksucker!' I did as he said; I sat on my ass with my knees level with my chest, hands raised in the air, level with my shoulders; I was struggling to sit upright with the train's movement. 'Now you're going to do exactly what I tell you, ya hear?' Travis screamed. I didn't answer, you don't engage with scum like him, and you don't give them a way into your mind. I needed to think quickly and calmly.

Travis was about to speak again when the girl said, 'He told Craig to jump off the train. That's how sick he is. Woulda—'

Travis snarled out his answer. 'Yeah, woulda bumped his head on the rocks. Well, who fucking cares? He's just a worthless piece of shit. Soon as we get rid of him, we can start to party.' Just then, he saw the guy Craig try to raise himself onto his elbows. He stepped forward and kicked him hard in the head, knocking him out cold. Then he blew a kiss in the girl's direction. 'I got plans for you, baby. Oh yeah. Big plans. But first, we send lover boy on his way.' He reached down, still pointing the gun at me, and tweaked her right nipple. She lashed out at him, catching him on the cheek. He whacked her, hard, around the side of the face with his balled fist. She slumped to the floor as the train swayed violently, rocking Travis back on his heels. That gave me a chance I needed. I lifted my right foot, knee to my chest, and fired the .38 from inside its holster attached on my right boot; I fired all six shots right at him.

He fell backwards, getting a single shot away as he hit the floor hard. It slammed into the roof of the wagon. I leaped on him, wrestled the gun from his hand, and pressed my knee on his neck while I got the nylon cable ties out from my backpack. I then ripped Travis's shirt open; I'd made a tidy group of six shots in a cluster in his bulletproof vest. None of them had penetrated. He was stunned, nothing more; he'd cut his head and knocked himself out as he fell. I removed his bulletproof vest, placed it in my backpack, retrieved my pistol, and placed it back into its holster. I went through his pockets and his backpack. Jesus, he really did mean to party. I pulled out several packets of pills, a bag of cocaine and a pair of syringes, packs of condoms, an enormous dildo, a bottle of Amyl nitrate, and lubricants. Then a large bottle of bourbon whiskey. This asshole was undoubtedly going to have some perverted party.

I put his gun and ammo into a plastic evidence bag, then I rolled him over and tightened the nylon straps, so his hands were behind his back; I also taped his ankles together with duct tape; I then opened the bottle of bourbon and poured some liquor onto his head wound. That brought him round.

'What the fuck ya doin'?' he grunted, struggling to free his hands.

'You don't point a fucking gun at me,' I said. 'Nobody does and lives.'

'Hey, c'mon, man. All I wanted was a bit of fun. Gimme my shit back. We can fix this; you can take a bigger share of the bounty money.'

I didn't answer. Travis rolled to one side and grimaced in pain. 'Damn you; you busted my fucking ribs.'

'You're fucking damned lucky you ain't dead yet,' I said. I picked up the duct tape and sealed Travis's mouth shut. I'd heard enough of the whining little shit.

217

I went to the open door and pulled out my cell phone. Just enough signal to contact Hanson and give him our position. The train was now climbing up the mountainside, and our speed must have been down to about fifteen miles an hour. With the aid of a map, he would be able to find a spot about a hundred miles further on where we faced another long climb. It would be safe to jump out there, and he'd be able to pick us up.

Travis had propped himself up on one elbow and was listening. When Hanson asked me how many of us there were, I said, 'It's just me and two skips.'

'What about the other bounty hunter?' he asked.

I looked at Travis and spelled it out, clear and slow. 'Bounty hunter?' I said. 'That fucking pricks a disgrace to the name. Anyway, no need to worry about him. He got fucking shit-faced, and yeah, he kinda fell off the train. I guess the coyotes are chewing on his ribs as we speak.'

Travis twisted his body around, trying to get to his feet; I could see the veins standing out on his neck as he tried to swear at me. I finished the call and ripped the tape off this ugly perverted bastard's mouth.

The words burst out of him. 'You fucking throw me off this train, you Limey cocksucker, and I'll hunt you fucking down. I'll hunt your fucking mother down and fuck her to death. And your fucking old man.'

'Too late,' I said, 'You're way too late for them.' and I couldn't resist whacking him across the face with the butt of my pistol, knocking him clean out again. Then I holstered the gun, grabbed him with both hands, hauled him towards the open door, and cut the duct tape from his legs. I swivelled him around so that his legs were hanging outside the wagon. I looked around and could see that my two skips were still unconscious on the floor. Travis was starting to come round.

'Hey, no. Please don't pleeze. What the fuck ya doing? C'mon, you can't do this to me. I'm your partner. We're the good guys, right?' He was whining like a spoilt kid, pleading with me. We were still trundling through a forest with a river raging along a shallow valley just below us; trees and bushes were zipping past. I kept my knee pressed into Travis's back, my left hand gripping his hair, then reached around for his whiskey. 'Here, you might need this,' I said, shoving the whisky bottle in his mouth and pouring it down his throat. While he was choking and spluttering, I cut his nylon hand-cuffs with my knife, then kicked hard with my right foot between his shoulder blades. He flew out and landed hard, then he rolled over a few times on the loose rocks, going over the side of the rocks and reaching out to grab at a scrawny sapling. He missed and went over the cliff edge. As the train lurched to the left, he disappeared from view.

I cleaned my prints from the bottle and tossed it out, then I sat with my back against the door frame, trying to catch my breath. I waited and watched the skips as they slowly regained consciousness. They weren't in bad shape after all, just groggy. As I cleaned them both up and gave them fresh water, and cuffed them both – hands forward – they asked where my partner had gone. 'That sonofabitch?' I said. 'Got fucking shit faced and jumped off the train. Not a damned thing I could do about it.'

First off, they wanted to thank me for rescuing them. Pretty soon, Donna and Craige started to plead with me. Maybe I could let them escape. I could have anything, the girl if I wanted, or all the money they were carrying. 'No dice,' I said. 'Be glad you're unhurt and still alive, but you got to face justice. That's my job. I'm taking you in,' we travelled the rest of the way in silence, the girl sleeping most of the time. About two hours later, we slid out onto the trackside at our agreed rendezvous, and there up ahead was Hanson – Mister reliable – waving to us from the trackside.

There was a strange ending to this episode. When I showed up at the bonding office to collect my fee, there was a question about the payment due to Travis, twenty grand. I told the bondsman what he'd done, explained how Travis got shit faced and had fallen off the train, and I made him swear he would never think about hiring the guy again – if he ever made it out of the forest. 'Tell you what,' I said, 'make half of Travis's share of the cheque out to Donna's old lady, and I will keep the other ten grand. She doesn't live far away. I'll take it round to her. And if Travis shows up, tell him I took his cut, and tell him I said to come and find me to get it back.'

I called on the old lady the next day. Boy, was she grateful – for everything. She thanked me for saving her collateral, and she thanked me for rescuing her daughter – not that I'd said a word about that, but it turned out the girl had called her to apologise for running off with Craig and told her the whole damned story.

When I handed her the ten grand cheque originally intended for Travis, it was too much for her. She flung her arms around my neck and sobbed helplessly. I don't get moved too easily when I'm about my business. A part of my professional conduct that I take pride in is never letting my feelings get the better of me. Still, when I left her house that afternoon – yes, I can admit it now, I had to stop and dab my eyes, but that may have been because I was starting to miss that fucking asshole Travis.

A City in Flames

I knew trouble was brewing in Los Angeles. Everybody did. All you had to do was look at the papers or switch on your radio or TV. The problem was, I wasn't in the habit of listening to the radio when I was driving in that town. It's too distracting. The traffic there is insane, and if you get lost once, you take great care never to get lost again. It's a nightmare.

For me, there was always a large-scale map on the seat beside me in those pre-Sat Nav days, and no car radio on all the same, in my room at night or if I was spending the evening in a bar, I watched the news reports. You need to have some idea what's going on. Like the time I went down there to collect a member of the LA Crips, the bulletins were all about corruption within the mainstream LAPD and CRASH, their anti-gang unit Community Resources Against Street Hoodlums. The story was those police officers were on the take. There was widespread use of violence and intimidation against ethnic minorities, and the police had effectively decided that specific neighbourhoods run by black and Mexican MS13[41] gangs were no-go areas. Welcome to the City of the Angels, everybody.

This sort of thing wasn't only happening down there, of course. If you believed what you heard, it was widespread in many other cities. In the whole of the USA in 1992, there were 23,760 homicides. In Los Angeles alone, there had been 2,589 homicides in that year – that's five times the total of 581 for the

[41] *glossary

221

entire UK in the same year. Around the country, from New Orleans in the south to Chicago in the north, from the east coast to the west, police officers were being arrested for perjury, money laundering, for pocketing the proceeds of the drug trade. Cops were accused of having Mafia connections for dealing in drugs, and incidents of brutality, murder, even torture were coming to light. The LA police had a reputation as the most corrupt and brutal in the entire country. Everybody had heard the stories. They'd been doing the rounds for years. They'd all seen the movie *Serpico*, about the cop who blew the whistle on a corrupt New York City police force. Okay, so that was way back in the 1970s, but why should things be any different? People were willing to believe any accusations the papers made.

But while there was widespread knowledge of these problems, most of the time, when an allegedly corrupt police officer was taken to court, the charges just didn't stick. There were rumours of bribes, witnesses being paid off or frightened away, or even murdered and buried, and a general acceptance that the judiciary was always going to side with the authorities. It didn't inspire confidence. In my work, I certainly didn't trust the police – even when I called them for backup. I'd come across corruption myself – cops who made an arrest, then called a bounty hunter, let him claim it, and split the proceeds with him.

But never mind what the cops were up to, I made it a point of pride always to do my job in accordance with what the law allowed. Sure, I'd had prisoners offer me money, drugs, cars, and sexual favours, so it stood to reason that some bail enforcers might be crooked. I'd had threats too, many times. But I can only recall one occasion when I let a skip go free, which was in LA, at the unrest's height.

The whole powder keg went up after a bunch of LAPD officers, who'd been caught on camera kicking the shit out of

Rodney King; the court found them not guilty of any crime. The only trouble was, it was a verdict reached by a majority white jury. The day the news broke, I was on the road, so, for the reasons stated, I wasn't listening to the radio. I had plenty on my mind. And I certainly had no idea about the extent of the trouble that kicked off as word spread around town. It travelled fast when it did, although nowhere near as quickly as it does today with everyone on their smartphones the whole time. Yes, I had a mobile phone, but it was merely for making and receiving calls, and you had to flip it open and pull an aerial up in order to use it. Then, as often as not, you'd find you had no signal. So, while the TV and radio stations were reporting widespread rioting, looting and burning, spreading stories about people being dragged from their cars and beaten, you needed to be tuned in to hear about it – unless, that is, you had the misfortune to stumble upon such an incident.

I was down in LA on several cases, but mainly to pursue a gang member named Horace 'Creeper' Burns. I can't even recall the charges against him, but I know it was a potentially valuable job. The boy was only twenty years old. He was proving elusive. I'd been in the area three weeks trying to find him and was getting nowhere. It didn't surprise me that he was so hard to trace. He was an active gang member with the south side Crips, so he would have had a massive network of supporters and many sealed lips. In the end, I spotted him the way I so often did find people – especially the younger ones: by keeping an eye on the homes of his relatives. I was watching his aunt's house. Only been there a few hours when out he came. He wasn't with a bunch of fellow gang members, in which case I might well have stayed in my truck, but with a buddy, and between the pair of them, I doubt they both weighed 250 pounds. It looked like I'd lucked out. My only concern was, both might have guns.

I decided I might as well grab my chance there and then. I sat and watched as they walked around the back of the house they'd left and gone down an alleyway. I drove quickly to the far end, maybe a hundred yards away, and backed my truck into a space to wait for them. I'd tried to call the cops for backup but got no reply. While I stayed there with the engine idling, I tried again, nothing. In fact, it sounded as if the line was dead, which was weird? I'd never had that happen before.

Maybe the fault was with my phone. Well, there was nothing I could do about that. I would concentrate on what I could do. This was gang territory, an all-black neighbourhood where they would kill me as soon as look at me. With the window wound down, I waited until I could hear their footsteps coming towards me, then jumped out from behind the fence, Taser in one hand, 9mm pistol in the other. I knocked the buddy down with the Taser, pointed the gun at Creeper, and bellowed, 'On the ground, mother fucker! Now! Or I'll fire.'

He was looking at me, probably asking himself what my full uniform and badges meant. Like, was I a cop? I didn't give him a chance to think it through. I cocked the gun and repeated it. 'Fucking down! Now! Or I fire!' He was still standing there, weighing up the odds. 'Your call,' I said, jerking the gun. That did it. He got down, just as his buddy got to his knees and tried to stand up. I gave him a few more volts, slapped the cuffs on both of them, and then frisked each in turn. They were both carrying. I unloaded both guns and threw them into the cab of the truck. I put duct tape over Creeper's mouth, then felt for my cable ties. Damn, I'd forgotten them. I then took the cuffs off his unconscious pal. Then I removed the laces from his shoes and used them to tie Creepers ankles. I lifted him and carried him to the truck, slung over my shoulder like he was a deer I'd just shot. Then I got in the cab and drove out of there.

I couldn't believe I'd been so lucky: no harassment from neighbours, no crowd of onlookers. I still had my pistol in my hand as I drove, and I decided to hang onto it. It was that kind of area. At the first red light, I tried calling the cops again. The line still seemed dead. What the hell was going on? I needed to tell them I was bringing someone in on a warrant.

I was heading towards the police precinct when I decided something big must be happening. I switched the radio on; reports were coming in that civil war had broken out, police stations were under attack from armed rioters, and gun shops raided. Shopowners were on the streets, firing at potential looters. Looking around, I now saw smoke billowing up from several points along the skyline, mostly in the area I was heading for, south-central.

I didn't have time to think about what to do. My hand was forced. I swung around a corner to avoid a jam of cars, trucks, and people, directly into a street where crowds of people, mostly youths and kids, were smashing windows and looting stores. Even as I wondered what the hell to do, I heard the reporter saying that police in one precinct had barricaded themselves inside and called in the National Guard. I slowed to avoid colliding with a car that was heading my way on the wrong side of the road. There must have been six or seven guys inside it, one of them waving a gun out the window. I slammed my truck into reverse, spun the wheel, and found myself facing a side street teeming with young men with guns, some brandishing baseball bats, several clutching goods they'd looted – TVs, microwave ovens, cases of beer. One had a trolley-jack and was trying to manoeuvre a giant washing-machine down the road. I took my gun off the dash and placed it on the seat, under a sweater I had there.

As I nosed the truck forward towards an intersection, I wriggled out of my black jacket, then removed my cap and dark glasses. I wanted it to look like Joe Schmoe driving a delivery truck. The only problem was, I didn't have a stack of lumber in the back. I was a white guy who had a black guy in the back, a Crips member, with tape around his – fuck!

A space opened up; I gunned the engine and accelerated through it, narrowly missing an old lady wheeling a trolley piled high with groceries. As she ducked out of my way, she dropped a gallon of red wine, which smashed on the kerbstone. I raced up the road a few hundred yards to a spot where there were no stores and consequently no crowd of looters, just a few curious onlookers heading towards the trouble, one or two pushing empty trolleys. I slammed on the brakes and went to the back of the truck; my skip was sitting upright and looking around him.

'This is your lucky day,' I said. 'I'm letting you join the fun. But first…' I pulled out the Taser, gave him one farewell blast, then released his ankle and wrists before pulling his leaden body off the truck bed and laying him on the sidewalk; I then put duct-taped over my licence plates.

Christ knows how I made it out of there. Three times and a fourth finding my exit blocked by rioters, I just gunned the engine into them, bodies flying everywhere. Once a kid got hold of the door handle and tried to wrench it open. I saw his mouth contorted in rage as he spat the words 'honky mothafucka' at me; he soon let go when I pointed my pistol at him. An iron bar crashed into the windshield but bounced off without causing anything worse than a star-shaped crack. Even when I made the highway, there were trucks roaring past with excited youths in the back, shouting abuse at any passing whites. A stray hubcap bounced off my fender. I sped along an overpass through a cloud of black smoke and saw below me a bus on its side, engulfed by flames. In all the miles I drove before finding my way out of there, I never saw a single cop car, just helicopters overhead and camera operators perched at the open doors, filming everything.

My cell phone rang. I picked it up, hands shaking, heart pounding.

'Yeah?'

'You okay, bud?' It was my bondsman. 'Been trying to get ya these past three hours.'

'I'm fine,' I said. 'Had a little trouble getting through, that's all.' I paused, then said, 'I had your skip in the truck, but I had to let him go. Never planned to, but no place to take him, and if they'd caught me with him, I was a dead man.'

'Hey,' he said, 'ya did the right thing.'

'So why were you trying to call me? Did you know what was going down?'

'Not really, just wanted to tell you what I was telling all my other bounty hunters in LA.'

'And that is?'

'Wrap it up, watch your back and take a rain check, yeah?'

'Oh,' I said. 'Well, that's good – cos I already did.'

Later I discovered that the riots had already been in full swing before I even ran into Creeper, and all the power lines had been taken out, the police had ceased to answer 911 calls, and all phone masts were destroyed. I decided that next time I was in LA, traffic or not, I'd keep the damned radio on.

Size Isn't Everything

I always carried a Taser. They're convenient, handy, and in 99.9% of cases, non-lethal. One of the Taser's great features is that you can disable your target without getting in so close that he can harm you. *I should say he or she* because I've tangled with some tough females in my time and given one or two an electric charge. A Taser is different from the old stun gun. It sends out a pair of electrodes on wires. Once they've attached themselves to the target, you can administer further electric shocks and induce further muscle spasm and paralysis until you are sure the subject is subdued. You can use a Taser effectively at about thirty feet, although it isn't easy to hit a moving target at that range. But, given that bail enforcers are only allowed to use a gun if you have good reason to believe that the target is armed and that someone's life is in danger, the Taser is a great asset—a necessary part of your arsenal. First, however, you have to take a test and get a licence to use one. The fun part is where they get you to experience it for yourself. They stand you up, make you take off your shirt, shout out 'Taser, Three-time and let you have a dose. A trainer is standing on either side of you to cushion your fall. Otherwise, you're down like a sack of potatoes.

Having felt the Taser's full impact, The trainers persuaded me that a Taser was a handy piece of equipment, and I started carrying one regularly. But then along comes my buddy Pete with a new toy. Pete was with a bonding company, who sent a fair bit of work in my direction over the years. You get to know these guys, you get to trust them, and from time to time, you get to work alongside them – especially if there's an ID issue. Like, they will know the guy you're after, whereas to you, he might be just a face in a crowd – just another black dude, or Hispanic, or Anglo.

I'm not sure why I called in at the company office that day. It was a Friday, around lunchtime, and I was looking forward to a weekend away. I had a hot date lined up, and a buddy of mine had loaned us a beach-front apartment, so I wouldn't usually have called in. Maybe they owed me money. What I do remember is that Pete was real pleased to see me.

'Hey,' he said, 'Ted, my ol' buddy. Great to see ya. Siddown.' He cleared a stack of papers off a sofa he had on there and motioned me towards it. 'Can I get ya something? A cup of coffee? Or hey, how about a nice panatella? My boy's just back from Costa Rica. They got some excellent cigars down there. Here.' He opened one of those wooden boxes and handed me one. I've never smoked in my life, but I recognised a decent cigar when I saw one. I put it in my shirt pocket. One of my buddies would appreciate it. Then I said, 'Okay, now cut the crap. You got some shitty case that nobody'll look at, and you figured I might be dumb enough to step in – am I right, or am I right?'

Pete, never even laughed. He just said, 'Y'know, it's hilarious you should say that 'cos something did come up.' Then he passed me my coffee and sat down beside me. Which in itself was odd because he was the kind of guy who generally seemed more comfortable if you were on one side of the desk and he was on the other. 'Listen,' he said, 'everything's falling into place. Number one, I gotta guy I really wanna pull in. I don't like him. Never did. I had a feeling he'd go AWOL from the get-go. Number two, I just had a call he's drinking in a bar downtown. Some guy has a beef against him – gave me the tip-off. And number three—'

229

I cut him short. 'Yeah, number three. In walks Muggins, aka Ted Oliver. I read you, Pete. I read ya real good.'

Pete did laugh this time. 'Hey,' he said, 'you're really on the ball, aren't you? You got a knack for reading the signs.' And then, before I could tell him to fuck off, he picked it up again. 'So listen, the bar's not ten minutes' drive from here. I can ID this guy, and you, my friend, can try out my new toy. Whaddayou say?'

'What new toy?' When it came to equipment and devices, I like to use my own gear exclusively. That way, I never have anyone to rely on anyone but myself. No one to blame, either, if things go wrong. Except maybe the manufacturer.

Pete got up and pulled open a drawer. 'You might like to give our man a little taste of this,' he said. 'My new bang-stick.' He was holding what looked like a black police nightstick or truncheon. It was about eighteen inches long, made of metal, and had two prongs at the end. Pete handed it to me.

'Christ,' I said, 'I've heard about these. Don't they use them to stun cows?'

'You got it, buddy.' He laughed again. 'Cows... and big sonsabitches who wanna argue with you.'

I squeezed the trigger and couldn't help giving a little jump as the end lit up, two blue arcs of light spanning the gap between the prongs. I handed it back to Pete, 'I don't get it, mate. With this in your hand, why would you want me?'

'Ah well,' he said and gave the trigger a squeeze himself. 'This is one big mother we're going after, right?'

'You tell me,' I said.

'Trust me; he's big. And leery. One of those bodybuilder fanatics. So suppose I stun him.'

'I still don't get it, Pete. You knock him out, slap the cuffs on, and Ker-ching! Payday. You keep your fee.'

Pete shook his head. 'Nah, the trouble is, they don't stay knocked out for long, maybe a few seconds, max. It depends on the guy. I mean, what if he's one of those guys who's immune to this shit? What if he comes for me? I mean, you – you're used to handling maniacs. You do all that Kung foo shit and what-all.'

'Oh, that's fucking great,' I said. 'Yeah, now I get it. You prod the sonofabitch, and if you don't give it enough volts and he recovers, I get fucked over. That's brilliant, that is. For you.'

That's when Pete started whining, pleading with me. 'Teddy boy,' he said, 'this one's right up your street. It's just a little job. And fuck, he ain't dangerous.'

'No? So why the cattle prod?'

He ignored the question. 'He FTA'd[42] on some vehicle charges. That's all. I beg your pardon – not *some* vehicle; it was a Corvette convertible. DWI. Listen, the job's yours if you want it. I got a $2,500 bounty fee on him. You could go right out and buy yourself one of these babies.' He was waiting for me to react. 'One hundred and fifty thousand volts, Ted. Think about it. It's some fucking backup. Better than that taser you carry.'

I felt the thing in my hand once more. It had a good heft, a nice feel to it. And I had to admit it, at a hundred and fifty thousand volts, it was some weapon. I pulled myself up from the sofa. 'Okay, you lousy sweet-talking fuckwit,' I said. 'Let's go.'

We went in Pete's car, which was a mistake he was to regret later. Within fifteen minutes, we arrived at the bar where our skip was supposed to be drinking. We cruised around the parking lot, nice and slow. They shared it with a discount grocery store on the adjoining lot, so it was pretty big. Even so, it didn't take but a few seconds to spot the Corvette. It stood out like a whore in a nunnery, nail-varnish red and glinting in the sunlight.

---

[42] See glossary

Pete was over the moon. The guy actually whooped out loud. 'Man, I been looking for that baby everywhichway. Nice set of wheels, doncha think?'

'You bet,' I said. There was no question about that. It was a beaut. 'So let's go grab our man, eh?' I'd already started on my usual checks – the badge around my neck, Taser, pepper spray, leg cuffs, handcuffs, hogties on my belt holders, pistol in my waistband holster – just in case. I zipped up my lightweight jacket and pulled on my baseball cap. Pete just stood there, watching. 'Shit,' he said, 'you really need all that stuff?'

'Sure,' I said. 'Now put this bulletproof vest on, just in case. It's called going prepared, distinguishes the pro's from the wannabe.'

I checked that Pete had his badge on too. The fact that he only carried his new bang-stick and the warrant was a matter for him. For me, the important thing was that I was ready to do things my way.

When we walked into the bar with our jackets done up, we could've been any couple of construction guys going out for a beer after work. The place was a real daytime drinkers' hangout. Lots of guys at the bar, perched on stools, shoulders hunched, baseball on the TV. We chose a table by a windowless wall. My ass had barely hit the seat when Pete whacked me in the ribs. He spoke out of the side of his mouth like he was a TV detective from the black-and-white days. 'Thass him,' he said. 'There at the bar. The jacked-up black dude, third from the end.'

'Yeah, sure,' I said. I waited till the barman came across, took our order, and then had a quick look around, real casual. Our guy was a monster. He was wearing a white singlet. What he had, you could see, every frigging inch of it, and it was all solid steroid muscle and covered with tattoos. Beside him was his girl, a Mexican, and a female version of him with an enormous pair of tits. 'A couple of steroid junkies, by the look of them.' I said. 'Where's his fucking neck?' I murmured.

'What's that?' Pete asked.

'Mister fucking no-neck,' I said. 'These bastards can be dangerous, y'know. You provoke em, and you got a serious case of roid-rage on your hands.'

'Road rage! I don't get it? Said Pete.

' No fucking Roid-rage?' I said Pete looked at me like he thought I was joking.

'Oh yeah,' I said. 'You get 'em all riled up, and they can blow. Then you've got big fucking trouble. All those steroids – makes 'em go fucking psycho.'

Pete put a hand up to his eyebrows and tried to steal a surreptitious glance at the guy, who had turned around and was now facing us. 'Check out the upper arms,' I said. 'Jesus, they're fucking bigger than the girlfriend's tits.'

'Gonna be a problem,' whispered Pete.

'Tight call,' I said. I paused as the barkeep placed our drinks on the table. Then I said, 'So here's how we play it. You take the guy out, and I'll deal with the *Chiquita[43].*' The look on Pete's face was worth it. 'Relax,' I said. 'It's a team effort.'

Back at Fenway Park, someone had hit a home run to the accompaniment of a few desultory cheers around the bar. Our man was now glued to the TV. 'Okay,' I said. 'Here's how it goes. We both approach the bar, nice and quiet. You walk up behind him; you hold out your badge and say 'Warrants.' At the same time, you give him a few volts, okay?' He nodded. 'That's when I slip the cuffs on him.'

'Okay,' Pete said. 'Sounds good to me. And you're gonna be right there with me, yeah?' I could tell he was all but crapping his

---

[43] See glossary

pants, and to tell the truth, I was nervous myself. When I told him about roid rage, I wasn't shitting. I've seen it happen more than once.

'Sure,' I said. 'I'll be there. Now, badges out. Just you do your part and leave the rest to me. I'm the kung fu expert.' I smiled with a wink.

We leave the table and walk across the room. Funny how big a place can seem when you go into action. I glance at Pete. He looks edgy, but he goes right ahead and does precisely what I told him to be fair to the guy. He carries out his end of things to the letter.

I see Pete reach out with his new toy, then look at the target. I have half an eye on the girl too, but she's fixed on the ball game now, same as our man. They both have bottles in their hands. As the guy raises his to his lips, there's a sharp crack, a flicker of electric blue, and Pete blurts out 'Warrants!' like he's suddenly remembered his lines.

The guy falls off his chair, spluttering beer down his nice white T-shirt. But instead of hitting the deck and lying still like he's supposed to, he's on his feet, moving like a big old bear and coming towards Pete, with his fist raised. Pete gives him a booster dose, and he stumbles, half falling. This time Pete holds the prod against the guy's midriff for several seconds, and finally, he hits the deck.

There's a sudden eruption of cheering from the TV, but as I glance up, I see everyone in the place is now watching us, except one guy who's on his phone calling the cops; we're all transfixed as our man gets to his feet again, Pete and I look at each other in shock. And now the chick's joining in, whacking Pete with her purse. I'm talking about a big leather bag, studded with brass. Christ knows what she has in there, but it sounds like lead as it whumps into Pete's chest, knocking him backwards. As she takes another swing, I grab it and pull her to the floor.

'Leave it!' I shout and draw my gun. 'Back off, or you're under arrest too!' Soon as she sees the pistol, she backs off. I pull out with my other hand my good old trusty X26 and shout 'Taser!' I aim the red dot at my skip's chest and fire. Two wired prongs hit him, bang on target. His legs buckle, and he falls in a heap. He lies there, shaking convulsively like he's having a fit, one arm still clawing the air. I keep the Taser trigger depressed. One Mississippi... two Mississippi... I count to six, and then when I can see he's no longer resisting, I throw the cuffs to Pete. 'C'mon, partner,' I tell him. 'You going to sit on the floor and gawk at me all night, or are you going to help? Put them on him, legs and wrists and if he gets up, whack him on the head with your new toy.' Pete just gawped and didn't answer; he just did what I asked. I could see his hands were trembling as he put the cuffs on our skip.

Once the skip was under control, I hogtied, searched him, and removed his car keys from his pocket. As I threw them across to Pete to bag up, the bar's door burst open, and the cops came in. These guys knew me, so there was none of that lying down and being cuffed bullshit. Pete showed them the warrant, they carried the skip outside, and we agreed to come down right away and make out a report. We weren't there for long, maybe an hour, after which Pete drove me back to the parking lot. He was like a dog with two dicks as we prepared to repossess the Corvette. 'My kinda collateral,' he said, as he ran a hand over the wing, hugging and kissing it!

'Hope you treat your wife that way,' I said. Then I reminded him that we'd come out in his car, and I needed to get home as I had a long trip to do. Reluctantly, he surrendered the keys. I opened the driver's side door and eased myself into the seat. Switched on and gunned the engine. It was a deep, throaty roar, the kind that's guaranteed to get a guy's pulse racing.

'You'll bring it right back tomorrow?' Pete asked as I gave it a few more revs.

'Sure,' I said. 'Monday – maybe, sometime.' I just had time to watch his mouth open as I took off. Just for the hell of it, I made a circuit of the parking lot, burning enough rubber to engulf him in a cloud of smoke. Last I saw, he was still gawping like a goddam codfish. 'Hey, and have my cheque ready!' I shouted before taking off for the coast. I'd got a hot set of wheels and a hot girl waiting. On the way to pick her up, I thought about Pete's new bang-stick. It might be okay for a gentle old cow, I thought, but no match for an enraged steroid junky. As they say, it's not the size that counts, but how you use it.

Meet Dan Durass

Whoever said life is a lottery got it dead right. All you need, when the numbers come out of the hat, is a bit of luck – and boy, I'd had my share. I'd done well for myself. I'd made good money, been my own boss, driven around in flashy cars, and bedded a string of good-looking women. But when I knelt on the ground and felt that lowlife gangsta holding the gun to my head, I felt cheated.

Whenever I'd thought about dying – and in my job, trust me, death is frequently on your mind – I'd imagined myself in a bed, with tubes coming out of a loving woman stroking my head and me, but on my knees in a goddam parking lot, with a sack over my head and my hands tied behind my back? No, that was never what I had in mind.

Neither was the waiting, the tensing of every muscle in my body, bracing myself as I waited for the bang, the blinding light. And then what? Darkness, I supposed. And even as the thought entered my head, I sort of shrugged. It would be a quick death, at least, and most likely a painless one.

I could hear the guy breathing—him and his buddy too. Everybody was breathing heavily – except me. I seem to remember holding my breath and screwing my eyes tight shut. But not my gangsta man. He was panting. It was that kind of day – hot, humid, limping to its end. So what's the hold-up? Was I thinking? Just get the fuck on with it. Pull the goddam trigger. He pulled okay – squeezed, I should say. And what I heard – what I can still hear to this day – was a single click, followed after a long silence by a second one. Then a muttered curse as he checked his gun and tried it one more time.

While part of my brain babbled thanks to a God I didn't believe in; the other part tried to figure out what had happened. Did he forget to load it? Had it misfired? Twice? Well, who cared? What mattered to me was, this guy had fucked up. Seriously. And when he whacked me over the head and left me there to regain consciousness in my own good time, he made another mistake, a big one. He signed his own death warrant.

Later, when I'd had time to think things over, I realised that my would-be executioner wasn't the only one who'd let his standards slip that day. And I was mad about that. Angry with myself because I should never have allowed the situation to arise. Think of a hunter. A hunter respects the animal he's going after, but if he's any good at what he does, he will have studied his prey. He will have prepared, down to the tiniest detail. He will make sure he has the upper hand. His life depends upon it.

Pretty much the same thing applies to a bail-enforcement agent. I was born to do this job, and I take pride in it. From the way I prepare for the day ahead to the way I conduct myself out there in the field, I aim to excel. Before I step out that door in the morning, I have to know I'm one hundred percent ready to face what's coming – whatever it is. And in the gun-crazy US of A, it could be anything, anything at all. By the time I carry out my final checks, I've done my homework and worked on my sources. I've got my uniform on, my weapons in place, guns, knives, Taser, cuffs – all of that shit. I have spare ammo; I look good and feel good. At that moment, I'd back myself against anybody – especially some lowlife piece of crap who deals in drugs.

A guy like that may have made the Ten Most Wanted list, but how much effort does that take? Not a lot. What he wants is a comfortable life. That's why he's a criminal. And a drug-dealer. Like most of them, he's a user too. So a lot of the time, he's stoned. Which means he overlooks crucial things. I mean important things like maintaining his weapons and using cheap crap reloaded ammo. All I can say is thank Christ. I still think that was what saved my life that day in the dirt and weeds, way out on the derelict fringe of Washington DC. That day.

This guy Leroy was one evil sonofabitch, but a pathetic one. He called himself 'Killa-Blood.' I guess it was the best he could come up with, a sorry name for a sad individual. At twenty years of age, this trigger-happy Crip[44] had racked up a couple of dozen arrests for turf-related violence involving firearms and trafficking. His stock-in-trade was to take out rival gang members – mostly if they were dumb enough or brave enough to venture into Crips territory. Personally, I never lose any sleep when some gang member gets his head blown off. It's one less problem for the rest of us to worry about, but the way Leroy went about things, he was a danger to anybody who happened to be in the vicinity.

The thing with Leroy was, he had this nasty habit of giving in to his animal instincts. Like that afternoon, he was cruising the hood in his Cadillac, smoking crack with his buddies. It was a lovely sunny day. People were walking around minding their own business. Men, women, and kids playing street basketball. They were all in the line of fire – as if he gave a flying fuck about any of them. I guess he wanted to show his homeboys how tough he was. So when he spotted a bunch of Bloods[45] on his turf, he got out of the car, opened his long black trench coat, pulled out a pair of fully automatic Uzi sub-machine pistols, and opened fire.

Five of them went down; a couple managed to run, and, as

---

[44] See glossary
[45] See glossary

anybody with a half brain would have predicted, one or two bystanders and kids were hit by stray bullets. But our boy Leroy wasn't bothered about them. He just strode around, calm as you like, preparing to dispatch the injured. The only thing was, his gun's jammed. It's the kind of thing that happens when a cheap-jack bastard puts third-rate ammo into an automatic weapon. The type of mistake that would later save my life.

So Leroy left the wounded, got back in the car with his buddies, and sped away. I heard about all this when I went downtown to hand over another skip. The cops were full of it. They were watching the news updates on TV. About two months later, I got a call from my FBI contact. Let's call him Troy. He had a contract for me.

I was lucky to have met Troy. Like many of the best things that come your way in life, it happened by chance. I was at an indoor shooting range. It was back in the early days when I was still pretty new to the country and wasn't as busy as I became later. So I was down there almost every day. Many police and Federal agents used the place, and, naturally, I got talking to them. The first thing I learned – and it surprised me – was that most of the cops do no more than a single day's training with a pistol, whereas Federal law-enforcement agents do a much more comprehensive course with every kind of firearm. Me, I'd done all sorts of practice back home on pretty much everything available. Guns are, after all, my life's passion.

This particular day I was going through a routine I'd taught myself. I'm talking about reduced FBI-QIT and CIR-2 targets. Half-inch dot targets, left-hand, right-hand, eight-second bursts, four seconds each hand from ten, fifteen, twenty-five yards, using a 9mm pistol, from concealment, aimed at a reduced QIT target, firing sixty rounds, changing clips and hitting fifty shots inside a mark the shape and size of a whisky bottle from all different positions: standing, kneeling, lying down. I even put up plastic face masks at the far end of the range and practised eye, mouth, throat, and headshots. I had in mind teaching myself to hit a hostage-taker who's hiding behind his victim because that's what the cowardly bastards do. And if I ever came up against such a situation, I was going to be prepared. It's the way I work, the way I conduct myself. You could call it professional pride. You could also call it self-preservation.

So, this guy Troy waits till I'm through shooting, then comes across and says, 'Pardon me asking, friend, but just where the heck did you learn to shoot? Because I can tell you right now, the FBI is always looking for guys like you.'

I explained to him that I'd been shooting in England for over twenty years, that I'd settled in the US, and working for the Feds wasn't on the agenda. We broke for a coffee. We talked. We became friends and what a valuable friend he turned out to be. Later through Troy, I became an undercover contractor for the FBI.

Okay, back to that sorry fucker Leroy 'Killa-Blood'. I went after Leroy for several reasons. One reason - that it was my job to bring in the guys that the police didn't have the time or the resources to chase. The second reason - I went after him was because I despise people like him. They're indiscriminate killers. They have no values.

Consequently, I have no use for them. Third, this was an FBI case, and there was big money paid at the end. When you're working for a twenty percent take, you don't want to spend all your time going after minor felons who've skipped a $2,500 bail bond. This guy had a massive price on his head, $1,250,000. And he was on the FBI's most-wanted list. Do the math, as they say over there.

I worked many long hours on this case – evenings mostly to

keep on top of my other contracts during the daytime. First, I studied Leroy's track record and his ugly mug – notable for the high forehead and a silver earring he wore, in the shape of a skull. Then it was the usual thing, the tedious business of checking out a long series of addresses including his favourite hang-outs, his family and friends, especially females. That particular evening, I went to one of the clubs he frequently goes to. It was in a run-down neighbourhood on a six-lane highway, about a hundred yards past a McDonald's. Washington DC I'm talking about, the nation's capital – and about the most deadly place in the entire US of A if you read the homicide stats. I arrived as it was about to get dark. Out front, a purple and green neon sign in the shape of a cocktail glass was flickering into life. In the window, they were advertising Miller Lite.

The club was a single-storey building with a parking lot on three sides. The lot was almost empty, just a few early customers parked up by the entrance. A couple of empty trash-bags were swirling around in the breeze. I slowly drove and chose a spot facing a line of bushes that ran along the sidewalk. It often pays to park with your back to the place you're watching and use your mirrors for a covert operation like this. It makes you way less suspicious. I switched off the engine, adjusted the rear-view, and sat there watching. People were arriving in ones and twos. Mixed, but plenty of whites, which put me at my ease. If I was going to walk in there, I didn't want to stand out like a sore thumb. Bad enough with my Limey accent, let alone the colour of my skin.

There was minimal illumination in the lot—just a single street-lamp over in the far corner; I parked near the exit. The place would soon be pitch black. I wondered whether the club would have an escort service to get females to their vehicles in safety.

After a while, I got out of the car and walked over to the entrance. I approached the doorman. Behind him was a printed notice, 'NO FIREARMS / WEAPONS INSIDE.' As the guy held out his metal detector, I stepped back. 'Hang about,' I said and patted my hip pocket. 'Looks like I forgot my damned billfold.'[46] Back at my car, I removed my badge, my gun, the holster, and my bail agent ID, and my bulletproof vest; I hadn't realised I was going to be searched on entry.

By the time I got back to the door, there was a line of people waiting to get in rednecks, a few blacks, and a few criminal types. It was that kind of place. I went to the bar and tried to order a drink. I had to shout; the music was so loud. Did I say music? I mean rap, and right behind me, a group of young guys joined in full volume. They knew every damned word.

When you go into a place like that, you try to blend in. You don't make eye contact if you can avoid it; you edge past people without touching them, and you look for an empty table. Suppose someone wants to talk, fine. You tell them you're over from the UK, that you're meeting some people. And you make it clear you've never been here before.

I sat there, alone, my ears ringing. After a while, I went to check out the food. Mexican, and it didn't look bad. I ordered a plate of tacos and re-fried beans, washed down with coffee and iced water. It was one of those places where, if you told them you were a designated driver, the soft drinks were free.

You can only sit on your own listening to that kind of racket for so long. When it got to around ten, I decided after chatting to a few punters that my skip wasn't going to show. I was sweating, I was bored, I was half deaf, and I was already running over a string of jobs I would be doing the next day. I might as well head for home.

Outside I stood and held my shirt away from my body, letting

---

[46] See glossary

the breeze run over my damp torso. My mind was all about getting home and into a cool shower. When I walked across to my car, I was half-aware of the blue Cadillac parked beside it. When I put my hand in my pocket, I noticed the licence plate, 258 CUZ, and the dent on the chrome fender – and the sticker. 'Yellow and Blue with the Stars and Stripes.' The car had a white leather roof. On the rear shelf were two large speakers. Fuck, I didn't like this. If my brain hadn't been half numbed by the racket in the club, I would've seen it halfway across the lot. I'd just got my key out when I heard the door behind me click open.

Whump! My midriff hit the side of my car, winding me. I felt the hand clamp onto my right shoulder as my face collided with the roof, a gun jabbing into the back of my neck. I quickly dropped my keys onto my boot and kicked them under the car.

'Keep yo' f-fuckin' mouth shut and d-don' turn around.' It was a black voice stuttering out the orders.

My first thought was this was a mugging. Then someone grabbed my hands and secured them with a nylon wrist restraint. Another guy tied a dusty hood over my head. Next thing, I was being dragged backwards and punched around the face. Blood seeped into my mouth. My right eye was stinging. Then I was in the car, face down on the back seat. The smell of leather hit my nostrils. Oh shit. These guys aren't muggers. No way, not with a quality car like this. They're gangsters – unless the vehicle's hot.

'Listen,' I said, spitting out a mouthful of dry cloth, 'I dunno what you fellers want, but I'm from England. I'm on vacation, for fuck's sake. Look, take my wallet. I got a couple of hundred dollars, maybe three. Come on, take it.'

The answer must have been another whack on the head because the next thing I knew, the car was speeding along, the radio was on full blast, and I was on the floor, squashed in under the rear seat with my head throbbing. As I tried to lever myself up with my elbows, I was shoved back down by a size twelve shoe between my shoulder blades. Next moment I felt the car lurch to the right and heard the sound of loose gravel pinging against the wheel arches. Where the fuck were they taking me? And why?

The answer to the second question was all too obvious. If these weren't muggers, they were fucking gangsters taking me out someplace to kill me. Was that what they were discussing? It was hard to tell above the radio's sound – the silky tones of Marvin Gaye, for Christ's sake – they weren't saying much at this point, but that was my best guess.

I felt a hand probing me and heard a grunt as it plunged deep into my trouser pocket. All I had in there was my wallet, no I.D., and a few odds and ends, along with the pain from my head; the sudden bucking of the car as it bumped its way through potholes was making me nauseous. The guy was leaning over me. The smell of his aftershave as his hand delved into my hip pocket had me gagging. 'Yuh, he's c-clean.' I heard that plain enough.

I needed a plan, but my mind was seething. An animal fear had got hold of me. If I had to die, I could think of a dozen better ways than this. Was I going to be dumped in the woods at the edge of town? A bullet between my eyes and left for the wild dogs to pick over my corpse? Surely not that.

The car stopped. The engine cut out, slicing the end of a plaintive love song. The door creaked open, and my abductors stepped outside. I listened carefully—two of them. I was sure of that now. For a moment, there was just the sound of the breeze rustling through the weeds. One of the guys lit a cigarette. Even when they started talking, it seemed remote, mumbled. Then the wind dropped, and two words hung in the sudden stillness. 'Cap him.'

Fucking Jesus Christ. I wrestled with the nylon ties that bit into my wrists. Damn, they were tight. Then, as the smell of tobacco smoke and weed wafted into the car, I thought, why the delay? What are they waiting for?

I clenched my ass muscles as their footsteps crunched towards me. One thing I was not going to do was shit my pants. When it's time to die, you do it with dignity.

So what the f-f-fuck you doing in the hood, whi-whitey?' They'd dragged me out, and I was lying on the ground, stones digging into my ribs, my face held tight against the dirt by the shoe pressed into my left cheek. 'Wh-who you lookin' for, huh?'

'I told you, man. I'm on vacation. You got to believe me. I just got off the plane. I got people waiting for me. My sister. If I don't show, she'll go to the cops.'

They pulled me up by my shoulders, onto my knees. They kicked my back. I was facing the car now, the lights full in my face and half blinding me – even through the hood.

'Don't gimme none o' that sister sh-shit. Who you after? Who you l-l who you looking for?'

'You've got it wrong,' I said. 'I'm a tourist. I'm just passing through town. I'm flying out to Disneyland tomorrow. My sister told me to meet her at the club. Gave me the address and—'

Whack. They caught me on the side of the head. 'You lying. Yooz, a mothafuckin' bounty hunter, is what you are.' Whack. 'And we dah — we don' like bounty hunters.' Crack. This time with the gun. 'We k-k we kill you s-s-sonsabitches.'

'No, no, no,' I said. 'You got it all wrong. Look, can't you hear my accent? There ain't any no such thing as a British bounty hunter.' Whack. That was the third or fourth blow, and for the first time, it occurred to me that they weren't really hitting me all that hard. If they were sure they were going to rub me out, they would have been laying it on.

'Quit shittin' us, white boy. We know you lookin' for L-

246

Leroy. You been askin' around the b-bars fo' him.'

'Who the fucks, Leroy?' I said. 'I don't know any Leroy. I'm a British citizen; I'm here on my vacation. Like I keep telling you.' Then I said, 'Maybe you heard me asking for my sister's husband. Lee. Lee Ronson. Except we call him Lee Ron.'

'You lyin' fuckin' honky.' That, too, was punctuated with a kick to my ribs. Then they backed off a few yards. I half turned away, ducking my head out of the glare of the headlights. They were talking, but once again, I couldn't make out the words, just a hint of uncertainty in their voices.

Crunch, crunch, crunch on the stones they were back. Standing over me, perfectly still now. Silence once more, just the clicking and whirring as one of them spun the chamber of his revolver. 'Okay, whitey, ya- you can tell us now. Tell us what you d-doing here, huh? You don' belong here, so what you do- what you doing, huh?' He pressed the gun against the side of my head. I heard the hammer being pulled back and braced myself. One thing I did know this wouldn't hurt. One big bang, and it was over and out. I opened my mouth to speak; part of me determined I wasn't going to plead with these lowlife fuckers. Another factor was babbling, begging for my life. I could hear the words tumbling out of me. The only thing I seemed in control of was my buttocks. I clenched as tight as I could.

He spoke quietly, and he said in a horrible, offhand manner. 'Hey, forget it, honky.' There was a pause, and then he pulled the trigger. That's when I heard the click.

And? I thought. Why no explosion? I don't know long it took, but part of my mind that had spent so much time handling guns and bullets and learning the damage they can do. That part had been taking me through it step by step, the blast, the nose of the missile ripping into my skin, penetrating the fragile bone, ploughing mercilessly through my brain. At what point, I wondered, at what point did the blinds come down? But…. why the click and no blast?

I was aware that my whole body was shaking. Then I heard laughter. The fuckers were laughing at me. What were they, off their fucking heads? Twice more, they shoved that gun into my temple. Twice more, I prepared myself for oblivion, taking a slow, deliberate final breath, determined to die like a man. Each time came the laughter, descending into giggles. And with each click, I felt the fear slowly loosen its grip as a venomous rage engulfed me. These fuckers were making the biggest mistake of their worthless lives. I felt a final, heavy blow to my head. Saw stars, then blackness.

The car had gone. I was sure of that. I lay on my front, buried in the darkness that rendered the silence around me all the more intense. Slowly I became aware of a noise in the distance and the hum of traffic. It seemed miles away at first. Then the pain took over. My head was throbbing. I could feel the hood, sticky and wet around my mouth, the blood now chilled by the night air. One or two drops of rain landed on the back of my hand. I lay still, listening, counting seconds in time to my heartbeat, which was slower than I expected. I reckoned I'd been there some time. Then a panicky thought struck me. Was I shot? In the head? Was I going to bleed to death anyway? In a vacant lot on the edge of town?

Some creature of the night came snuffling about nearby. I kept counting. By the time I'd got to a hundred, I was sure they'd gone – and confident that I wasn't shot and that I was going to live. It only took that long for the rage to retake hold of me. I was going to hunt those fucking bastards down like dogs if it took me the rest of my life. They were dead men walking.

I needed to be free. I realised my legs too were tied, and stiff, and numb. As I twisted and tried to roll over onto my back, I felt a stab of pain in my neck. But at that moment, I got lucky. I distinctly heard a glass bottle roll away from me if I could grab that.

I managed to get myself upright. I mean, sitting up. Now I was able to wiggle my way over the rocky ground. There was a stale, yeasty smell. It must be near a trash can. As I squirmed backward, I reached out with my fingers, and there was the beer bottle that was what I'd smelled. It took a while, but I got a grip with my thumb and forefinger that enabled me to swing it against a rock a few times and shatter it. A few minutes later, I'd got hold of a shard, worked it into position, and was able to saw through the nylon ties. It took some time, and it took a couple of slices out of my thumb, but I managed to release my hands, work some movement into them, and rip off the hood. Then I felt in my pockets. No wallet, no nothing. Well, all I had in there was a couple of hundred bucks and some junk. The personal stuff was back in my room at the motel.

As my eye's night vision kicked in, I was able to make out the ground, bare and rocky. It was like a little clearing with weeds around the edge and what looked like a long-abandoned factory – a tall building with blank spaces where the windows used to be. To one side, I could see the orange glow of the city, reflected by a bank of low clouds, and below that, a few trees tossed by the wind. The raindrops were coming faster now. Further over was a highway. I couldn't see it, but I could hear it. A siren wailed briefly, then faded away. I reached forward and hacked at the nylon strap that held my legs. Standing up, I immediately felt dizzy. There was a lump on the back of my head, a cut over my right eye, still oozing blood. The weird thing was, I suddenly felt good. Not long ago, I'd been preparing myself for the most squalid of deaths at the hands of a piece of trash. I raised my eyes to the sky and let out a yell that was part ecstasy, part rage.

I looked around for something to defend myself with. Christ

knows who I might meet as I made my way home; I felt naked without my weapons. I found a jagged piece of metal, the kind of thing they bale pallets with. I put that in one pocket, the broken bottle in the other, and set off along the track, the one those sons of bitches had driven me down earlier that night.

I was in one hell of a hurry now, anxious to get back to my car before those bastards found my keys, searched it, and found my guns and ID, but with my stiff legs and aching head, it was more shuffle than run.

When I hit the highway, I got lucky. The third vehicle that came by was a police car. As it slowed, I jettisoned the makeshift weapons. I told them no more than I wanted them to know. I said that I'd been kidnapped, robbed, and beaten up by unknown assailants and explained where my car was. They looked at my head, called an ambulance, and within twenty minutes, I was in the emergency room.

The guys at the hospital stitched up my head and put a bandage around it. An hour or so later, the police came back and took me to the precinct.

They'd said they'd found my car but no keys and had it in the pound. I wrote a statement; then they fired a lot of questions at me. For all, they knew I could be in some other gang. I wouldn't go into details about who I was. I told them I had no desire to go after my captors or press charges, and all I wanted was to go home and forget about it. Take a look at me, I said. I'm traumatised. It didn't take much acting on my part. So they released me, I called a cab, and I returned to my motel.

It must have been about three in the morning by this time. I had to wake up the night manager for a spare key. Soon as he saw me, he got edgy. If I looked as bad as I felt, I couldn't blame him for that. After I'd paid the cab driver from the spare cash I had hidden in my room, I locked myself in my room and took out my backup gun, a Smith & Wesson .38 caliber. Then I loaded up my shotgun. I still didn't feel safe, but I needed to sleep. I tied a string line from the door handle to a vase on the shelf, so if the door opened while I was asleep, the vase would fall and smash to the floor. I then made the bed look like I was sleeping under the cover, took the spare bedding, and made a bed in the corner on the floor, so I would get a clean shot at the door if they came in, my gun and shotgun loaded beside me. If they decided to come for me, they would have to weigh up whether the price was worth paying.

I woke up and reached for my watch—eight o'clock. I felt stiff and sore, but at least the head wound seemed to have dried up a bit, and the lump had reduced in size. I showered, using a flannel to wipe my sore, bruised face and almost black eyes, then checked out of the motel. I got a cab to the car rental office downtown, got a spare key, which I had to pay for, then I went to the police pound to collect my car. Before I laid a finger on it, I had a good look around on my hands and knees to see whether the guys had been back and stuck a beeper on it. Just because PI's and agents have them doesn't mean gangsters can't get hold of them too. It was clean. I paid the cops what I owed them for towing and storage and took off, but before I'd gone a mile or so, I pulled over and made a more thorough inspection, this time with my bug-sweeper, to see if any electronic devices were attached to the car. I also checked the glove box; my gun and gear were still there, also my ID, untouched, and checked the trunk, nothing touched. Even so, I drove around in circles for a while to make absolutely sure there wasn't a tail on me. I'd fucked up with that Caddy in the parking lot the previous night. I wasn't going to fuck up again.

When I felt safe, I put in a call to Mitch, the guy I dealt with at the bonding company who had been continuously calling me. I used a payphone in case anybody was scanning my cell phone calls. I told him I was out of action for a while that I was fishing for a big one. He didn't ask any questions. Next up, I called Troy from the FBI to update him on what had happened. His advice was straight from the hip. 'You're being taken off the case, bud. You are to leave this one to us. We don't want to be picking up a body bag with your name on it. Just let it go bud, we'll get him.'

'Sorry,' I said. 'You know I can't do that. I put a lot of blood, sweat, and tears into this case. I'm going to nail these bastards once and for all. Remember Troy,' I said, 'it was your agency that fucking made me take that DNA test. When you took me on, you informed me I had the "MAOA" (Warrior Gene)[47] gene. You stated that one day it might help get me off a murder rap. You, Troy of all people, know I cannot stop what I cannot control! So you understand what I must do?'

Troy never answered my question; he just wanted to know if I could tell him anything about them. 'No,' I said. 'They jumped me blind didn't even get the fucking license plate number on the car. Can't even tell you what make it was.' I knew I could track the vehicle's registration. If I let the Feds in on it, they might get there before me. They would take the credit, and I wanted this one as payback for myself. 'All I can tell you,' I said, 'Is there were two guys' voices I heard. Black. That's all I remembered.'

Again Troy reinstituted angrily that the agency had ordered that I was off the case; no exceptions, my authorisation was revoked. 'Fine, fuck the lot of you,' I said, before throwing the phone down and smashing it in pieces.

After I'd spoken with Troy, I drove across town, threw the broken phone into the lake so they couldn't track me, then checked into another motel. I chose one with a parking lot out back where I could leave the car unseen from the highway. Then

---

[47] See glossary

I got a new phone from the store and arranged for another rental. I chose a maroon Dodge Shadow with tinted windows and got them to deliver it to me. They had it there within the hour. I went out, got some breakfast, and then made my way to a place I knew that sold wigs. I bought two or three pieces and a pair of sunglasses. Then I went to a thrift store and bought a selection of old nondescript clothes – cheap, everyday stuff; the kind of clothes that turned you into a person nobody would stop and look at.

I called all my contacts back in my room, trying to get a lead on this Caddy, 258 CUZ. Nobody had anything positive for me. When I'd exhausted every possibility, I took a drive out to the abandoned factory where they'd left me; I looked around for ages, trying to find something, anything that would give me a lead. There was nothing there. The rain had messed things around pretty well, and then some kids had been down there with trail bikes tearing the dirt up.

All this time, Mitch was calling from the bonding company. Was I free yet? They had a stack of jobs piling up. Every time I told him the same thing. 'Too much work on my plate. Give me a few days.'

The days soon turned into weeks. Every time I put the local news on, they said the police and the Feds were still after the guy. The latest was that he'd left the state, headed to California. If that turned out to be accurate, I was in for a lot of work. I had no desire to head out west, but at the same time, I was obsessed with the need to track this guy down, him and his stuttering sidekick. This had become personal; they had made it personal; I wanted revenge. I was hooked on it.

My obsession with Leroy was costing me a lot of time and money; I was like a man possessed. There were the expenses associated with life on the road, and there was all the work I was

253

turning down – easy jobs that would have netted me a regular series of small cheques. As to Leroy's supposed flight to California, I had no way of knowing how reliable that was. The Feds could easily be laying a false trail – partly to feed the news media and give the public something to chew on, somewhat to put the fugitive at ease, make him think the authorities were getting insufficient information.

As to my own sources, they were slowly starting to address where Leroy was supposed to have been seen or was known to frequent. I dutifully surveyed them all. I spent long cold nights watching, waiting. I lined the car's rear window with black plastic trash-bags, as even in the dark, your silhouette can easily be spotted.

Along the way, there were a lot of false leads. I got very excited when I got an address to which the Cadillac was registered. But that came to nothing. Then, at last, I got a call from an informant to tell me that this new information he had was going to cost me big bucks, stating that Leroy was holed up in someplace out of town with a bunch of homies[48]. I just agreed to pay whatever he wanted. Also, that Leroy was getting regular visits from a girlfriend. Better still, my informant had her name, address, and car registration. It was a dark blue Nissan 280ZX, a sports car with three gold lines painted along the side. Very high profile.

I felt I was starting to make progress, but it was slow. Slow as cold molasses. I found the girl and spent days following her – around town, to the shops, the hairdresser's, back to the shops, then to her family out in the suburbs. All the glamour and excitement of detective work, and every day having to swap the car and pay for a fresh one. Why did I do this freaking job? If I

---

[48] See glossary

didn't nail Leroy soon, I would be thousands of bucks out of pocket.

What kept me going was the specific knowledge – knowledge gained by experience – that if I stuck at it, the girl would, in the end, lead me to the man. Late one afternoon, I followed her to Walmart, not for the first time that week. She met a friend at the entrance, and I watched them go into the store together. I took up a parking lot position, from where I could see her come out of the store and get into her car. And just when I figured I could predict her every move, she
surprised me. She came out holding two brown grocery bags in each hand, her friend beside her. So far, so humdrum. But then my girl went to a silver Metro, leaving her friend to drive the Nissan.

I was on full alert now. Something was up. I watched the girl dump the bags in the trunk and get in. I turned my key in the ignition. As she moved towards the exit, I followed, pausing to motion another car out in front of me for cover.

I followed her along the road. It was a divided highway flanked by retail outlets, diners, and an occasional gas station. She didn't go far. She stopped at a bar, some sort of Irish tavern joint all decked out in green. She parked up and went inside. I grabbed a tracking device, got out of my car, and walked casually towards hers. As I passed it, I stopped as if to pick up something I'd dropped, quickly placing the tracker under the wheel arch. Then I circled back to my car and checked that it was transmitting okay.

She came out about half an hour later with another girl; it looked like a waitress coming off her shift. The pair of them got into the Metro. I followed them out of the parking lot, my heart thumping this had to be the break I'd been waiting for.

They made their way to the freeway and headed south for several miles. They were cautious, driving at a steady sixty-five.

255

When they came off at an intersection, they headed west for half a mile then did a U-turn. Had they seen me? I'd been hanging well back. I pulled in behind some parked vehicles and watched the tracker on the dashboard. I couldn't let them get too far ahead, but I needed to remain out of sight. I gave them a count of twenty, and then I set off after them. The road was wide, with not much traffic on it. I could just see them, way off in the distance. When they made another turn about an hour later, I followed, tucking myself in behind an eighteen-wheeler. Then they swung off onto a county road, kicking up a big old trail of dust. I pulled over once more hidden by bushes and waited, watching the dust-cloud as far as a cluster of trees. The signal was getting weaker by the minute. I knew I'd soon lose it, but there was no way I was going to risk being spotted. The sun was setting, and it would soon be safe to move on.

When I did go, I drove without lights. The road led into a forest. I stopped, put on my night vision goggles, and then continued. I was worried now, fearing that I might not get the signal back, that they'd gone off up some farm track and lost me.

Bee-ip bee----ip, beep beep beep. Suddenly I was getting it, and it was coming stronger. They couldn't be far away, and it was looking as though they'd got to wherever they were going. I slowed down to a crawl, lights still off, scanning the road ahead and trying to see through the densely packed trees. The signal was now so strong I knew I was within a few hundred yards of my target. I pulled off the road and into the woods and parked in the middle of some high ferns. I got out and covered the car with branches and a camouflage net. Then I kitted up weapons, a ghillie suit, night vision goggles. In my right hand, I held the tracking device. On my back, I had a pack loaded with water and food as this could take some time.

Pretty soon, a farmhouse came into view through the trees.

There were yard lights around it, showing up its dark red walls and black roof. I could see the Metro parked right alongside a double garage that stood a few yards to the left. I hoped that the girls were still in there for the night. There was no way I would approach the place in darkness, and if I had to wait six hours or more for the sun to come up, I would need some sleep.

There was a drive that led from the forest road and up to the house. Crouching low, I crept towards the point where they joined up. Moving with great stealth, I crossed to the far side and tied some fishing line around the wooden post base where the mailbox was. I threaded it through a bunch of keys, stretched it tight, and tied it to the trunk of a tree on the near side, a proper high-tech alarm system. Then I settled down, back against the tree. I could doze if I wanted. The keys would wake me.

The new day was grey and overcast, with a light drizzle falling. First thing, I checked the line. Still tight. I took out my binoculars and scanned my surroundings. The Metro was still there. No other vehicles. After making sure there was no movement from the farmhouse, I wormed my way forward and removed the makeshift alarm. Hidden away behind my tree, I breakfasted on water and the first of the MREs I had with me. Some of my oppos call them 'Meals Rejected by Ethiopians.' (The joke was that the food is so unpleasant that even someone starving hungry would reject it). They're not what you'd choose, but they give you what you need. I also had a flask of coffee, but I decided I'd better save that for later in the day. It would be cold, but it would give me a lift. There was no way of knowing just how long I might be stuck out there.

Three hours later, I ate again. You get like that on a stake-out. I was bored, cold, hungry. I knew I would have to go into the woods and dig a little hole at some stage. The day passed without incident. Night fell, and still no movement. Then, around nine, I heard a car door slam. As I swept the night vision goggles around, I saw one of the girls re-entering the farmhouse. Shit, I'd never seen her leave. What else had I missed? At least the yard lights did not come on; maybe they were not on a sensor; I think they had switched them off. So as not to attract attention, which was great news for me. Then nothing for ten, fifteen, twenty minutes. I was cold and damp, and a breeze was getting up. I took another look at the house and noted that the windows out front were the old type. Tall, the lower sills no more than eighteen inches from the level of the veranda. When I was thinking about grabbing a bite to eat, I heard a car door slam once more. Looking up, I saw the garage doors opening, and there inside was the blue Cadillac with the white roof. Even with the night vision goggles, I couldn't make out the registration, but there was no doubt in my mind. I was at the right place, okay, and I was about to get a positive ID.

Two men came out of the house and went to the Caddy. A moment later, I heard it startup, and here it came, along the drive towards where I was lying, on my belly, peering through the rank grass. There were two black guys in front, one girl in the back, and the plate, 258 CUZ.

I needed to get a closer look at the house; I could see the garage was still open, so I knew they would return between where I was lying, and the porch was a clump of bushes; it couldn't have been fifteen yards from the front windows. I made that my first objective. I pulled my balaclava over my head. I moved swiftly from tree to tree but soon saw that I would have to break cover to make the last few yards. I checked the road twice and then made a dash for it. I was halfway across when I heard the Caddy emerge from the wood, slow down and make the turn into the drive. Already its lights were sweeping across the clearing. I jumped and fell face-first into a little hollow and froze. They pulled up alongside the Metro.

I heard them get out, and I heard voices. More importantly, *the* voice, the stutterer. 'In the fu-fuckin' house, bitch!' As if I'd ever forgotten that or the feel of the gun against my hooded temple. I risked a peek over the top of my little hollow. Two more males emerged from the house, helping carry a stack of pizzas – so close I could smell the damned things – and a few packs of beer. It looked like it was party time.

Soon as they'd gone inside, I took out the night vision goggles and studied the place again; there was little to see. The blinds were down the lighting low. I weighed up the situation. Yes, I would have the element of surprise, but if it came to a shoot-out, what about the girls? People get hit. They're bound to. But then, what if they were armed too? And the four guys I'd seen. Was that it? Or were there more of them?

The door opened, and one of the guys stepped outside. He put a wooden chair on the veranda and went back in. A few minutes later, he re-emerged with a pizza box and a beer. Then in again and back out, this time wearing a coat against the night air and carrying in his right hand a Ruger semi-automatic rifle. He sat on the chair, cracked open the beer, and ripped the box apart. That smell again. Pepperoni, the son of a bitch.

I lay where I was, cold, stiff and cramped, for a good half hour, wondering how to play this. I was almost dozing when the door opened, sending a pool of light across the rough ground that separated my hiding place from the veranda. Out came the two girls, stumbling on their high heels, arms wrapped around the middle of their skimpy dresses. The lookout guy got to his feet, brushed the girls aside as they made their way to the car, and walked to the door to greet another guy. I now had the night vision goggles on them, and what I saw sent my pulse rate through the roof. Leroy. There was no mistaking the guy. I'd spent long enough looking at his picture, with that forehead of his – and the

259

dangling silver skull earrings.

The two girls were already in the Metro and were on their way, their tyres chewing up the wet dirt as they sped towards the highway. Leroy went back inside. I distinctly heard the critical turn in the lock. Lookout man finished his beer, then got a flashlight and started to check around the house.

It was now time to go to work. The girls had gone, and most likely, the guys would be nice and relaxed in there. My gloves were already on. I again pulled the balaclava over my face and flicked the safety catch on the MP5, tightened up the silencer, and squirmed into the dirt, securing a steady, comfortable position. The lookout was coming closer, clearly intent on looking around the bushes just in front of me. I waited until he stood still for a moment picking his teeth, then, very slowly and carefully, aimed and fired off a double-tap[49] at his head. He made no noise, just a rustle of leaves and a thud as he fell, face down. With my knife in my hand, I crept forward to make sure he was out. I didn't need it. He was stone cold dead. I started to sing and hum that tune by Bon Jovi. 'Woah, Woah, we're halfway there, mmm mmm…'

Crouching low, I now made my way to the veranda. Choosing each footstep with care, I stepped over the warped boards and approached the window where a narrow crack of light suggested I might get a peek inside.

The view I got told me everything I needed to know, I could see four guys seated around a table: my two kidnappers, Leroy, and some other guy, a heavy-set, broad-shouldered six-footer. On the table was a wad of cash, three or four guns, and several lines of coke. Loud music was blasting from a player on the far wall.

I crept to the front door and carefully turned the door handle, it was locked, I thought about kicking it in, but it looked pretty

---

[49] See glossary

solid. If it needed a second kick, that might give the gang the vital split second to react. It wasn't worth the risk. It had to be the window. I made my way back there and had another look inside. Leroy had a pack of cards out. The stuttering guy was leaning forward over the coke-line, one hand to his nose. Nobody else had moved. I closed my eyes and checked that I'd got their positions fixed in my mind. I had twenty-eight rounds remaining.

I stood ready, then opened fire, screaming at the top of my voice before emptying the clip in one continuous burst. Above the sound of breaking glass, I heard screams and a couple of gunshots as they returned fire. Then the ghetto blaster cut out, and so did the main light. Somebody groaned. I pulled out an SW .45 semi-auto throw-down pistol and let them have a blast from that. There was no silencer, and it sounded like the fourth of July. Putting a fresh clip in the gun, I clambered in through the smashed frame of the window, crunching the glass under my feet, holding my pistol in the Centre Axis Relock (CAR) Stance[50] (like the way you see John Wick holding his weapon in the movie with both hands on the gun slightly tilted). Three of them were injured and on the floor, backs against the wall. The big guy lay in the corner in a pool of blood, stone dead, the one small light on the wall, swinging but still on.

I stood over Leroy, pointing the pistol at him, almost touching his forehead. 'Do not fucking move, mother fucker!' I shouted. He was watching me, wondering who the hell I was, to one side of him, his buddy stirred, I swung the gun around, but he was only putting his finger in the hole in his jaw, from which blood was pouring from.

I turned back to Leroy and pulled my balaclava off. Leroy looked puzzled. The guy on his other side said, 'Bludclut'! We

---

[50] See glossary

shoulda fucking killed you when we had the chance.' I smiled and started to holster my gun, it was already cocked, but they didn't see that. Then I began to dance and sing like a maniac, glass was crunching under my feet, 'Whoa we're halfway there, whoa you're living on a prayer, take my hand... Someone shouted, "He's a crazy mother fucker." I saw one, then two of them raise their weapons. I let them have it—Blam blam blam, right into their heads.

I don't know how long I stood there looking at them, my ears ringing from the temporary deafness from the .45 caliber pistol shots in a small confined room. It was like I was waking up from a dream and now coming back to reality, the blood and fragments of brain tissue slipping slowly down the wall and puddles of blood flowing from their lifeless bodies into the baseboards. Thirty seconds, forty-five, who knows, the sound of distant sirens jolted me out of it. Through the gaping hole that used to be the window, I saw the flashing blue and red lights coming out of the woods at high speed. Christ, I thought. Where the fuck did they come from? I glanced outside. It was two or three unmarked black SUV trucks, not the cops, but the feds.

That's it, I thought, I'm well and truly fucked now. I looked around me at the scene. It was like something out of *Taxi Driver*. Did I have to do that — could I justify it — or was I screwed? I took the throw-down weapons and quickly wrapped the dead guy's fingers around one weapon, and another dead guy's finger on the other, then placed the guns on the bare wooden floor near the dead guys. It's called planting evidence, and it's illegal—just a thing you sometimes have to do. Then I took the Sig Sauer from my belt and placed it in the holster, held my hands high, and turned so that I was facing the window.

'On the floor, now!' Four of them, screaming orders with balaclavas on, exploded into the room, two at the door, pointing their pistols at me, the others launching themselves through the window, semi-automatic machine-guns at the ready, almost landing on top of me. Red laser lights came from their guns.

Someone said, 'Christ, what a fucking mess.' Then I felt a knee in my back as someone grabbed my hands, dragged them down, and put the cuffs on. One of the officers was on the radio already, the others scouring the rest of the house. 'Jesus,' one of them called out. 'Must be at least a few million bucks' worth.' I guessed he'd found the rest of the drugs.

What else was said I didn't hear? I was being dragged outside and shoved in the back of a black SUV. A familiar voice greeted me from the front seat. 'Okay, Dan, it's me.' For a moment I was about to tell him that's not my name, Then I remembered. Dan Durass, the code-name Troy and the agency had given me. Their little play on words. Dan-gerous. 'How the hell did you survive the carnage in there, what a fucking mess, five dead?'

I didn't answer at first. I was in the shit, and I knew it. I could be facing a homicide rap. Instead, I asked Troy. 'How did you know?'

'How did we know you were here?' he said. 'We've been tracking you for weeks; we knew you would find them and finish it, saved us a lot of hassle.'

I was hardly listening. 'Troy,' I said, 'just do what you gotta do – yeah?'

I knew I was fucked. I could be facing anything up to twenty, thirty years, or life in jail for murder.

Troy didn't answer at first. He got out of his seat, came around to the rear door, and got in beside me. He took off my cuffs. What the fuck, I was thinking, they going to kill me, plant evidence, and leave me at the scene? What the fuck is going down here?

'Listen,' he said, 'the DEA and ATF are gonna be here any

time soon, and this place will be swarming with federal agents.'
He leaned forward and lifted something from the front passenger
seat. 'Here, take your backpack. We found it in the bushes over
there.' Then he handed me my guns – the registered ones, not the
throw-downs. Without another word, he returned to the driver's
seat, and we set off down the driveway. I was still in a state of
confusion. When we got to the woods, he pulled up right beside
my car. They'd taken away all the camouflage. 'We got the two
females in custody,' he said. 'As for you – you don't exist; you
weren't here. Ever!' He reached into the glove box and pulled out
an envelope. 'It ain't what you would've normally got, but there
are fifty thousand big ones in there.' He handed it over to me.
'Okay, now get the fuck outa here. This place'll be crawling. Just
disappear, you got that? I'll find you and be in touch.' As he put
his fist out, we bumped fists. Then he said, 'Remember same
blood bud.'

We shook hands. I thanked Troy – for being a good friend. Then
I loaded all my gear into the rental car and quickly headed back
along the highway. A few minutes later, passing a bunch of police
and paramedics, lights blazing, sirens full-on, and a helicopter
buzzing overhead.

I later stopped and slept a few hours, then headed for home.
Somewhere along the way, it must have been in a diner
someplace; I saw it on the news my story, but the official version.
It spoke of a gang-related incident involving a joint operation
between the FBI. ATF*[51] and DEA. Vast amounts of cash, drugs,
and weapons were recovered, and five men on federal warrants
were shot dead at the scene in a shootout. When I'd had time to
think about it, I realised I was deeply in debt to Troy, and the
agency, and one day, down the line, I knew they would find me
and be calling in that favour.

---

[51] * see glossary

It's Your Thanksgiving.
Not Mine.

When you're going after a skip, there are two main elements to the process. One is locating the skip. That's the tedious part, all the hours, days, sometimes weeks, of staking out premises and talking to potential informers whose company you'd rather not keep, then sitting in the cab of your truck cold, or roasted half to death on a diet of stewed coffee and stale burritos. But in the end, persistence pays off, and you locate your skip. Then you embark on part two of the process, taking them in. Sometimes it's merely a question of placing a hand on a shoulder and telling them they have are under arrest. You'd be surprised how many do 'come quietly.' Other times, of course, the whole thing can get messy. Shots are fired and people die – and you're just praying that this isn't your turn. So whenever you move in, and whatever your method, it's usually within your power to claim the one massive advantage I've mentioned more than once. You cannot underestimate the advantage of surprise. Go for them when their guard is down, when they least expect you, and you will minimise the risk to yourself and others.

Most Brits have no idea just how big a deal Thanksgiving is in the States. It's huge, way more important than Christmas. Christmas in the USA consists of a day off on the 25th of December, and then back to work. There's no Boxing Day, and certainly no seven or ten-day lay-off from lunchtime on the 24th through to January 2nd or whenever. Basically, the Yanks don't do holidays – certainly not paid holidays from work, not in the way we do in Europe. Labor Day, yes, that's a big deal, and of course, July Fourth. But Memorial Day, Martin Luther King Day, Easter – they don't take them all that seriously they're just meticulously observed by the public sector, the mail service, government agencies, schools, and so on, but for most people, they're little more than a damned pain in the neck.

But then along comes Thanksgiving, and that's different. Thanksgiving matters. It's at the heart of what it is to be an American and live the American life. On that fourth Thursday in November, all across the nation, families get together and eat together. And on that particular day, that sacred day, if there's one thing that's not on your mind, even if you happen to be a criminal on the run, it's getting arrested, because, come on, even bounty hunters go home to their families for their turkey dinner, sweet potatoes, and pumpkin pie. Don't they?

If they're true Americans, sure they do. But if your local neighbourhood bail enforcer just happens to be a Brit, well, tough shit. Because we heathen bastards don't give a damn about Thanksgiving, so every year, around the middle of November, I would contact a few bonding companies to see whether they had any urgent, outstanding cases, I'd manage to get a few nickel and dime jobs, where the bonds might be as low as $2,500, although there would be a big one from time to time. Mostly they were simple FTAs, (Failure to Appear). They'd be local, close to where I was living in the downtown Seattle area. In nearly every case, the bondsman would tell me to lighten up, wait until after the holiday, and my answer was always the same. I had nothing to celebrate, and this was the one time of year when the average skip would return to the bosom of his family. On a good day, I could round up a dozen, maybe twenty. A nice little earner, as we say in England.

Before drawing up a plan for my Thanksgiving Day blitz, I would have to organise a good team. It wasn't easy finding Americans who shared my lack of interest in the festivities, but I knew one community who did. Over the years, I'd got to know a couple of Native American bounty hunters, who were perfectly happy to pick up a bit of extra work over the holiday. As one of them said to me the first time, I asked him, 'Sure. What have we got to celebrate? Those Pilgrim Fathers, man, you don't see many statues of them on the Rez.'[52] As well as these two, I usually rounded up two or three guys who were desperate enough for a spot of extra cash to postpone their family get-together for a day or two.

It was a special day, and I wanted the guys to pay particular attention to their appearance. I wanted them to be like me and put a uniform on, to look thoroughly professional. That way, people were more likely to think we might be the feds. Anyway, I was paying them $500 each, no matter what the outcome, so, like it or not, they would have to wear full black uniforms and vests marked with the words 'Fugitive Recovery Agent'. If we made all the arrests on my list, they would earn a bonus payment.

On this particular Thanksgiving Day, I'm thinking there were at least a few dozen cases to settle, some of them quite lucrative. The total recovery fee I stood to gain was around $40,000. Subtract the costs for my assistants – two Native, three white – and I was going to clear a reasonable $30,000 – which is a decent daily rate in anybody's language, although a few soccer players might scoff at it nowadays. Once I'd got a team recruited, I had to find a couple of tow-truck drivers. That wasn't a problem: those guys will work any day you care to send for them.

Two of the bounty hunters would travel in one of the tow-

---

[52] See glossary

trucks, one in each. Their job was to transport the skips to jail and to protect the recovery drivers when they re-possessed cars, motorbikes, boats, or caravans had been placed as collateral on the bond. They ran a ferry service more or less because on a day such as I was planning, they'd be taking vehicles to the pound, turning right around and heading for the next address we were raiding. Sounds easy, but it was potentially dangerous work. People are remarkably free and easy about putting up their treasured possessions as collateral for a family member who's in trouble, but, boy, do they get pissed off when the law tells them they have to surrender said goods and chattels. That's why the drivers needed protection. You might ask, why take the goods when we've got the skip? The answer is, there are expenses to be met. Some bondsmen make a killing at that. I knew one who had collected a whole portfolio of houses and apartments. They were dumps, mostly, but he rented them out to people who couldn't afford anything better and made a decent second income.

So, we had two members of the team riding shotgun with the tow-trucks for protection. The other three would assist me in the actual arrests and, where necessary, the house searches. Before we started, I rang all the police departments in the areas where we would be operating and gave them our names, licence plate numbers, and the addresses we were going to hit. We also informed them that we would need cell spaces. I had a couple of empty cells in the office I used, but we were expecting quite a round-up on this day.

You need a thick skin and sense of humour to go around on this holiest of days in the US of A, barging into people's houses and clapping the handcuffs on a guy who's halfway through his turkey and sweet potatoes. You're going to catch a lot of flak. We had knives and forks poked at our chests – some with slices of meat and potato on them, we were all cursed in English, Spanish,

Russian, Navajo, and a couple more languages I couldn't identify. We had people telling us they would pray for us because what we'd done was a sacrilege. Some of the places we broke into called the cops, but when the cops showed up, they ignored the protests, read the warrants, and helped us remove the wanted person.

We worked our socks off, going from one house to the next, while the backup team ferried the captives to the lock-up. We nearly – but not entirely – lost one. The moment we burst through this guy's front door, he was through the rear window, out into the yard, and onto his motorbike. He would have got away, but unfortunately for him, I'd run to the side of the house. He was only a little skinny fellow, and as he roared past me, I held out my arm. Caught him right across his face, and off he came. While the other guys cuffed him, I collared the bike as a collateral repo.

It was a day of domestic mayhem. We dragged husbands, sons, and daughters from the dinner table in front of their startled mothers. I remember one old lady wagging a finger at me and saying, 'Do you know what day it is? Have you no compassion?' Others were more aggressive. 'I am going to hunt you down and kill you for disrespecting me in front of my family.'

'Yeah yeah yeah,' I said. 'Yadda yadda yadda.' After you've been subjected to these threats a hundred times, you hardly even hear them.

The day took a bizarre turn when we bust into a house and saw our skip getaway through a window and into an alleyway. It was a residential neighbourhood with a lot of kids on the street. There was a bunch of them playing on their bikes. I was through the side door and after the guy when I saw him grab hold of a kid, yank him off his bike, and ride it away. I looked around for the truck, but it was out of sight around the front of the house. One of the little boys had a mountain bike, child-size but bigger than what the skip had taken. I ran up to him and reached into my hip pocket. 'I need to borrow your bike for a few minutes,' I said. 'I'll give you…' I opened my wallet. There was nothing in it but a clip of one-hundred-dollar bills. I peeled one-off. 'Here,' I said, 'I'll give you this. Quick. I need to get after the thief. Back soon.'

The kid never spoke. He just snatched the bill and stood there with his mouth open, staring at it as his buddies gathered round. I stood on the pedals and took off after my skip. I spotted our truck at the end of the street, about a hundred yards away, I signalled to the team. The guys chased after the fleeing cyclist, but when he made a ninety-degree turn and disappeared up an alleyway, they had to slam on the brakes. It was far too narrow for them.

'I'll get the fucker!' I shouted, and I followed him as he made a right turn into another alley, then he crossed a road, then turned again. I was gaining on him but struggling. The bike was way too small for me.

When the skip made a third turn to the right, I stopped and watched him. He crossed another road, then swerved along an alley that ran parallel to mine.

This was my chance. I pedalled like crazy for forty or fifty yards, then took a right turn, darting across the road and skidding to a halt as I arrived at the next junction. I leaped off the bike and pulled out my retractable baton. Even before I peered around the corner to catch sight of him, I could hear him panting towards me. The alleyway sloped slightly, and over the final few yards, my skip gathered speed. I timed my move to perfection, leaning back and holding the baton like a spear. When I let fly, it went straight through the spokes of his front wheel and stopped it dead. The bike flipped over, and he flew over the handle-bars head first, skidding across the rough surface until his head smacked into the fence.

270

I rushed up to him, pistol drawn. He was still lying there, groaning, when I cuffed him. Looking around, I saw my baton, wedged between the buckled front wheel of the bike and the front fork but otherwise undamaged. Then I radioed to my oppos[53] in the van to come and pick up the skip and the bikes.

When we got back to the street corner where it had all kicked off, the kids were still there, along with one or two adults who'd come out to see what the fuss was about. I returned my bike to the lad I'd got it from and told him to keep the money. Then another other kid piped up. 'What about me, mister?'
'Was that your bike the bad guy rode off on?' I asked. His father answered for him. 'Yeah, I saw him do it.' I pulled out another $100 bill. 'That ought to fix it,' I said. Then I ruffled the kid's hair. Hey, happy Thanksgiving day, mate.' His dad looked at me, clearly puzzled by the sound of my accent. 'Say, where you from, buddy?' he asked. I rolled my eyes and said, 'I come from another land, far away across the sea.'

We left them standing there with their mouths open, took the skip to jail, and carried on with our day's work – which was soon to take another strange turn. I'd already warned the crew we would all have some heavy lifting to do. They were thinking of a boat or something. But no, this was a fat man. He was one heavy sonofabitch – massively overweight and confined to a wheelchair. His rap sheet had him at 450 pounds, and I don't think it was far wrong. He was a mound of flab, and when we went in there, he was sitting with a big old napkin tucked under his chin and an enormous tray of food sitting on his knees. As his family hurled abuse and threats at us, we cuffed him to the wheelchair. He just carried on eating. I guess he'd been looking forward to his turkey dinner and wasn't going to give up on it; we sat the plate back on his lap, took the knife and fork from his hands, and

---

[53] See glossary

replaced them with a large spoon from the table. Then the four of us grabbed a corner each and carried him out into the yard. It was a struggle, but luckily there were no stairs to negotiate; we soon had him in the truck secured. Then I searched him, took the keys for his van, and repossessed that.

As we worked through my list, I got a call from an informant, about a guy I'd been after for some weeks had been spotted at a country club. He was a known drug-dealer facing a homicide rap, and the word was that he was out playing a round of golf. I had a think and decided I could manage this on my own. The other guys could carry on rounding up strays, so long as I gave them the relevant warrants.

I showed up at the club in full uniform. It was a classy place, and all the people I saw were elegantly dressed. The parking lot would have had the average motor-head drooling. I found the manager and told him I was there to arrest one of his members, and he'd better call the cops. He never batted an eyelid – it was like this sort of thing happened every day. I guess the last thing he wanted was to have any fuss. When I gave him the guy's name, he checked some list he had in his pocket and told me he was out on the golf course. 'Should be around the ninth,' he said and snapped his fingers to some valet guy he told to drive me out there in a golf buggy, at my request he loaned me a white coat to cover my uniform, and I set off. I didn't want to be conspicuous

The guy had just holed out at the eighth. He was standing by the next tee with a couple of heavies, waiting for the party in front. They were still on the fairway, so there was no rush. He pulled a big cigar out of this pocket, and one of his sidekicks immediately stepped forward with a lighter, with my white coat on, I was able to walk up to within a few yards of him without anybody taking any notice of me. Maybe they thought I was a waiter or something. By this time, he was placing his ball on the tee. I pulled out my pistol, flashed my uniform, and told him to freeze, as he was under arrest. He glanced up at me, adjusted the ball's position, and shaped it to make the shot. 'Hold it right there!' I shouted. 'You are under arrest fucking dickhead.'

The guy was either extremely cool or stark raving mad. There I was with my gun pointing at him, and he continued to ignore me. His heavies were standing with their hands half raised, looking from me to the boss, but he was all about sending his ball down the fairway. As he swung, I fired my gun. Don't ask me how, but I managed to hit the ball dead in the centre. –It flew off to one side and landed about 10-12 yards away. He swung at thin air and lost his footing.

Mister Cool was now ready to engage with me. More than ready. With his club held at shoulder height, he lunged at me. I fired again, hitting his hand and knocking the club to the ground. He gasped and shook his wounded hand, spraying blood down his pale blue trousers, "I'll fucking kill you... you son of a bitch", he shouted.

'Okay,' I said, 'that time you got lucky. I was aiming at your fucking head.' I swung around, pointing the gun at all three of them in turn. 'Now,' I said, 'who wants it?'

They got the message. All three lay face down on the perfectly manicured turf, I quickly zip tied the heavies hands behind their backs and tied their ankles together, then searched them for weapons, but they were clean, then I cuffed the skip and wrapped a towel around boss mans wounded hand while he cursed me. All this time, my valet had been watching me from the golf cart, his mouth open. I led my captive across to him and told him to take us to the clubhouse. By the time we got there, the cops had shown up,

I told the cops that the heavies were secured and still lying on the lawn. They took the skip from me, then checked the heavies, told me they had warrants for the other two guys as well. I arranged to call in at the precinct later to complete the paperwork, as these would be a bonus, then went back to my hired men to see how they were doing on the great Thanksgiving Day round-up.

The team was doing great, by the time finished, we had arrested fifteen skips, repossessed one boat, eleven cars and trucks, one disabled modified Dodge van, and one 250cc trail bike. I'd made my thirty grand, and the guys had all got their bonus. But we were all, to a man, weak with hunger. As I stated, 'You'd think someone might have offered us a turkey leg, a slice of pie. Jesus, it's Thanksgiving Day, is it not? What happened to the spirit of hospitality?' I don't think they ever saw the irony in that remark. I had a nice little treat planned for my team; I had booked us all into a swanky restaurant at my cost for my Thanksgiving day thank you treat.

My Thanksgiving round-up had been an enormous success. I decided, there and then, that it would become a regular feature of my year-end, whichever state I worked.

A Few Facts about Bounty Hunters

Even in the USA, few people don't realise that bounty hunters even exist. They see us portrayed in westerns and imagine we're fictional creations dreamed up by Hollywood. Or that we used to exist in frontier days but died out once the West was settled. For a lot of people, the first they know about us is when they commit an offence, skip a bond, and find us on their doorstep. We are virtually invisible as far as the general, law-abiding public is concerned.

Bounty hunters have always been looked down on as a necessary evil. They have a history dating back to medieval England when there was often a long delay between a person's capture and the arrival of a travelling judge to try him. In that case, a relative, perhaps a brother of the offender, would be asked to stand as surety. If the accused failed to show, the surety would stand in his place and take whatever sentence was handed down. In return for the risk undertaken, the surety was given sweeping powers to hunt down the offender – including the right to break into his home.

The tradition was adopted in the United States, but the personal surety was replaced by a commercial surety. Rather than another person, a sum of money or property items were offered up against the offender's non-appearance. If the accused could not afford the court's sum, he could hire a bail bond agent to put it up, usually for a fee of 10%. So now you had a third party, the bondsman, risking a large sum. If the offender failed to show, the bondsman would hire a bounty hunter – again, for a fee. And that's pretty much how things operate to this day.

In the USA, most bounty hunters work on county bail bonds – that is, locally. Once I got established, I preferred to work on Federal bail bonds. These are the most severe and risky kind, involving criminals sought by the Federal authorities and therefore likely to be more desperate, reckless, and dangerous. Their bail is set very high on the plus side, meaning a correspondingly high return when you bring them in. Before I became a contractor for the FBI, I also worked on warrants issued by the FBI (Federal Bureau of Investigation), the DEA (Drug Enforcement Agency), and EPA, or Environmental Protection Agency.

In most states, bounty hunters in the USA do not require licences. So we're a mixed bunch. Some are highly professional, and I count myself among that kind. Others range from the amateurish to the downright sloppy, to egotistic thugs and borderline criminals. I have known bounty hunters assault prisoners, steal their drugs, and, in the case of a female suspect, commit rape. I have never heard of a bounty hunter being successfully prosecuted for such offences.

Bounty hunters have wide-ranging powers. In essence, we are doing the police and Feds dirty work for them. We do not need a warrant to enter a suspect's property to make an arrest. In that way, we have more extraordinary powers than the police.

Thousands of bailed suspects fail to appear in court every year. Ninety percent are brought in by bounty hunters, five percent by regular law-enforcement officers; the other five percent remain at large.

Bounty hunters now wear an identifying uniform and carry documents, including their personal ID and the warrant they are about to serve. We work hard at making ourselves known to the police: if they arrive at a situation and mistake us for the criminals we are pursuing, we could end up being shot, and on top of that, most of the police hate us.

Our only income derives from successfully capturing and bringing in wanted men and women. No matter how long we spend on a case, if we don't bring the wanted person in there's no reward to claim.

A bounty hunter is virtually unsupervised. He is a self-employed businessman. He wants to make a profit, and he wants to get the job done as quickly and efficiently as possible. If the bounty is high, he will spend a lot of time and money hunting down his prey. He regularly pays informers.

When we've done our job and placed the defendant in custody, we leave the police to get the credit. Then we return to the shadows, quite happy to be ignored by the media and the public. The fewer people who know who we are, the better that suits us.

In order to survive, bounty hunters will take courses in weapons training, self-defense, martial arts, and other skills relevant to their work. Over thirty years, I have taken courses in all aspects of gun use. The list includes gun placement, holster draw, taking multiple shots while on the move, shooting with both hands, low light and night vision shooting, and a whole range of other refined skills. I have also taken and passed an advanced sniper course. I also did high-risk security courses, including advanced weapon skills, basic land warfare, open-air rescues, tactical driving, unarmed combat, and radio procedures.

I took basic SWAT courses I and II, as this was a requirement to work for the FBI, as well as a SERE (Survival, Evasion, Resistance, and Escape) course – everything from jumping from a moving vehicle to the techniques required to break free from nylon hand-ties or loosen your wrists from duct tape.

Other courses taught me survival skills. On one, they took you by helicopter to a wilderness location and left you. For three weeks, I slept in the open and ate what I could find on the land. I hunted and trapped, and when I couldn't find a rabbit or wild boar, I resorted to insects, worms, snakes, and frogs. At times I had to drink my own urine.

In 1988 I took and passed the private investigation course with Burns and Pinkerton Security. I also completed a polygraph course.

I have been a member of the NRA since 1988 and the North American Hunting Club since 1990.

As well as these mainstream courses, I have spent forty-three years acquiring advanced skills in the martial arts. In 2016 I became a Schichidan (7th Dan) with the formal title of 'Kyoshi' samurai.

Interesting facts:
How drugs were spread in the USA

It was a known fact that during the Reagan Administration and for nearly a decade, the CIA helped spread crack Cocaine in black ghettos across America. For years, writers, authors, activists, gang members, and many others have implicated the U.S. government in the deadly crack cocaine-gun trade. Now evidence has surfaced linking the U.S. Central Intelligence Agency to the introduction of crack cocaine into black neighbourhoods with drug profits used to fund the CIA-backed Nicaraguan Contra army in the early 1980s.

This new evidence that came forward has given credence to the long-held suspicions of the U.S. government's role in undermining black communities. There are thousands of young black men who are serving long prison sentences for selling cocaine. Crack cocaine was virtually unobtainable in black neighbourhoods before members of the CIA's army started to bring it into South Central in the 1980s at bargain-basement prices. It's also well known that in the San Francisco Bay Area, a drug ring comprised of CIA and Drug Enforcement Agency agents and informants sold tons of cocaine to the Bloods and Crips street gangs of Los Angeles. Millions of dollars in drug profits were then funnelled to the Nicaraguan Democratic Force, the largest of several anti-Communists commonly called the Contras.

The five thousand men of the FDN Group were also known

as the Nicaraguan Democratic Force, which is a terrorist group. The FDN was created in the mid-1980s and run by both American and Nicaraguan CIA agents in its losing war against Nicaragua's Sandinista government, which were the Cuban-supported socialists who had overthrown the United States backed Dictator Anastasio Somoza in 1979.

According to testimonies and facts that later came to light, this CIA-backed drug network opened the first pipeline between Columbia's cocaine cartels and black neighbourhoods of Compton and Los Angeles. The cocaine that flooded Los Angeles helped spark a crack cocaine explosion in urban America and provided the cash and connections needed for the Los Angeles's gangs to buy Uzi sub-machine guns, AK-47 rifles, and other assault weapons that would fuel deadly gang turf wars, drive-by shootings, murders, and robberies all courtesy of the U.S. government. While the FDN's war is barely a memory today, black America is still dealing with its poisonous side effects. Urban neighbourhoods are today still grappling with legions of homeless crack addicts.

Even although there were detailed activities of numerous Nicaraguan and American informants and government ties involved in the drug-gun trade, only three men were cited as crucial players: Norwin Meneses; a Nicaraguan smuggler and FDN leader, Danilo Blandon; a cocaine supplier and a top FDN civilian leader in California, and Ricky Donnell Ross: a DEA informant also known as 'Freeway Rick,' a South Central Los Angeles high school dropout and a drug trafficker who was also Danilo Blandon's biggest customer. The trio was, directly and indirectly, responsible for introducing and selling crack cocaine as far away as Cleveland, Cincinnati, Dayton, Indianapolis, and St. Louis. Drug trafficker Ricky Ross's street connections and his ability to obtain cocaine at low prices and deals that allowed him to receive drugs from Contra-CIA operatives with no money upfront helped him undercut other dealers quickly spread crack wholesale to gangs across the states.

Most of the information surrounding the Contra-CIA's involvement in the crack trade came from testimony in the drug trafficking trial of Mr. Ross, along with two other men, who were all convicted of cocaine conspiracy charges in San Diego. A federal judge indefinitely postponed Mr. Ross's sentencing to grant his lawyer time to try to show that federal authorities misused DEA agent, Mr. Blandon, to entrap Mr. Ross in a reverse sting. Mr. Ross could receive life in prison without the possibility of parole, the records later showed that Mr. Ross was still behind bars in Cincinnati in 1994, awaiting parole, when San Diego DEA agents targeted him for the reverse sting, one in which government agents provide the drugs, and the target provides the cash, and although Mr. Blandon has admitted to the crimes that have sent others away for life, the U.S. Justice Department turned him loose on unsupervised probation in 1994 after only 28 months behind bars and has paid him more than $166,000 since his release as the court records show.

When Blandon testified in a 1996 trial against Ricky Ross, the Justice Department blocked any inquiry about Blandon's connection to the CIA. Although Norwin Meneses is listed in the DEA computers as a major international drug smuggler implicated in 45 separate federal investigations since 1974, he lived conspicuously in California until 1989. He was never arrested in the U.S. Senate investigators and agents from four organizations complained that the federal government has been aware of the illegal cocaine dealings since at least 1974.

Many have charged the U.S. government with supplying gang members with these tools in an effort to undermine and eradicate the black community through wanton murder, drug addiction, and crime, and some believe crack did not become an "American problem" until the drug began hitting white neighbourhoods and affecting white children.

Los Angeles City Council, responding to pressure by the Los Angeles Chapter of (BAPAC). Black American Political Association of California asked the U.S. Attorney, Janet Reno to investigate the government's involvement in the alleged sale of illegal street drugs in Los Angeles' black community, to support the CIA-backed Contras, the BAPAC vice chairman Glen Brown told that a federal agency monitored by a civilian advisory board was one way the government could investigate the matter because "we can't have people who are responsible for this investigate them-selves." BAPAC, a state-wide coalition of political activists, had also demanded that the U.S. government provide the necessary funding, materials, and labour to rebuild urban areas destroyed by the flow of crack cocaine, as well as the required medical care, education, counselling, and vocational training to restore shattered lives. A long-term Los Angeles activist Chilton Alphonse, the founder of the Community Youth Sports & Arts Foundation, which aids former gang members, said he briefly assisted Ricky Ross when the drug dealer was paroled from prison in 1994, Alphonse said that Rick was a legend on the streets. After serving about half of a ten-year prison sentence in Cincinnati in exchange for his testimony against corrupt Los Angeles police detectives, he came back to Los Angeles and tried to get his life together. Still, he flipped when he testified against law enforcement officers, he said they used him to skim money from him and testified against Los Angeles Police Department narcotics detectives, who had been fired or indicted along with dozens of deputies from the Los Angeles County sheriff's elite narcotics squads for allegedly beating up suspects, stealing drug money and planting evidence.

Alphonse stated that he had warned the authorities for many years that the flood of crack cocaine and assault weapons into the black community was not the doing of the 'Bloods and Crips' gangs, as the inner city youth did not have the resources to manufacture cocaine or ship in guns.

While the head of the NAACP Los Angeles Chapter, Anthony A. Samad, aka Anthony Essex, announced his findings that some Bloods and Crips members had implicated the U.S. government, in the ruthless crack and assault weapons trade among Los Angeles street gangs, Samad said that he learned this after extensive interviews with gang members housed in Los Angeles County Jail. But he was largely ignored by black elected officials, who sided with law enforcement. Gang members claimed that the police and the government were perpetuating gang rivalry and drug wars. African American males didn't have planes and boats to move the guns and narcotics into the black community.

Stuckey also said that Black and Latino youths must be appraised of the government's involvement in order to understand that their communities will continue to be the dumping grounds for guns and drugs unless the youths do something for themselves and that the blame that was laid on the gangs was wrong Stuckey said. But you can't say that it vindicates them for their actions because they had a choice in the matter. But it was the government that targeted our youth."

Roland Freeman, a former member of the Black Panther Party. The BPP was targeted and ultimately nullified by FBI counterintelligence programs. Freeman said he knows first-hand of the deceit of which the government is capable of. A government, he said, that tries to set itself up as if it's higher than God when really it's lower than the devil they put smallpox in the Indian's blankets and gave them fire water and they make drugs available to Blacks and other minorities. It only surprises me that the CIA got caught out in the acts.

Note: Part of this article was originally published in 1996 by the then Final Call News West Coast Bureau Chief, Rosalind Muhammad.

***

Gary Webb.

Based on a year-long investigation, Gary Webb, a reporter, wrote a similar story; wrote a series of three articles called "Dark Alliance." That claimed during the 1980s, the CIA helped finance its covert war against Nicaragua's leftist government through sales of cut-rate cocaine to South Central L.A. drug dealer Ricky Ross. The series unleashed a storm of protest, spearheaded by black radio stations and the Congressional Black Caucus, with demands for official inquiries. Many in the media have also postulated that any drug-trafficking contras involved were "rogue" elements, not supported by the CIA. But these denials overlook much of the evidence of CIA complicity.

For example, The CIA-supplied contra planes and pilots that carried cocaine from Central America to U.S. airports and military bases. In 1985, Drug Enforcement Administration (DEA) agent Celerino Castillo reported to his superiors that cocaine was being stored at the CIA's contra-supply warehouse at Ilopango Air Force Base in El Salvador for shipment to the U.S. The DEA did nothing, and Castillo was gradually forced out of the agency.

Webb also wrote that Senate investigators and agents from four government organizations had all complained that their contra-drug investigations "were hampered by the CIA or unnamed 'national security' interests." In the 1984 "Frogman

Case," for instance, the U.S. Attorney in San Francisco returned $36,800 seized from a Nicaraguan drug dealer after two contra leaders sent letters to the court arguing that the cash was intended for the contras. Federal prosecutors ordered the letter and other case evidence sealed for "national security" reasons. When Senate investigators later asked the Justice Department to explain this unusual turn of events, they ran into a wall of secrecy.

Gary Webb was found dead in his Carmichael home on 10th December 2004 with 'two' Gunshot wounds to his head.

His death was ruled a suicide by the police and the Sacramento County coroner's office?

***

Bo Gritz.

Lt. Col. James 'Bo Gritz' had fought in Vietnam and was in command of the Special forces, where he came across a US Government drug deal under the code name of Operation Watchtower, this he alleges was the setting up of clandestine communication sites from Bogota to US Army airfields, the aim of this he stated was to flood the USA with drugs to keep the FBI and DEA in business. A telephone interview was arranged with Lt. Col. 'Bo Gritz,' one of the most highly decorated Green Beret's, and was now giving a testimony about the United States government's drug smuggling. The Bush administration was fighting his efforts to do this. Gritz explained how he came across this operation called 'Watchtower,' a CIA program that erected three South American navigational towers to help cocaine smuggling. Gritz named 3 American officers who had been killed in order to keep this story under wraps. Gritz was eventually arrested and imprisoned by the US Government.

Later he stated that in 1986, after a trip to Burma (now Myanmar), he went to interview drug kingpin 'Khun Sa' regarding possible locations of U.S. Prisoners of war. Gritz returned from Burma with a videotaped interview of 'Khun Sa' with evidence supporting to name several officials in the Reagan administration involved in narcotics trafficking in Southeast Asia. Among those named was Richard Armitage, who most recently had served as Deputy Secretary of State during George W. Bush's first term as president. The footage, also shot by a film team for Italian television, produced and directed by Patrick King and Tudor Gates in Burma, features in a new documentary "Erase and forget." Gritz believed that those same officials were involved in a cover-up of missing American POWs. During the 1980s, Gritz undertook a series of private trips into Southeast Asia to locate United States prisoners of war, which as part of the Vietnam War POW/MIA issue, some believed were still being held by Laos and the Socialist Republic of Vietnam at Nhommarath.

Those missions were heavily publicized, controversial, and widely denounced as haphazard by most people; for instance, some commentators stated; few successful secret missions involve bringing to the border towns women openly selling commemorative POW-rescue T-shirts.

During this period, Gritz established contacts with the Christic Institute, a progressive group that was then pursuing a lawsuit against the U.S. government over charges of drug trafficking in Southeast Asia and Central America. Clint Eastwood and William Shatner fronted up cash for Bo's preposterous rescue-adventures in return for the "movie rights," thus creating an overwhelming temptation for this big talker to return with Hollywood tales of derring-do (but no POWs). Gritz was widely considered to be the model for Sly Stallone's Rambo, but Gritz was already the star of the movie in his own head. Later he would run for office as an anti-establishment populist, although Gritz genuinely served in dangerous war zone situations.

***

Frank Serpico.

'The police are still out of control, I should know,' said in 2014 by the Whistle-blower Frank Serpico, a former New York City police detective in the 1970s who exposed rampant bribery in the New York Police department.

Serpico, a cop himself, ended up getting shot in the face when fellow officers wouldn't come to his aid when confronting a suspect. He eventually testified before a special commission set up to investigate corruption in the NYPD.

Serpico said he just wanted to do his job and uphold the law and protect the public, he said he loved being a cop, and he valued public service, which made it hard for him to witness and accept corruption and abuse of power in the force.

In the opening scene of the 1973 movie "Serpico," you see him shot in the face or, to be more accurate, the character of Frank Serpico, played by Al Pacino, is shot in the face.

Frank Serpico had only recently been transferred to the Narcotics division of the New York City Police Department. They were moving in on a drug dealer on the fourth floor of a walk-up tenement in a Hispanic section of Brooklyn. The police officer backing him up instructed him, since he spoke Spanish, just to get the apartment door open and leave the rest to us. One officer was standing to his left on the landing, no more than eight feet away with his gun drawn; the other officer was to his right rear on the stairwell and his gun drawn. When the door opened, Serpico pushed his way in and snapped the chain. The suspect slammed the door on him, wedging in his head and right shoulder and arm. He couldn't move, but he aimed his snub-nose Smith & Wesson revolver at the perp (perpetrator of the crime). From behind him, no help came from his fellow officers, and at that moment his anger got the better of him he stated. He made the almost fatal mistake of taking his eye off the perp and screaming to the officer on his left: "What the hell are you waiting for? Give me a hand!" he turned back to face a gun blast in his face. He had cocked his weapon and fired back at the perp, almost in the same instant, probably as a reflex action.

When Serpico regained consciousness, he realised he was still lying on his back in a pool of blood; he tried to assess the damage from the gunshot wound in his cheek, which was in this case of small entry, big exit, as often happens with bullets? He then checked to see if the back of his head was missing? He thought he heard a voice saying, "Don't worry, you be all right, you be all right," and when he opened his eyes, he saw an old Hispanic man looking down at him just like Carlos Castaneda's Don Juan. His backup was nowhere in sight. They hadn't even called for assistance. He never heard the famed "Code 1013," meaning "Officer Down." They didn't call an ambulance either; He later learned that the old man did call the police for help. One patrol car responded to investigate, and realizing he was a narcotics officer, rushed him to a nearby hospital with one of the officers who was with him on that night who said, "If I knew it was him, I would have left him there to bleed to death,"
The next time he saw his "back-up" officers was when one of them came to the hospital to bring him his watch. "What the hell am I going to do with a watch?" He told the officer. "What I needed was a back-up. Where were you?" The officer answered, "Fuck you," and left. Both his "back-ups" were later awarded medals for saving his life.

There was never any investigation into what took place that

day. But years later, Patrick Murphy, who was police commissioner at the time, was giving a speech at Alma mater (University, school, or college that one formerly attended) the John Jay College of Criminal Justice, and Serpico confronted him and said, "My name is Frank Serpico, and I've been carrying a bullet in my head for over 35 years, and you, Mr. Murphy, you are the man I hold responsible. You were the man who was brought in as commissioner to take up the cause that I began rooting out corruption. You could have protected me; instead, you put me in harm's way. What have you got to say?" Patrick Murphy just hung his head and had no answer.

Nobody knows exactly why Frank Serpico was left trapped in that door by his fellow police officers. But the Narcotics division was at that time rotten to the core, with many officers taking money from the very drug dealers they were supposed to bust. Serpico had refused to take bribes and had chosen to testify against his fellow officers.

Glossary of Terms

AC: Air Conditioner.

ADOBE: This is a building material made from light brown earth and organic materials. Adobe is Spanish for mud brick, but in some English-speaking regions of Spanish heritage, the term refers to any kind of earth construction. Most adobe buildings are similar in appearance to cob and rammed earth buildings. Adobe is amongst the earliest building materials and is used throughout the world.

AK-47: *Kalashnikov.* A gas-operated automatic 7.62x39mm assault rifle was developed in the Soviet Union by Mikhail Kalashnikov.

APPALACHIA: Named after the Appalachian Mountains. Appalachia is a cultural region in the Eastern United States that stretches from the Southern Tier of New York to northern Alabama and Georgia.

AR15: A lightweight semi-automatic rifle.

AR16: The AR-16 was developed shortly after ArmaLite's previous rifle, the AR-15. It was a gas-operated, selective-fire rifle battle rifle that utilized a rotating bolt.

ATF: Bureau of Alcohol, Tobacco, Firearms, and Explosives. Is a federal law enforcement organization within the United States Department of Justice.

BACKCOUNTRY: Very remote, undeveloped, isolated and difficult areas to access.

BAIL: A recognized guarantee for the court appearance of a defendant. By posting bail, which is a determined amount of monies set by the court, the surety or sureties who secure the release of an individual from legal custody will thereby be held responsible for the appearance in court of the said defendant when scheduled to do so.

BAIL BOND: A surety bond; is money or property offered or deposited by a defendant or other persons to ensure the defendant's appearance at their trial; a written declaration of the bail undertaking releasing a defendant from detention.

BAIL BONDSMAN/WOMAN: A person who acts as a surety or gives bail for another, which is usually referred to as 'bail bondsman' or 'bondsman.'

BAIL EXONERATION: The term used by the court to describe a bond that is free and clear of any liability; to release from liability the sureties on a bail bond either by the surrender of their principal to the proper authorities or by a surrender of themselves before the day stipulated in the bond. It is sometimes necessary to file a motion designed to exonerate a forfeited bond on a technicality and not based on the defendant's surrender.

BARKEEP: A person who owns or serves drinks in a bar.

BILLFOLD: A traditional pocket wallet.

BINS: Binoculars.

BLACKFOOT RESERVATION: The Blackfoot Nation, also known as the Blackfeet Tribe of the Blackfeet Indian Reservation, is an Indian reservation.

BLACKTOP: A bituminous material (Tar) used primarily for surfacing roads.

BLOODS: The name of one of many street gangs in the USA. The name Bloods is an acronym for "Brotherly Love Overcomes Overrides and Destruction." The Bloods was initially formed to provide members' protection from the Crips in Los Angeles that dates back to the 1960s. Since then, a powerful gang called the

Crips dominated the city. They targeted and harassed smaller gangs like the Pirus and Black P. Stones Jungles. Eventually, dozens of smaller gangs in Los Angeles formed an alliance to fight back against the Crips, creating what's known as the Bloods, a gang with a reputation for its relentless violence and drug-dealing, which has expanded throughout the US. (See Crips).

BOHICA: (Military slang) Bend Over Here It Comes Again.

BOMBER JACKET: This is also known as an MA-1 jacket; the jacket is also worn in North America, where it is commonly known as a bomber jacket, especially in areas with cold weather. These jackets became popular in the late 1960s with punks, mods, and skinheads. It was a flight jacket created for pilots and eventually became part of popular culture and apparel.

BONDING OFFICE: An office where a person writes a bail bond to release defendants that have had a court set their bail.

BOONIES: Is short for boondocks. A place out in the sticks or wilderness, in the middle of nowhere, or remote areas and locations outside of towns and cities.

BOSQUE: Spanish word for woodlands. A Bosque ecosystem encompasses a riparian forest and floodplains that surround a river. In the US, this ecosystem is found almost exclusively in the arid Southwest, mostly along the Rio Grande.

BRACKEN: Any large, tall or coarse fern with lobed fronds or leaves, Ferns can cover vast areas.

CADDY: USA Slang. For a large luxury car manufactured by the US Cadillac motor company.

CANNED LAUGHTER: A fake laughing track, made to be inserted into the show. A separate soundtrack for a recorded comedy show containing the sound of audience laughter.

CANTINA: It is a Mexican bar, a place for eating, games, and drinking.

CANDYMAN: American term for a drug dealer or a person who sells (Candy) drugs.

CB RADIO: Citizens' Band Radio. A system of short-distance radio communications between individuals typically selects 40 channels within the 27 MHz.

CENTRE AXIS RELOCK (CAR) STANCE: You assume an aggressive martial arts-type stance with the support side foot well forward. Think of it as a fighting position from which you can quickly press forward or withdraw as needed. With the CAR technique, your firing hand is actually about half or maybe two-thirds of the way extended, so the sights are relatively close and in the ideal focal range of 12 to 16 inches. The pistol is canted towards your support side so that the sights are more in front of your support side-eye. The canted position also prevents having to cock your wrist in an unnatural position and aligns the wrist with the forearm to absorb recoil better.

CELL PHONE: Cellular mobile phone.

CHIQUITA: A Cutie, honey, or little girl.

CICADAS: Cicadas are a large swarming winged insect. They are the only insects capable of producing such a unique loud courtship sound.

CLANNISH: A close-knit family, concentrating on people in your own family or group, not wanting other people to join it.

CORNDOG: Is a sausage/hot dog on a stick that has been coated in a thick layer of cornmeal batter and deep-fried.

CORRAL: A pen or enclosure put or keep livestock, especially cattle or horses in on a farm or ranch.

CREE GIRL: Native American Indian Girl. The Cree are one of the largest groups of First Nations in North America.

CRIPS: (One of many street gangs in the USA). The name had no political, organizational, cryptic, or acronymic meaning, though some have suggested it stands for "Common Revolution In Progress." The Crips are one of the largest and most violent associations of street gangs in the United States. With an estimated 30,000 to 35,000 members in 2008, they have been involved in murders, robberies, and drug dealing, among other crimes. The Crips have had a long and bitter rivalry with the Bloods. (See Bloods).

CROSSHAIRS: A pair of thin wires crossing each other at right angles in a gun sight or other optical instrument device, for use in positioning, aiming, or measuring.

CURRYCOMB: A comb or brush, having rubber or plastic teeth, used to groom horses.

DC: Washington, D.C, formally the District of Columbia.

DEA: Drug Enforcement Agency. Formed during the summer of 1973, the DEA is a federal law enforcement agency responsible for dealing with drug smuggling and drug abuse within the United States. The Drug Enforcement Administration is responsible for inhibiting drug trafficking within the United States of America.

DECREPIT: Worn out or ruined, dilapidated, because neglect, derelict, rickety.

DEFENDANT: Is a person in a court of law who is accused of having done something wrong.

DOUBLE TAP: This is a controlled shooting technique, where two well-aimed shots are fired in rapid succession at the same target.

DRIVE BY-SHOOTING: A drive-by or drive-by shooting is a type of assault that usually involves the perpetrator firing a weapon from within a motor vehicle and then fleeing. Such shootings are associated with gang violence in urban areas of the United States

EAVESDROPPING-BUG: Covert secret listening device.

FBI: Federal Bureau of Investigation. Operating under the United States Department of Justice jurisdiction, the FBI is also a member of the US Intelligence Community and reports to both the Attorney General and the Director of National Intelligence.

FEDERAL BAIL: Federal charges originate in federal court. Federal bonds use no middle-man and require assets to be pledged directly to the federal court. A federal judge has the ability to set a bail or bond amount, just like a state judge does. Those facing charges in a federal court may be met with a higher bond amount than a state court may have charged for a similar offence.

FEDERALES: The Federal police or security forces operating under a federal political system in Mexico.
Sometimes called the Mexican feds by US agents.

FENDER: This is the American English term for the part of an automobile, motorcycle, or other vehicle body that frames a wheel well (the fender underside). Its primary purpose is to prevent sand, mud, rocks, liquids, and other road spray from being thrown into the air by the rotating tyre of a mudguard.

FIDDLE: A violin.

FLUNKEY: A liveried manservant or footman, lackey, steward, butler, footman, valet, attendant.

FORFEITS: To lose the right to do or have something because you have broken a rule.

FTA: Failure to appear is a person charged with a crime and did not appear in court on a date and time set by the court.

FUBAR: Fucked Up Beyond Any Repair. Military slang

GANG INVESTIGATORS: Are specially trained law enforcement professionals trained to address gang activity and crime problems within their jurisdictions.

GHB: (Gamma-hydroxy-butyrate). Also known as a date rape drug called liquid ecstasy. The person or user taking it becomes physically weak or passes out entirely and cannot be woken; the effects can last from 6 to 24 hours.

GHILLIE SUIT: It is a type of camouflage clothing designed to resemble the background environment such as foliage; it is a net or cloth garment covered in loose strips of burlap (hessian), cloth, or twine, sometimes made to look like leaves and twigs, and optionally augmented with scraps of foliage from the area.

GIST: The main point of it, or to understand something.

GIZMO: A gadget, or any small device with a particular purpose, especially one whose name the speaker does not know or cannot recall.

GRITS: Coarsely ground corn, traditionally served with other flavourings as a breakfast dish.

GOPHER: A North American animal that lives in holes that it makes in the ground.

GUFFAW: Belly laugh, loud and hearty short laugh at something stupid that someone has said or done.

GUMSHOE: A detective.

HEX: A curse, jinx, spell, or malicious wish.

HICKORY: Is a tree of a genus Carya species, of the North American hardwood trees of the walnut family, that often have sweet edible nuts.

HILLBILLY: An unsophisticated country person, that dwell in remote rural regions of the Appalachia and Ozarks. The stereotype of a hillbilly is a person who is a White Southerner who owns a shotgun, goes barefoot, wears a worn-out floppy hat, drinks moonshine and whiskey which he makes himself, plays the banjo or fiddle, drives an old beat-up pickup truck, has bad teeth, is poorly educated, has long a beard, wears worn-out clothes and hand me downs, and is happy and content with what they have.

HOEDOWN: A redneck gathering or community dancing party typically featuring folk and square dances accompanied by lively hillbilly tunes played on the fiddle.

HOG: A pig, especially one that is allowed to grow large so that it can be eaten.

HOGTIED: To secure a person or animal by fastening the hands and feet or all four feet together.

HOMIES: Slang for homeboy, meaning a male friend from back home, or an acquaintance from one's town, city, or neighbourhood, or a member of one's peer group or gang.

HORN DOG: Sexually aggressive man or a man with strong sexual desires.

INTEL: Intelligence.

KINFOLK: Family or friends.

KNUCKLE DUSTER: A weapon made of metal worn around the knuckles that strengthen the impact of a punch.

LA.: Los Angeles

LACONIC: Using or involving the use of a minimum of words.

LICENCE PLATE: Car number plate.

LIMEY: A word Americans use to describe a British person.

M16: A gas-operated semi and fully automatic rifle.
The original automatic rifle was a United States military adaptation of the ArmaLite AR-15 rifle, Calibre 5.56 mm, with a 20-round magazine.

MAOA GENE: Monoamine Oxidase-A gene. This was named "Warrior Gene" in 2004. It is a survival gene that is passed down by family generations. Studies have linked the "Warrior Gene" to increased risk-taking and retaliatory behaviour. One emerging aspect of recent advances in Neurocriminology is discovering possible links between violent criminal behaviour and genetics. Men with the "Warrior Gene" are more likely to respond aggressively and violently to a perceived conflict.

MIDNIGHT RUN: In bounty hunter slang – It's an easy job or to get a skip into custody by midnight before the bond is forfeited by the court the next morning.

MOCK ABODE: Not authentic, imitation, artificial, human-made residence; a house or home.

MOONSHINE: This is illegally distilled homemade whisky or rum, usually with a very high alcohol content, that is made in secret to avoid the high taxes.

MOUNTS: A horse or other animals.

MRE: Meal-Ready-to-Eat, is a self-contained, individual field ration in lightweight packaging bought by the U.S. Department of Defense for its service members for use in combat or other field conditions where organized food facilities are not available. Later they added a Flameless Ration Heater (FRH), a water-activated exothermic reaction product that emits heat, allowed a service member in the field to enjoy a hot meal. Each meal provided about 1,200 calories and was also made available to civilians. They are also nicknamed: Meals Rejected by Ethiopians. Meals Rejected by the Enemy. Meals Rejected by Everyone.

MS-13: Mara Salvatrucha - 13. The name's origins are still disputed, but "**M**ara" is a Central American term for gang. "**S**alva" refers to El Salvador. "**Trucha**" is a slang term for "clever" or "sharp." And **13** is the position M occupies in the alphabet. MS-13 is one of the largest and most dangerous International criminal gangs in the United States. It originated in Los Angeles, California, in the 1970s and 1980s, and they still operate today. Initially, the MS-13 gang was set up to protect Salvadoran immigrants from other gangs in the Los Angeles area.

MTV: Music Television. An American pay channel.

OFFGRID: Are a system and lifestyle. You are not using or depending on public utilities or electricity.

ONE HORSE TOWN: A small town in the middle of nowhere with few and inadequate facilities.

OPPO: A colleague or friend, a military friend.

PACK HORSE: A packhorse or pack horse refers to a horse, mule, donkey, or pony used to carry goods on its back, usually in side-bags or panniers.

PALEFACE: A name used for a white person, often used in

fictional representations of the speech of Native American Indians.

PAPELES: Spanish/Mexican for papers or documents

PARKING LOT: A car park is also known as a car lot; it's a cleared area intended for parking vehicles.

PCP: Also called Phencyclidine, also known as angel dust among other names, it's a drug used for its mind-altering effects. PCP may cause hallucinations, distorted perceptions of sounds, and violent behaviour. As a recreational drug, it is typically smoked but may be taken by mouth, snorted, or injected, also an anesthetic that can stop people feeling pain but also cause hallucinations

PEEP-HOLE: A small telescopic hole that may be looked through, especially one in a door through which callers may be identified before the door is opened.

PEN: Penitentiary, jail, prison.

PHIAL: A small cylindrical glass bottle, typically used for medical samples or potions or medicines

PIMPING: The action or practice of a person controlling hookers or prostitutes, arranging clients for them, then taking part of their earnings in return.

PINK: In the United States, it's the certificate of title for a vehicle, also known as a car title or pink slip.

PINTO: A horse has a coat colour consisting of large patches of white and any other colour.

POMMEL: The upward curving or projecting part of a saddle in front of the rider for holding onto.

POSSUMS: American possums are called opossums. They're the only marsupial found in North America. Opossums are easily identified due to their long tails, pointed faces, and large, hairless ears. They are generally gray or a cinnamon colour and look like a large rat. It is a solitary and nocturnal animal about the size of a domestic cat. Their diet includes all types of bugs and insects, including cockroaches, crickets, and beetles. They love snails. They also eat mice and rats. So if you want to try and eat a possum, it's best to feed it a lot of corn for a few weeks to clear out its stomach to avoid catching diseases.

PRECIPICE: A very steep rock face, a vertical side of a cliff.

PRINCIPAL: A defendant that has been accused of a crime and has been released on a bail bond.

RAGTOP: A car with a soft or convertible roof.

RED NECK: In America, it is a derogatory term name for a poor, white person without education, especially one living in the countryside in the southern US, who is believed to have prejudiced unreasonable ideas and beliefs; they disapprove of him because they think he is uneducated and has strong, irrational opinions, and regarded as ignorant, and violent.

RESERVATION or REZ: A reservation or reserve is a place where North American Indians live. A tract of land set apart by the US government for the use of Native American Indians.

RESOLUTE: Purposeful, determined, and unwavering.

RETARD: Stupid or foolish people who are slow or limited in mental development, have no Intellectual understanding and awareness, etc.

REVERSE DIRECTORIES: A reverse telephone directory is also known as a gray pages or a criss-cross guide. These manuals were costly to buy and where a collection of phone numbers gave you the name and the address the telephone number was associated with.

REVERSE TACTICAL PEEPHOLE: It reverses the effects of a door viewer or peephole, meaning it allows you to see the inside from the outside.

RIDGE: A long elevated strip of land or a long narrow hilltop or mountain range.

RIDGELINE: A-line formed along with the highest points of a mountain ridge. An area of higher ground separating two adjacent streams or watersheds

ROADKILL: Animals hit by cars and found dead along roads.

SAPLINGS: A young tree, especially one with a slender, skinny trunk, a small tree not over four inches or about ten centimetres in diameter, about breast height.

SATURDAY NIGHT SPECIAL: A pistol .32 caliber. It was also known as a suicide special or junk gun with constant bullet jamming. It is a term used in the United States to refer to any inexpensive handgun pistol or revolver.

SENSEI: A martial arts teacher.

SHEBANG: All of it; the whole thing.

SHTUM: To be or become quiet and non-communicative. Stay silent, quiet, not speaking.

SIDEWALK: Pavement or pedestrian path beside a road.

SKIP(S): A fugitive that can't be found at their place of residence or usual hangouts.

SKIP TRACER: Skip tracing is an industry term used to describe the process of locating a fugitive that can't be found at their place of residence or usual hangouts. The act of skip tracing is most often used by bail bondsmen, bounty hunters, repossession agents, private investigators, debt collectors, and even journalists.

SMOKE: (her or him). Slang is used by a gang member who wants to shoot someone; the word came from the ghettos; smoke comes out of the gun after being fired to kill someone.

SNAFU: (Military slang) Situation Normal All Fucked Up.

SNIPING/SNIPER: The action of shooting at someone from a hiding place, especially accurately and at long range.

SOMBRERO: A broad-brimmed felt or straw hat, typically worn in Mexico and the southwestern United States.

SPAS-12: 'Special Purpose Automatic Shotgun-12' made by

Franchi. This was a semi-automatic 12-gauge shotgun, noted for its variable-mode firing method. The weapon could be fired via a gas-operated, semi-automatic mode (featuring self-loading) or a manually-actuated, pump-action, or slide-action system.

SPIT: This is a roasting style where meat is skewered on a spit – a long solid rod used to hold food while being cooked over a fire in a fireplace or on a campfire.

SPONDOOLICKS: **(Spondulix. Spondulicks).** A term for money, particularly cash acquired in a profitable exchange.

STAIRWELL: A shaft in a building in which a staircase is built.

SUPERS: Superintendent – The manager of a building or a person who directs and manages an organization.

SUSFU: (Military slang) Situation Unchanged Still Fucked Up.

TARFU: (Military slang) Totally And Royally Fucked Up.

THERMOS: Vacuum flask. It is an insulating storage vessel that significantly lengthens the time over which its contents remain hotter or cooler than the flask's surroundings.

TOPO MAP: Topographic map. These maps are detailed, accurate graphic representations of features that appear on the Earth's surface. These features include roads, buildings, urban development, railways, airports, names of places and geographic features, administrative boundaries, state and international borders.

TRACKER: This was a magnetic device attached to a motor vehicle's underbody to track its location. The United States government created the system, maintains it, and makes it freely accessible to anyone with a GPS receiver. The GPS project was launched by the U.S. Department of Defense in 1973 for use by the United States military and became fully operational in 1995. It was allowed for civilian use in the 1980s.

TRACKER MONITOR: This was a handheld device that received the device's signal attached to the motor vehicle.

TRANSGRESSOR: A person who breaks the law.

UNDERBELLY: A hidden, unpleasant part of society.

VET: A veteran (from Latin 'Vetus' means "old") is a person who has had long service or experience in a particular occupation or field. A military veteran is a person who has served and is no longer serving in the armed forces.

VIGAS: Often, builders use logs, or rough timbers called vigas as beams, with sticks laid over and between them under the roofing. Some people use adobe mud as roofing.

VUCSA: Violation of the Uniform Controlled Substance Act. This also includes possession, distribution, and the manufacture of controlled substances. Controlled substances can be illegal drugs as well as prescription drugs.

WIDE RECEIVER: Is an American or Canadian football key player, they are among the fastest players on the field. The wide receiver has to be smart and strong. Practice catching, speed, agility, tackling, and reading plays. He also functions as the pass-catching specialist and is an offensive player positioned away from the line, primarily as a pass receiver.

ZEE's: Going to sleep or sleeping

ZILCH: Nothing, zero.

ZIP-TIES: Normally is made of nylon, it has a flexible tape section with teeth that engage with a pawl in the head to form a ratchet so that as the free end of the tape section is pulled, the cable tie tightens and does not come undone, they are for holding items together, primarily electrical cables or wires but also can be used as handcuffs when steel handcuffs are not available.

YANKS: A term used by the British to describe Americans.

Coming Soon:

**Cases to read in Book Three
'Dead or Alive'
The Warrior Gene
The Ghosts and the Demons.**

**These are just a few of the chapters that
you can read about in the next Book.**

The Ghosts and the Demons
  Inside the Warrior Gene
  We do Bad Things to Bad People
  Risky Business. (Dirty work for the feds)
  Drugs, Guns, Contracts, and Hits
  The Minute of Angle Accuracy
  Teen Sicario a No Mercy Kill
  Shooting an Agent
  The Hano and the Halo
  Ojo Por Ojo, Diente Por Diente
  The B.M.O.'s, Doppelgangers and Boogeymen
  Almost Black Toast
  The Curare and the Dead Drops
  Embrace the Suck. (The point of no return)
  Gookin the Spook
  Gaggle 'N' Cluster Fucks
  The Mustang Sally Deluxe
  The Snowmobile Incident
  Many more cases to follow in Book 4